THE GUINNESS BOOK OF

MOTORCYCLING

FACTS AND FEATS

THE GUINNESS BOOK OF
MOTORCYCLING
FACTS AND FEATS

L J K SETRIGHT

GUINNESS SUPERLATIVES LIMITED
2 CECIL COURT, LONDON ROAD, ENFIELD MIDDLESEX

ACKNOWLEDGEMENTS

The publishers wish to record their gratitude for particular help given by:
Auto-Cycle Union
Beaulieu Motor Museum (Mrs Vera Russell)
London Borough of Enfield Libraries (Mrs Sheila Thacker)
Joseph Lucas Group Services Limited (H J McMillan)
The Manx Grand Prix Riders' Association (Harold M Rowell)
The Motor Cycle Association of Great Britain Limited (C H Smart)

Editorial: Beatrice Frei and Stan Greenberg
Design: Bernard Crossland Associates

Published in Great Britain by
Guinness Superlatives Ltd, 2 Cecil Court, London Road, Enfield, Middlesex
Set in 10/11 Times Roman
Colour separation by Newsele Litho Ltd, London and Milan

Printed and bound in Great Britain
by W & J Mackay Ltd, Chatham, Kent

British Library Cataloguing in Publication Data

Setright, Leonard John Kensell
  The Guinness book of motorcycling facts and feats.
  1. Motorcycling
  I. Title
  796.7   GV1059.5
  ISBN 0–85112–200–0

CONTENTS

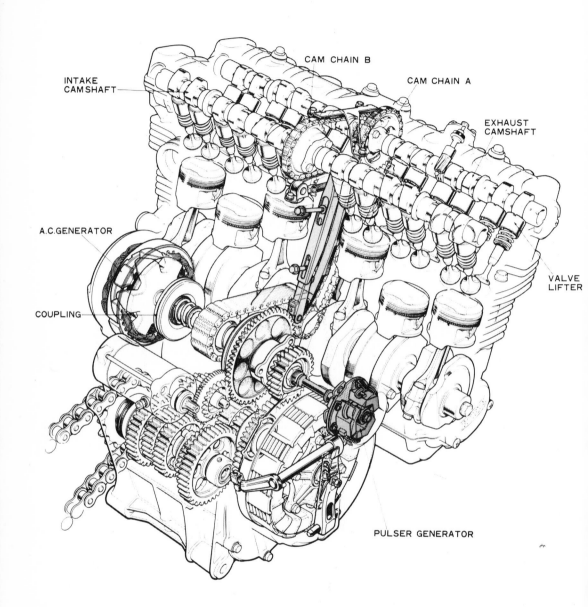

INTAKE CAMSHAFT

CAM CHAIN B

CAM CHAIN A

EXHAUST CAMSHAFT

A.C.GENERATOR

VALVE LIFTER

COUPLING

PULSER GENERATOR

The most elegantly complex motorcycle engine in production at the time of publication, this Honda CBX six-cylinder four-stroke with its profusion of carburettors and proliferation of valves provides the most complete imaginable contrast to the primordial powered three-wheeler opposite. But with 103 years and as many horsepower separating them, the story of technical developments is a long one. . . . (Honda Motor Co Ltd)

SECTION I

TECHNICAL ACHIEVEMENTS

The simplest way to define a motorcycle is as a bicycle propelled by a heat engine; and if we accept this, we must go on to admit that its prototype is unidentifiable, shrouded in the mists of industrial antiquity. There are bicycles, tricycles, and quadricycles or carriages driven by steam engines all milling about in that primordial chaos: for if indeed there were bicycles before ever there were petrol engines, so also were there steam engines before either, and so it followed naturally as a consequence of man's innate curiosity and perpetual dissatisfaction that steam power was the first kind to be applied to the motorisation of the bicycle.

There were some unnatural devices, too, the object of which was merely to achieve a powered vehicle, as distinct from a motorised one. There was for example the Cynophère, invented by Huret in France in 1875: this was a dog-cart, but in a sense that no carriage builder would have envisaged. It was in fact a tricycle, its single steering wheel foremost and its two driving wheels of even larger diameter: attached to each of these was a cylindrical cage, in which a dog could be imprisoned. The dogs then ran within these drums, turning them like squirrel-cages or the old penal treadmills and thus turning the wheels. There was a large version of the Cynophère calculated for propulsion by Great Danes, a lesser one appropriate to poodles; but the Society for the Protection of Animals considered the whole idea singularly inappropriate, and its protestations led to the idea being abandoned — though it is doubtful if it was ever meant to be taken as seriously as the Society took it. Even more ingeniously absurd was the horse-driven tricycle of 1906, in which pedals adapted to hooves were connected to the two rear wheels: pedalling with its fore legs and keeping up as comfortably as it could with its hind legs, the horse could thus propel this surely rather superfluous vehicle, while the rider steered it by means of a tiller controlling the front wheel. The device was presumably not an engineering experiment so much as a philosophical one to illustrate the old Greek principle of *hysteron proteron* (ιστερον προτερον), or literally putting the cart before the horse.

The Cynophère. (National Motor Museum, Beaulieu)

A hobby-horse. (National Motor Museum, Beaulieu)

Much more germane to the evolution of the motorcycle was the hobby-horse. The earliest single-track form of two-wheeled transport, it amounted to little more than a beam carrying an idler wheel at the rear and a steerable wheel in forks at the front: the rider straddled the beam and paddled himself along the road with his feet. It was a German, Carl von Drais, who invented the seminal vehicle in 1817, whence the name by which the French knew it, *Draisienne*. The alternative name of *vélocipède* appeared as efforts were made to provide some more efficient form of propulsion, usually by means of treadles or levers rotating the rear wheel, but there was not much velocity involved and the English nickname of 'boneshaker' was perhaps more apposite.

A way was found eventually of getting the rider's feet off the ground when, in 1861, Pierre Michaux followed the analogy of a handle on a grindstone and fitted cranks and pedals to the front wheel spindle of one of the *Draisiennes* that he and his sons Ernest and Henri manufactured commercially (along with perambulators) in a little workshop at Bar-le-Duc, France. So popular

was the Michaux velocipede that the annual output grew to more than 400 and others quickly copied it, not only in France but also in Britain and America.

This, then, was the vehicle for which mechanically motive power was sought; indeed the idea preceded the pedals, for an artist's impression of a steam-driven boneshaker appeared in a coloured engraving published in France in 1818, only the year after von Drais produced his invention. According to the caption, the device had been invented in Germany and was capable, in the event of the horse becoming extinct, of replacing the animal and assuming its servitude. Given the zany title 'Vélocipédraisiavaporianna', the contraption was virtually a foot-propelled hobby horse carrying a large boiler on its tail (and attended by two coalheavers and a stoker), but any other expected mechanical detail such as the steam engine itself was carefully suppressed by artistic plumes of smoke and steam apparently emanating from the hubs of both wheels. It all looked singularly imaginative, and yet the caption states quite categorically that the first trials were conducted on Sunday 5 April 1818 in the Jardin du Luxembourg, Paris — four days late, it would appear.

There was more realism abroad in the 1860s, and once the Michaux velocipede was in production the application of steam power to it was earnestly studied. By 1867 Ernest Michaux is supposed to have fitted a light steam power unit to one of his two-wheelers. In the same or the following year (the authorities are vague and inconsistent) a steam-powered bicycle was ridden at a number of fairs and circuses in the eastern United States of America by W W Austin of Winthrop, Massachusetts. This machine had a twin-cylinder engine, the cylinders flanking the frame backbone and linked by connecting rods directly to cranks on the rear wheel spindle; steam was fed from a coal-fired boiler, carried beneath the chassis beam between the wheels.

It seems likely that this machine was built not by Austin himself (who claimed to have covered about 2200 miles (3500 km) on it) but by Sylvester Howard Roper of Roxbury, Massachusetts; at any rate Roper built another that was virtually identical in 1869.

Still preserved in the Smithsonian Institution in Washington D C, Roper's steamer was based on a rather elegant hickory-framed boneshaker made by the Hanlon brothers, who were stunt riders or 'velo-gymnasts' doing the rounds of the same fairs as Austin attended. Roper's machine was probably capable of a fair turn of speed, for the cranks and pedals were removed from the front wheel and simple footrests put in their places: he claimed that his steam velocipede could be driven up any hill and outspeed any horse in the world — which implies something in excess of 40 mph (60 km/h), improbable though that seems. Roper may have built as many as ten steam-powered cycles and he used to exhibit them for a 25 cents fee. The last of his steamers were four-wheelers, but it was while demonstrating one of the bicycle types at the Charles River track at Cambridge, Massachusetts, that he collapsed and died, evidently having had a heart attack.

Contemporary with the pioneering work of Austin and Roper was that of Pierre Michaux and the engineer L G Perreaux whose previous inventions had included a six-chambered firearm, a river lock system and — perhaps most relevant — a powered circular saw. Perreaux developed,

at the urging of Michaux, a light single-cylinder steam engine fed by an alcohol-fired multi-tube boiler and driving the rear wheel of a front-pedalled Michaux velocipede by means of twin belts and pulleys. Perreaux patented his design in December 1868, and it was built and ridden in the following year. It evidently had a rather limited range but was ridden from Paris to Saint Germain, a distance of 15 km (nearly 10 miles) and was claimed to have reached a speed of 15 km/h (9 mph).

A year later in France the brothers Chapuis built a single-cylinder steam bicycle which also featured a multi-tubular boiler and belt drive, but its engine was set between the wheels. Experiments followed in Britain, but in that hippocracy all horseless carriages were remorselessly pilloried, and the steam tricycles of Meek (1877) and Parkyns & Pateman (1881) were effectively repressed by the legislation that had been designed to cramp all mechanically-propelled road vehicles in Britain. Under the Locomotive Acts of 1861 and 1865 even Sir Thomas Parkyns, who sponsored the Pateman steam tricycle, was charged and convicted of improperly riding his machine: such vehicles were not allowed to exceed 4 mph (6 km/h) on open roads and 2 mph (3 km/h) in towns, and were obliged to carry at least two people while a third walked 60 yd ahead carrying a red flag to warn of the vehicle's approach. An amending act of 1878 repealed the red flag provisions, but local by-laws often preserved them; and in a land where a pedal cyclist ran the risk of prosecution for furious riding if he overtook a horse going at more than a trot, there was no hope of a motorised cyclist being shown any mercy.

In the Land of the Free there was literally and metaphorically much more room for progress, and it was in 1881 that experiments with an auxiliary power unit for a bicycle were begun by Lucius D. Copeland of Phoenix, Arizona. He started with a high-wheeler bicycle, the 'old ordinary' or 'penny-farthing' type that had by then supplanted the boneshaker; but he found the project difficult and the results dangerous, so he turned to the unorthodox Star bicycle, a sort of farthing-penny with the large driving wheel at the back and the small front wheel doing the steering. A very light engine was made to hang just below the handlebars, driving the rear wheel by belt and pulleys, while a slender boiler was mounted on

the frame over the front wheel. Variously said to have achieved a top speed of 12 or 15 mph (19 or 24 km/h), Copeland's machine was first exhibited at the Maricopa County Fair at Phoenix in 1884, and was then put on show in San Francisco and later in New York as Copeland searched for commercial backers. Eventually he found some — Sanford Northrop, Dr Starkey and Dr Palen — and the Northrop Manufacturing Company of Camden, New Jersey, was established to put Copeland's designs into production. Soon he had built a steam tricycle with substantially automatic control systems, and on it he made many convincing journeys including a round trip of 120 miles (about 190 km) to Atlantic City. A steam bicycle followed in 1888, and later Copeland added a third wheel on an outrigger to make the first identifiable ancestor of the modern motorcycle-and-sidecar combination. All told, about 200 steamers of various sorts are believed to have been built from his designs, but he lost his faith in the project and faded from the scene.

Left: The 1884 Copeland steamer. (National Motor Museum, Beaulieu)

Below: This elegant scene was photographed in the USA late in the 19th century and shows one of Copeland's numerous steam power vehicles. (Orbis Publishing)

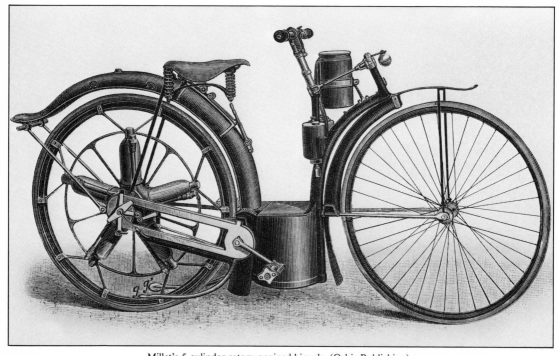

Millet's 5-cylinder rotary-engined bicycle. (Orbis Publishing)

Other experiments with steam propulsion continued — indeed they have never really stopped — but by the time that Copeland had enlisted the support of Northrop, the European scene was being enlivened by proposals for other kinds of engines. Clockwork, compressed air, carbon dioxide and hydrogen had all been suggested as propellants, hydrogen (in the form of coal gas) having been used by Etienne Lenoir in his gas-engined four-wheeler on which, in 1862, he drove the 10 km (about 6 miles) from Paris to Joinville. Then in 1879 Giuseppe Murnigotti of Bergamo, Italy, patented a combustion engine — specifically suitable for use in a motorcycle — which burned a gas mixture of hydrogen and air. His design never actually materialised, but was remarkable for its first specification of the 4-stroke internal combustion engine in any vehicle.

Murnigotti had not invented the 4-stroke principle itself, which had been proposed by the scientist Alphonse Beau de Rochas as early as 1862. Fourteen years after that, Dr Nicolaus Otto and Eugen Langen, of Deutz, near Köln, Germany, had patented a working application of the principle; and it was their assistants, Gottlieb Daimler and Wilhelm Maybach, whose experi-

ments finally bore fruit in a working 4-stroke stationary gas engine which was marketed by the Deutz Engine Company. This engine ran on town's gas, but Daimler recognised the possibility of carrying a more conveniently portable supply of combustible fuel on a moving vehicle; whereas Murnigotti's hydrogen gas had to be carried in unwieldy containers that would have imposed a severe practical handicap on his proposed motor bicycle (his expression 'bicicletta a motore' was almost certainly the first to foreshadow our modern 'motorcycle' usage). But Daimler had thought of the immense practical advantages of a liquid fuel of high volatility, which would make it possible for a large amount of chemically latent heat energy to be carried in a quite small tank. The fuel he most favoured was the petroleum distillate then generally known as benzine, commonly used for cleaning clothes. Otto and Langen disapproved of these experiments being conducted in their factory, and so Daimler left Deutz in 1882 to pursue his research full-time. His visionary persuasiveness soon had Maybach answering the summons to join him. In the garden shed behind Daimler's house at Canstatt, the two set to work to perfect their engine — and it must be emphasised that it was the engine that

VÉLOCIPÉDRAISIAVAPORIANNA.

First concepts of the motorcycle
French caricature of 1818 (above) and English of 1827 (below). (National Motor Museum, Beaulieu)

Steplessly variable transmission gear ratio by belt and adjustable pulleys was an idea vigorously pursued in the early days, beginning with the Rudge Multi built for the 1911 TT and followed for many years by the Zenith Gradua system shown here. (All Sport/Don Morley)

1917 Harley-Davidson eight-valve. (All Sport/Don Morley)

The Douglas racing twins of 1923 onwards featured a superb layout, with the engine as low as could be, the gearbox above the rear cylinder, and the weight and frontal area minimal. Details varied quite a lot from one racer to another, according to the needs of the riders. (All Sport/Photographic Ltd)

This 1937 Manx Norton displays the plunger rear suspension, familiarly described as the 'garden gate', which was not replaced until the McCandless trailing-fork suspension inspired the more kindly nicknamed 'featherbed' Norton of 1950. (All Sport/Photographic Ltd)

The Ariel Leader, a 250 cc two-stroke twin-cylinder engine hung beneath a pressed steel box frame, preceded by trailing-link front forks, and surrounded by weathercheating fairings, was one of the first and last modern motorcycles, but was a commercial failure within a couple of years of its 1959 introduction. (All Sport/Don Morley)

The Dunstall Suzuki GS1000CS ridden by the author to prove itself in early 1979 the fastest street motorcycle in production at a speed of 154·2 mph (248·1 km/h).

The Honda RCB 4-cylinder 16-valve racer completely dominated endurance racing in the 1976/7/8 seasons; many of its technical features found their way into production. (All Sport/John Starr)

concerned them, the idea of using it to power a motor bicycle being entirely subservient.

Because Otto's patent had been preceded by 16 years in the theoretical work of Beau de Rochas, Daimler did not have to worry about licensing obligations and was free to pursue his development of the 4-stroke engine. Recognising that a higher rate of crankshaft rotation would compensate for a smaller cylinder displacement, all other things being equal (a feat of no great intellectual accomplishment, but nevertheless one that was to prove beyond the mental abilities of sporting or political legislators decades later), he aimed to make an engine that ran at high speeds by the stationary gas-engine standards of the time.

His first was therefore of only 264 cc displacement, a little single-cylinder air-cooled engine with automatic inlet valve, developing about $\frac{1}{2}$ hp and running at 700–800 rpm. Lacking confidence in electrical ignition for such speeds, Daimler spoiled his project by relying on hot tube ignition; on the other hand the carburettor that Maybach devised for it was a good deal better than some of the contraptions used by rivals later.

At any rate the engine was completed within a couple of years of Daimler leaving Deutz, and the time came to mount it in a test vehicle. Daimler's thoughts were always directed towards a full-size multi-passenger horseless carriage, but his engine was not powerful enough for that, being merely a working prototype, and this was why he and Maybach decided to build it into a bicycle. Although the old ordinary or penny-farthing bicycle was then commonplace, the first 'new safety' bicycles, with two equal-sized wheels with drive to the rear, were already in fashion in England, where they were invented, and Daimler may have been aware of and encouraged by this

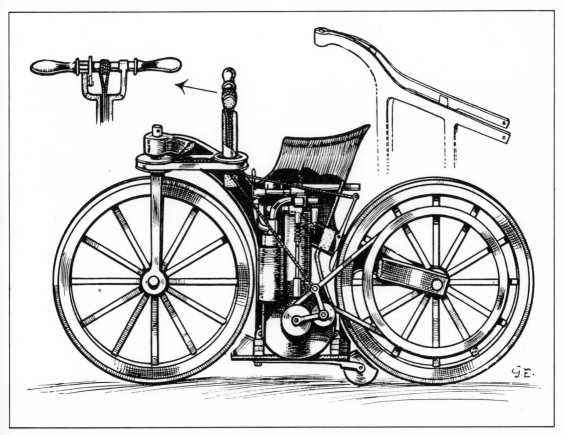

The original belt-drive version of Daimler's primordial motorcycle, with detail drawings showing the basis of the wooden chassis frame and the crude twist-grip control on the handlebars, which are linked to the steering wheel by belt and pulleys. (National Motor Museum, Beaulieu)

development. At any rate a roughly similar bicycle was built in his Canstatt workshop, mostly of wood, and the engine was installed with its cylinder upright between the wheels, a tall saddle roofing it over. The saddle was so high that the rider's feet could not easily reach the ground, and so a pair of small outrigger wheels were added to the chassis to give it lateral support, although the machine had been christened the *Einspur* or one-track.

Another snag about the saddle location came literally to light on 10 November 1885, the day when Daimler's 17-year-old son Paul rode the Einspur from Canstatt to Untertürkheim and back, a distance of about 12 km ($7\frac{1}{2}$ miles). The engine, devoid of cooling fins and relying upon a fan-induced draught to keep its temperature under control, grew hot enough to set fire to the saddle.

Fire was to be the end of the Einspur, which was destroyed in a big blaze at the Daimler factory in 1903; what may now be seen in museums such as that of Daimler-Benz are only replicas. Long before the final conflagration, the machine had been abandoned, having served its test-bed purpose which only lasted to 1886. Development works in the intervening winter had included the replacement of the original belt drive by a two-stage, two-speed transmission in which the primary drive was by belt to a counter-shaft with pinions engaging a final drive ring gear cut into the rim of the rear wheel. It was an altogether rude device, but it had a strong claim to being the ancestor of the modern motorcycle, if we think of that in terms of one propelled by a petrol engine.

However, there is an alternative claim that may be staked for the English three-wheeler created by Edward Butler in 1884. The selection of one or the other depends to some extent upon prejudice, whether arising from nationality or from numeracy, and taking into account the essential difference between designing something and actually making it work. It is admittedly confusing that we should have to consider the tricycle with the bicycle in this era, for the usual three-wheeler had more in common with the conventional four-wheeled car than with the bicycle. Such, at any rate, was the theory; but in practice the tricycles of the day owed their shape and constructional details almost entirely to contemporary bicycle practice, making it arguable that

they should be recognised as having played their part in the evolution of the motorcycle. As already pointed out, both kinds were treated indifferently as mere test-beds for the petrol engines that were the obsessing objects of so many experimental engineers' ambitions.

Daimler was one of these men, and another was Butler who had on paper before Daimler's bicycle his own designs for a tricycle which, if we admit three-wheelers (and many authorities, whether governmental or sporting, still bracket them with two-wheelers today), must be the first of them all. Those drawings were on display at the Stanley Cycle Show in London in 1884, following the grant of a patent to Edward Butler, a man then employed by F B Shuttleworth, a firm of marine engineers in Erith, Kent.

Butler, born in 1863, was a Devonshire man of a quiet and retiring disposition. Yet he has another claim to fame besides his tricycle, albeit one that is commonly dismissed by those who prefer the rival and perhaps less justifiable claim of Frederick Simms: he was the originator of the word 'petrol'. Neither this piece of inspired coinage, nor the ingenious work put into his tricycle patents of 1884 and 1887, earned him any kind of fortune: mainly due to lack of financial support, he never really got anywhere with his project, but he did make a brave start.

Unlike Daimler, Butler apparently considered Otto's 4-stroke patents binding, and he therefore decided to adopt the 2-stroke principle that had been expounded by Clerk some years earlier. The 1884 drawings show a short-wheelbase chassis with three tall spindly wheels, the singleton being at the rear. On each side of that stern wheel was one of the two cylinders of an horizontal 2-stroke engine, driving through connecting rods to cranks on the wheel spindle.

As in the case of Daimler's bicycle, Butler's patented bicycle was not built straight away, and several quite important alterations were made before he committed his designs to metal in 1887, by which time he had taken out further patent cover. One of these changes was to subsitute a 4-stroke engine with some astonishingly advanced features. Remember that at this time Daimler's engine was staggering along with hot-tube ignition, a surface carburettor, and an automatic inlet valve; in precocious contrast, Butler's had chain-driven rotary valves for exhaust and inlet,

Edward Butler's 1888 Petrol-Cycle. (Orbis Publishing)

electrical ignition, and a surprisingly modern float-feed jet carburettor which antedated the effective pioneer of the type (another piece of inspired work by Maybach) by 5 years. Alas, there was one respect in which Butler's design was less modern, this being the direct connection between pistons and driving wheel, a transmission arrangement that was guided by steam practice and was quite unsuitable for the faster-running petrol engine. In due course Butler interposed an epicyclic reduction gear between the cranks and the rear hub, and thereafter the tricycle worked quite well.

In fact it worked too well. The police stopped Butler from riding it, for although by that time the need for a man to walk ahead of any self-propelled vehicle, carrying a red flag, had been eliminated by 1878 legislation, there remained a mass of costive acts and by-laws which included a speed limit for such vehicles of 4 mph (about 6 km/h). Butler's tricycle, which had been called The Petrol-Cycle and was to be marketed by a company formed with Shuttleworth's assistance, The Petrol-Cycle Syndicate Ltd, was broken up for scrap.

Developments were by this time coming thick and fast. Even in 1887 there was another 4-stroke tricycle built with chain drive, this by one E H Owen. A year later J K Starley, son of the man who devised the modern wire-spoked wheel and became known as the father of the English bicycle, built an electric tricycle which he took to France where he could ride it free from persecution: at Deauville this machine maintained 8 mph (13 km/h), but its battery range was very limited. In 1892 another Briton, J D Roots, devised a 2-stroke oil-engined tricycle which was apparently sold in France in small numbers. Its engine followed the principles patented by Joseph Day in 1891, introducing the crankcase compression phase which was afterwards an almost universal feature of motorcycle 2-stroke engines.

Another 1892 newcomer was the Millet, in which the most unusual power unit was derived from an experimental steam engine. It was called a 'stellar' engine, and was suitable for building into either the front or rear wheel, being of a layout that later became familiar as the rotary engine of early aviation. Felix Theodore Millet

The initials are those of Felix Theodore Millet, designer of the 5-cylinder Stellar rotary engine incorporated in the rear wheel. (National Motor Museum, Beaulieu)

had taken out his first patent for such an engine in 1888; the 1892 machine featured a further novelty, an elastic wheel intended to give some measure of springing to cushion the mass of the engine against the dreadful bumps of contemporary roads. A series of spring blades between the heads of the five radial cylinders and the rim of the wheel provided this elasticity. However, the development of the pneumatic tyre, patented by John Boyd Dunlop in 1888 though originally invented by R W Thomson in 1845, promised a much more satisfactory solution to that and other problems, having already been demonstrated convincingly in pedal cycles.

Two or three further steam-powered machines occurred at about this time, all of interest in various ways. In 1893 the German engineer von Meyenberg built a steamer with two-speed transmission and a spine frame acting as a fuel tank. In the same year the Dalifol steam cycle was built by Georges Richard, a Frenchman who later became famous as a partner in the Richard-

Brasier car firm which won the Gordon Bennett races of 1904 and 1905. Perhaps more important than either of these was an earlier steamer made in 1889 by the Brothers Heinrich and Wilhelm Hildebrand of Munich: they started with a steam unit in a duplex-framed bicycle, mainly because they were keen cyclists until (as was the frequent and strenuous case in their native Bavaria) it came to going uphill! Later the brothers had teamed up with two other Bavarians, Hans Geisenhof (who had previously worked with Karl Benz, the pioneer of the motor-car), and Alois Wolfmüller. In 1892 Geisenhof built a small 2-stroke petrol engine for the brothers, but it was to prove a bit feeble, and so he and Wolfmüller got together to build a much larger parallel-twin 4-stroke, and then all four men got together to devise a frame strong enough to carry it. This was based on that of the 1889 Hildebrand steamer, and the resulting amalgam proved competent enough on the road to justify being patented and put into production by a generously financed new company. The Hildebrand & Wolfmüller (or

The Bernadi motor attachment for a petrol bicycle, dated about 1893. Note the large flywheel. (National Motor Museum, Beaulieu)

The Hildebrand & Wolfmüller of 1894. (National Motor Museum, Beaulieu)

The 1897 Holden. (National Motor Museum, Beaulieu)

H. & W.) was the first motorcycle to have pneumatic tyres — which were made by Veith, a firm near Darmstadt who had conducted suitable negotiations with the local Dunlop representative and who in more modern times have been closely associated with the Italian tyre manufacturer Pirelli. Much of the machine was crude, however, and it attained its results — 28 mph (45 km/h) on $2\frac{1}{2}$ hp — partly by virtue of having the largest engine capacity of any production motorcycle in history, the two cylinders having bores and stroke of 90 and 117 mm respectively, giving a displacement of 1489 cc. Despite some successful demonstrations and performances in races in Italy and France, the manifold crudities of the H. & W. doomed it to failure, and the enthusiasm that prompted an initial production batch of 100 machines eventually evaporated as the company collapsed in 1897.

The first race for motorcycles in America had been staged earlier in November 1895 in Illinois, the route running from Chicago to Waukegan. However, the word 'motorcycle' was at that time used indifferently in America to describe any mechanically propelled vehicle, regardless of how many wheels it might have, so the fact that 100 'motorcycles' were entered for this event should not be misconstrued. In any case only two of them started, and when a re-run was ordered later there were still only six.

One of the two-wheelers entered was particularly intriguing in embodying a spring drive not unlike that of a clockwork motor. This was the Lybe, the spring motor of which was designed to recover on downhill sections some of the energies dissipated on the level or uphill. Arm and foot power assistance were involved and were justified by the inventor D I Lybe, of Sidney, Iowa, on the grounds that it would 'afford a mild and pleasing form of exercise in addition to its speed advantages'. The speed claimed was no less than 30 mph (48 km/h), and in 1893 Lybe is supposed to have attained that speed while travelling a distance of about 770 yd (700 m). After that the spring had to be rewound, and according to comment at the time this demanded more energy and time than it took to cover the distance on foot.

The Marquis Albert de Dion on an 1888 steam-powered tricycle. (National Motor Museum, Beaulieu)

Clearly this was no way to ride from Chicago to Waukegan, but while in the USA progress in motorcycling hung fire, in France and England important developments took place. The year 1895 saw the creation of the first 4-cylinder motorcycle, designed by the civil engineer who in the following decade designed the race track at Brooklands, Colonel Capel Holden. His machine had a water-cooled flat-4-cylinder arrangement, with only two connecting rods pivoted from cross-heads pinned to what were in effect double-acting pistons; the connecting rods were linked by cranks to the spindle of the small-diameter rear wheel, thus condemning the bicycle to the same sort of jerkiness and control difficulties at low speeds as were material in bringing about the downfall of the Hildebrand & Wolfmüller. Holden's motorcycle did go into production, the Motor Traction Company of London adopting his design in 1899; but it was not generally avail-able for another couple of years, by which time it was hopelessly out-of-date.

The engine that did more than anything else to set future patterns and fashions was the little high-speed petrol engine introduced by the French firm De Dion Bouton, also in 1895. Originally this company was a triumvirate including not only the Marquis Albert de Dion and the commoner Georges Bouton but also the latter's brother-in-law Trépardoux, a steam specialist who guided the firm in its brilliantly successful manufacture of steam vehicles for more than 10 years. In the early 1890s, however, de Dion and Bouton saw a future for a high-speed petrol engine that Trépardoux could not, and his furious dissension led to his resignation from the company in 1894. In the next year Bouton produced a little petrol engine capable of 1800 rpm — a figure that surprised him almost as much as

Georges Bouton in 1935. (National Motor Museum, Beaulieu)

everyone else, for it was without precedent. The fact that the engine was only of 120 cc displacement made the figure less immoderate, perhaps, but the main thing was that this little engine, mounted behind the axle of a pedal tricycle and driving it through exposed bevel gearing, proved extraordinarily popular. The company sold hundreds of examples to other firms making cars, tricycles and motorcycles, not only in France but

The Components De Dion engine was built under licence in Birmingham. (Orbis Publishing)

also in many other European countries, and the design was pirated by many more, particularly in England. One of the first English firms to use the De Dion-Bouton engine was Excelsior, whose machine appeared in 1896; later they made their own engines, going to the other extreme in cylinder size with a 1913 model which, with a displacement of 810 cc, was one of the biggest singles ever made outside France.

The French were particularly notorious for making huge engines, sometimes of more than 2 litres displacement, with which to power crude motorcycles used for pacing pedal-cyclists racing on the small banked tracks that had become popular in or near many of the large centres of population in France and, to a lesser extent, in

H N 'Kork' Ballington, double World Champion in 1978.

The New Werner in 1902 form with a 2 hp engine. (National Motor Museum, Beaulieu)

England. It was from these grotesque monstrosities that the first true racing motorcycles evolved. The Frenchman Buchet was the leader of these megalomaniacs, his best known engine being a 4245 cc twin which he fitted into a tricycle. He is not to be confused with another French racing man of a similar name, Bucquet, who in 1902 won the race from Paris to Vienna riding the New Werner.

The Werner only became 'New' in 1901; prior to that, it was Werner *simpliciter,* the name being that of a couple of journalist *émigrés* from Russia, the brothers Eugene and Michel Werner who, in Paris in 1897, successfully motorised a bicycle by fitting an engine of De Dion type above the front wheel, which it drove through a twisted rawhide belt. It was no better than many of the others, and it was no worse than some, but it kept the brothers in business until they should perfect a new kind of engine location that was to set the pattern for generations to come.

They were very nearly beaten to it by a Yorkshireman, Joah Phelon, who in 1900 fitted a De Dion type of engine in place of the front downtube of a pedal cycle. Indeed Phelon's idea endured for a long time, for he later became associated with one Richard Moore with whom he founded the P. & M. concern whose Panthers were famous amongst other things for having no front downtubes in their frames, the sloping single-cyclinder engine doing the job of holding the front end together.

The brothers Werner, a year later, hit on the arrangement most favoured thereafter. In their bicycle, a single-cylinder 262 cc engine took the place of the normal bottom bracket where the pedals were usually to be found. Special lugs there embraced the aluminium crankcase of the engine, which thus became an integral part of the whole machine. In this fashion they created a motorcycle which really was a motorcycle, and was also a fabulous success.

It was not only the integration of engine and frame that made it attractive, but also the tremendous improvement in the general handling and controllability of the motorcycle. The engine,

FN (Fabrique National d'Armes de Guerre) made a long succession of in-line four-cylinder motorcycles, of which this 1905 example was one of the earliest, simplest and prettiest. (Orbis Publishing)

midway between front and rear wheels, and as low as was convenient, kept the centre of gravity desirably low and the balance of weight distribution fore and aft reasonably equal; and these virtues were sufficient for the layout to be copied everywhere, and to inspire scores of new manufacturers. The new Werner had a number of other modern features: there was a spray carburettor, rider-controlled engine lubrication by hand-pump, and a pedal-operated rear brake.

As far as most motorcycles are concerned, the engine is still where the Werner brothers put it. Perhaps nothing so revolutionary has happened since, in all the obscure and entangled technical history of the motorcycle: we have seen only evolution, and considering the passage of nearly 80 years we have seen surprisingly little of that. Year by year, ideas emerged for doing things better — or, at least, doing them differently: and according to the competence of their proponents, the conservatism of their customers, and the exigencies of their times, they either succeeded or failed, sometimes only disappearing to be revived years or decades later in new guises when the times were ripe for them.

The novelties and oddities of the 20th century make a fascinating chronology, but it is not one that can easily be guaranteed, so obscure, confusing and vaguely worded are the early references. Take the disc brake, for example: it is generally accepted that Honda were the first to put a disc brake into production in their epoch-marking CB750 4-cylinder machine of 1969, but Douglas built some machines with a form of disc brake produced by the Research Association in 1923, and mechanically-operated disc brakes can even be traced back to the Imperial motorcycle made in England in 1901. Nevertheless, the disc brake with modern spot-type calipers, albeit electrically actuated, can be traced back to an extraordinarily sophisticated design for an electric vehicle patented in or about 1888 by the American Elmer Ambrose Sperry, who was later to become famous for his work with the gyroscope.

Another feature of 1901 included the use of chain for the secondary transmission of the Royal, made in the USA.

The first V8 motorcycle, built by Curtiss and timed at 136·36 mph (219·45 km/h) on Ormond Beach, Florida. (National Motor Museum, Beaulieu)

In 1902 the French firm Bichrone was the first to make a V-twin 2-stroke, while a water-cooled crank-started V-twin was built in England by Iris.

In 1903 Roessler-Javerning of Austria made motorcycles with both wheels sprung. Another suspension development was telescopic front forks featuring in the Minneapolis made in America, a single-cylinder machine that had a two-speed gearbox with secondary drive by chain. There was a three-speed gearbox in the Raglan, made in England. The other way to achieve flexibility was with more cylinders, and 1903 was an outstanding year for developments in this direction, the most famous being the in-line, air-cooled, 4-cylinder engines introduced and destined to remain in production for many years by the Belgian armaments firm FN. Another 4-cylinder engine was produced in England by Binks, one of a family famous for carburettors, first under their own name and later as the Amal. Also in England, Herbert Dennell modified a JAP engine to make an in-line three, while in America Glen L. Curtiss the aviation pioneer took an interest in motorcycles and, starting with singles and V-twins, went on to make a V8, the first motorcycle to have a single engine of so many cylinders. No single engine for a motorcycle has ever had a larger number, although drag racing machines using multiple engines have featured as many as twelve cylinders resulting from three 4-cylinder engines being combined in one chassis.

1904: the four-speed gearbox became more common, with British examples from Roc and Zenith leading the trend.

1905: the $2\frac{1}{2}$ hp engine of the Howard, made in England, was given a rudimentary form of fuel injection (which had already featured in aviation 2 years earlier in the engine of the Wright brothers' first Flyer). Also in England the Fée (meaning fairy) designed by J F Barter was the first motorcycle to have a horizontally opposed twin-cylinder engine fitted with its cylinders lying longitudinally. This was later developed by Douglas and copied by BMW. In Germany, Grade built 2-stroke motorcycles with 1, 2 and 4 cylinders which were quite successful in racing.

The original open-frame Scott two-speeder, built for A A Scott by the Jowett brothers who were to have pursued a licensing agreement. (National Motor Museum, Beaulieu)

1907: A foot-operated gear lever featured in the New Era built in the USA, while pneumatic front and rear suspension was a feature of the ASL. This was also the year in which the high-tension magneto became the norm for providing the necessary sparks for ignition: Butler's tricycle engine was sparked by something like a little Wimshurst machine, the H. & W. and Holden by coil-and-battery systems that were most effectively popularised by De Dion Bouton. Frederick Simms patented the low-tension magneto in 1897 and it was made in Stuttgart by Robert Bosch, to be used in a few motorcycles. Boudeville invented the high-tension magneto in France in 1898, and again it was the Bosch firm who redesigned it, when it quickly became popular for motorcycles because of its efficiency and because it relieved the rider from depending on the fragile batteries of the day.

1908: Scott pioneered the water-cooled 2-stroke twin and the triangulated bicycle frame.

1909: Wilkinson built water-cooled in-line fours of 676 and 844 cc in England. These had three-speed gearboxes and shaft drive, the latter also featuring in the Pierce of America.

1910: James produced in Britain a super-charged flat-twin 2-stroke.

1911: Scott introduced rotary inlet valves for racing versions of his 2-stroke. Rudge-Whitworth introduced a variable-ratio belt drive to cope with the hill-climbing demands of the new Isle of Man 'Mountain' circuit being used for the first time for the Tourist Trophy races. Models based on this, known as the Rudge Multi, remained popular for many years thereafter, and the system of expanding and contracting pulleys was later emulated by Zenith in their Gradua models. In the same year the Militaire, an extraordinary 4-cylinder heavyweight built car-style in the USA, had a gearbox containing three forward speeds and a reverse: this provision was very useful in a sidecar machine, and for the same reason the in-line 4-cylinder machines that were to be built by William and Tom Henderson in Detroit from 1912 were also to be fitted with a reverse gear.

1913: In Australia several single-cylinder 500 cc machines with four overhead valves were built by Rova-Kent. In France, Peugeot applied their twin-overhead-camshaft design principles (convincingly demonstrated in their winning Grand Prix racing cars of 1912) to their racing motorcycles. In the USA an overhead-camshaft V twin of 1000 cc was built by Cyclone.

1914: The Indian twin was marketed with an advanced electrical system that not only catered for all necessary lighting and ignition but also turned the engine over for starting: this was done by a dynamotor which was wound to act as a dynamo at 6 volts or as a starting motor at 12 volts. By this time the simple dynamo figured frequently in the specifications of the better motorcycles; earlier, electric lighting had depended upon accumulators or dry batteries, and many motorcycles clung to the acetylene lamps that had been significantly improved in 1912. In Britain, Seal produced an unusual sidecar combination in which the passenger did the steering by means of a wheel controlling not only the front wheel of the bicycle but also the outrigger wheel.

1919: Krupp of Germany built a motorised scooter with front-wheel drive. Black Prince in England built a 500 cc flat-twin 2-stroke machine in a pressed steel chassis frame with a sprung rear wheel.

1920: Pressed steel was also used for the frame of the Nimbus made in Denmark. In Belgium, Gillet-Herstal made a 350 cc 2-stroke single with a rotary scavenge pump. In Germany, Ziro made a 150 cc machine similarly charged. In Britain the 998 cc Superb Four had a belt-driven single overhead camshaft and a single overhead camshaft also featured in some fours built in France by Train.

Megaphone-ended exhaust pipes were employed as early as 1920, when they were fitted to a racing ABC.

1921: SAR of France used oil-cooling for 350 cc singles. Megola produced in Germany a motorcycle with a car-style half-reclining riding position, made possible by incorporation of a 5-cylinder radial engine in the front wheel: the entire mass of the engine rotated with the wheel, although it was not a rotary engine in the strictest sense. Car principles were carried much further in the Neracar, devised by an American named Neracher, and featuring a very low pressed-steel chassis with gearbox or variable-ratio friction drive behind and in line with the crankshaft of the small single-cylinder engine. The most significant feature of the Neracar was its front suspension and steering arrangements, the front wheel pivoting about a hub-centre king-pin for steering and in leading-link pivoted forks for springing, the conventional bicycle-type steering head being completely eliminated. The Neracar was noted at the time, and has remained famous ever since, for exceptionally good steering and stability. It was later made in England by Sheffield-Simplex.

1923: The introduction of the first complete BMW motorcycle to carry the name, the R32 model which made its debut at the Paris show, confirmed the appeal of the transverse-cylindered flat-twin engine, which had previously enjoyed only a limited success (most notably in the ABC made in Surrey, England, by the Sopwith aircraft firm and designed by Granville Bradshaw). Also in Germany a 3-cylinder 2-stroke was first made by Grote, while in Italy a 4-cylinder water-cooled 1000 cc machine was built by Garbello.

The first disc-braked motorcycle to win a race was the 1923 Douglas, which scored victories in the Senior and Sidecar TT races of that year and was fitted with Research Association disc brakes.

1926: Three-valve engines with two inlet valves and a single exhaust per cylinder were built in England by McEvoy and in Germany by WMR. A mechanically operated exhaust valve was tried in the 2-stroke made in Germany by Schliha in the following year, long before exhaust poppets proved so successful in the 2-stroke diesel engines of General Motors and Foden.

The first motorcycle to have inlet valve larger than the exhaust valve was the 1924 AJS model built for the TT. The feature was afterwards incorporated in AJS production models.

Pictures of the Neracar with sidecar attached are rare, but this RAC patrol outfit at least reveals the hub-centre steering and front suspension, and the head of the 350 cc Blackburne engine of a 1925 model. (Orbis Publishing)

1928: The Ascot-Pullin, designed by Cyril Pullin who was also associated with Douglas, had an horizontal single-cylindered ohv 496 cc engine, an enclosed secondary chain, and an hydraulic brake. In Italy the 4-cylinder DPRA engine was designed by the engineer Remor, who was later responsible in turn for the 4-cylinder racers built by Rondine, Gilera, and M V Agusta.

A year later, in 1929, the designer Edward Turner produced the Square Four for Ariel. At the same time P. & M. were marketing their little 246 cc Panthette, a transverse-cylindered V-twin. Technically also a V-twin was the Matchless Silver Arrow, but the cylinders were set at the unusually narrow included angle of 26°, so narrow that it was possible to combine them in a single casting so that in appearance it came close to looking like a vertical twin. At the other extreme, Guzzi built a 500 cc V-twin with an included angle of 120°. Perhaps the most important development of 1929, however, was the introduction of the loop-scavenge 2-stroke engine devised by Dr Schnuerle and put into production

in Germany by DKW. A close rival for the honour would be the positive-stop foot-operated gearchange introduced, initially in racing, by Velocette. In production terms the German influence was probably the greater: in that year Germany produced 195 686 motorcycles compared with the 164 000 made in England.

1932: Brough Superior built a motorcycle specifically intended for sidecar haulage, powered by the water-cooled 796 cc Austin 7 car engine and driven by twin rear wheels.

1933: The designer Valentine Page, earlier responsible for the first overhead-camshaft JAP engine, produced for Triumph a 649 cc overhead valve vertical twin with gearbox in unit.

1935: At the Berlin Show, BMW had hydraulically damped coil-sprung telescopic front forks on their latest models. Zündapp displayed a machine with all-chain transmission, the usual cogs within the gearbox being replaced by sprockets on main and lay shafts connected by chains. Imperia exhibited a 500 cc horizontally-opposed 2-cylinder 2-stroke with its air-cooled cylinders projecting transversely and supplied with mixture from a supercharger. This Imperia had no gearbox: instead, a converter coupling or hydrokinetic 'torque converter' was built on to the tail of the crankshaft, with shaft-drive thence to the rear hub. The maximum speed claimed for this machine was 140 km/h (87 mph). In England a 4-cylinder racing AJS was designed by Bert Collier, a V4 with double overhead camshafts for each bank of cylinders. At this stage it was air-cooled and unsupercharged, though it was altered in both respects in 1939. Much the most significant 4-cylinder engine of 1935 was, however, that of the Rondine, an in-line transverse water-cooled supercharged 4-cylinder machine which was the ancestor of the famous and brilliantly successful Gilera.

1936: In Italy, Galbusera made a 250 cc V4 and a 500 cc V8.

The 1000 cc V-twin engine of the post war Vincent was so rigid a structure that it was able to be used as part of the machine's chassis, hence the absence of a front down tube such as might be found in more conventional motorcycles of the time. (L J K Setright)

1945: Torsion bar suspension in the 350 cc flat twin Douglas. Frameless stressed-engine construction, with taper-roller pivots for the rear suspension, four brakes, servo-aided clutch, and numerous niceties of detail in the 1000 cc V-twin engine of the Series B Vincent HRD Rapide.

1946: Cast crankshaft and flexible engine mounts in the 500 cc in-line twin Sunbeam, which also featured fat 4·75 in (120·65 mm) tyres on small 16 in (406 mm) diameter wheels. A sprung rear hub was announced as an optional extra by Triumph.

1947: At the Geneva show the new utility Motosacoche, designed by Douglas (otherwise known as Dougal) Marchant, a British Engineer commissioned for the purpose by the Swiss firm, had many unusual features. Its 200 cc side-valve engine had a fuel metering device replacing the conventional carburettor, was started by hand, and drove by belt through a transmission that relied for ratio variation on an expanding pulley whose dimensions were controlled hydraulically by high-pressure oil delivered from an engine-driven pump. Later in the year, Dowty oleo-pneumatic front forks were adopted on new machines by EMC, Panther and Velocette — all in England, where rear suspension struts of similar principles had been supplied by Dowty to Velocette for pre-war racing.

> Torsion-bar springs were used for the rear suspension of the 350 cc Douglas models introduced after World War 2. The original design envisaged torsion bars for the front suspension too, but helical coils replaced them before production began. The last 350 Douglas, the Dragonfly, had a new frame design and reverted to helical rear springs as well.

1949: Girdraulic front forks, combining telescopic springing and damping units with traditional girder fork geometry, and actually made by the Bristol Aircraft Company (the handsome fork blades were immensely stiff forgings of high-duty aluminium alloy), appeared on the Series C Vincent HRD. The Velocette LE model appeared with 149 cc transverse flat twin engine driving through a car-type clutch and unit-construction

The Honda 297 cc 6-cylinder GP racer in the 1967 TT, ridden
by Hailwood. (National Motor Museum, Beaulieu)

Above: This version of the 1000 cc Vincent is the racing Black Lightning, an example of which was timed in the USA at over 150 mph when ridden by Roland Free making it the fastest standard motorcycle in the world at that time. This pictured specimen dates from 1949. (All Sport/Don Morley)

Left: Engine and driveline of the 750 cc BMW R75. (Christian Lacombe)

Right: Claimed by its maker, Kirk D Wright of Arizona, to be the world's smallest rideable motorcycle, this tiny device has a wheelbase of 8 in (20 cm).

The production motorcycle engine with the largest number of valves is the Honda CBX, the 6 cylinders of which each have four valves to give a total of 24. The same number was contained in several Honda racing machines of the 1960s, the next highest number being 20 valves in the Honda 125 cc racing engine of 1965. No other manufacturer approaches this figure, the nearest being Guzzi with 16 valves for the 8 cylinders of their racing 500 cc machine in the 1950s — but that V8 Guzzi enjoyed the distinction of having the largest number (eight) of carburettors and of exhaust pipes for a single engine. In these it is now matched by the 1979 Honda GP 500 cc V4 which has 32 valves above elliptical pistons.

earbox to an universally jointed shaft. The frame as a pressed steel monocoque construction, the eather shielding and foot boards emphasised the ir of gentility and utility already suggested by andlever starting and optional manual gear-hange, and all doubts and distaste were finally ispelled by the machine's virtual silence — which is what particularly endeared it to the olice in subsequent years.

Since 1950, motorcycling has blossomed, died nd been born again. Astonishingly little that was

genuinely new can be identified as having appeared for the first time in the next decade: even the four-valve combustion chamber so brilliantly exploited by Honda in racing after 1959, and the rotary disc valve that wrought similar wonders for the 2-stroke in the 1960s, had been seen before, albeit in ruder and less ambitious forms. There were some important tyre developments taking place in the early 1960s, but the most significant of these — the adoption of high-hysteresis polymers in place of natural rubber to give far better grip on wet roads and abrasion resistance on dry ones, and the development of superior man-made fibres for carcass construction — were inherited from work done on behalf of the car industry. The same applies to the disc brakes which began to appear in racing during the 1960s and in production on the Honda 4-cylinder 750 of 1969. The same indeed is true of most other subsequent developments including electronic ignition, constant-velocity carburettors, automatic transmission, hydraulic brakes, coupled front and rear brakes, tubeless tyres, electronic instruments, and so on. Even the brief use of the Wankel engine by DKW-Hercules, Suzuki, and Van Veen in the 1970s was based on passenger-car developments. Possibly the only true exception to this general rule was the technique employed by Honda, first in the GL1000 Gold Wing of 1974 and then later in the CX500 of 1977, of incorporating into engines with longitudinal crankshafts a counter-rotating mass (alternator or clutch) that would negate the torque reactions and gyroscopic precessions that otherwise impaired the stability of motorcycles with the crankshafts thus disposed.

The most powerful motorcycle in quantity production to date (excluding purely racing machines, which are also produced in quantities by the major Japanese manufacturers) is the 1979 Kawasaki KZ1300-A1, the 6-cylinder water-cooled 4-stroke engine of which develops 120 bhp at 8000 rev/min and has a displacement of 1286 cm³.

The fastest catalogued production road-going motorcycle to date is the 1979 Dunstall Suzuki GS1000CS, road tested by the author at a speed of 154·2 mph (248·2 km/h).

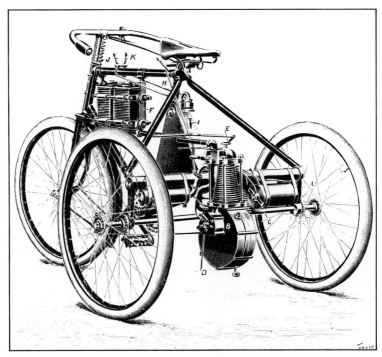

The De Dion motor tricycle, showing the location of the high-speed single-cylinder engine that became so universally popular in the early days of effective motor-cycling. (Orbis Publishing)

SECTION II

PERSONAL ACCOMPLISHMENTS

Johnson — first rider on a hobby-horse. (National Motor Museum, Beaulieu)

In a class of his own, and deservedly number one: Giacomo Agostini on an MV Agusta. (All Sport/Don Morley)

ABERG, BENGT: Born at Bolnas in Sweden on 26 June 1944, Bengt Aberg became world champion in the 500 cc motocross category in 1969 and repeated this success in 1970. He began his rough riding career at the age of eleven on a converted 98 cc Husqvarna and at the age of 16 won his first motocross race at Edesbun. That was in 1960, but progress thereafter was slow and not until 1966 did he win a race of national status. His career prospered thereafter, Aberg achieving his first important victory in 1968 at the Sittendorf course in Austria where he won the first leg and finished third in the second which was won by the then reigning world champion Paul Friedrichs. At the end of the following season, Aberg himself was champion and when he retained his title in the following year it was with overall victory in four of the twelve rounds, the Grands Prix of Switzerland, West Germany, Austria and Luxembourg. These victories were achieved when Aberg was riding a 2-stroke Husqvarna, although many of his early successes had been on a 4-stroke Matchless-engined Metisse. Later Aberg contracted to ride a Bultaco.

AGOSTINI, GIACOMO: Born at Lovere, near Brescia, in Italy, on 16 June 1942, Agostini is one of the very greatest and undeniably one of the most successful road racing riders in history, with no less than 15 world championships to his credit as well as a record of more than 120 Grand Prix victories.

He began his competition career in 1961, riding in hill climbs, entering road racing for the first time the following year when he rode a 175 Morini at Cesenatico. His ability was recognised promptly and he was soon engaged to ride factory-entered Morinis, which he rode creditably against the overwhelming might of Japanese opposition, doing particularly well to finish fourth in his first Grand Prix, the Italian, at Monza in 1963. The following year he won a major 250 cc event at Modena, and in 1965 came his first Grand Prix victory when, for the first time, he rode one of the works MV Agusta machines. This was the 3-cylinder 350 cc model, with which Agostini won the class at the difficult Nürburgring at the German GP meeting. With Agostini's inspired riding, MV Agusta were extremely competitive in that season, and Agostini only lost the championship by four points to Jim Redman as a consequence of a contact-breaker spring failure in the last event of the season in Japan. He also finished in second place in the 500 cc world championship tables that year, but succeeded in capturing the title in 1966.

> The rider with the greatest number of wins in world championship races is the Italian Giacomo Agostini who, in the eleven years from 1965, won 54 Championship events in the 350 cc class and 68 in the 500 cc class to amass a total of 122 victories. His nearest rival is the English rider SMB ('Mike') Hailwood, whose total of 77 is made up of 37 wins in the 500 cc class, 16 in the 350, 21 in the 250, and one Formula 1 TT.

Thereafter he seemed to lead a charmed life riding the MV Agusta entries, seldom against equally redoubtable opposition so that from 1968 to 1972 the 350 and 500 cc titles were his exclusive province. Rivalry only presented itself seriously when the British rider Phil Read was engaged as a team mate for him: although Agostini kept the 350 cc title in 1973, Read took the senior championship from him; and with this exacerbating the already considerable personal rivalry that existed between the two riders, Agostini left MV Agusta for the Yamaha team. For years afterwards, he and Read made great use of the publicity media in fermenting their quarrel — so successfully and determinedly that it looked almost collusive; but in fact Agostini was scarcely more successful in retaining a satisfactory relationship with his Yamaha team mate Lansivuori. This was a period when, encountering stiffer opposition than he had been accustomed to meeting in the past, Agostini became particularly provocative in such contentious matters as the boycotting by top-class riders of the Isle of Man races (following the death of his friend Gilberto Parlotti there in 1972) and the riders' strike at the West German Grand Prix of 1974 at the Nürburgring. He also took an individual stand against inadequate start money by boycotting the Swedish TT; but it would have been a mistake to treat this as evidence of cupidity rather than concern for matters of principle, for by that time Agostini had already raced to considerable riches, invested in a variety of Italian business interests including property and fertiliser manufacture.

Being also blessed with natural good looks, he was able to diversify his activities in other unusual ways: he is the only motorcycle racer of champion class to be a film star in his own right. Money apart, Agostini could afford to be a controversial figure in any case because his riding prowess could never be questioned: he has race and lap records galore to his credit at cirucits all over the world, and in 1975 he recaptured the 500 cc world championship while riding for Yamaha. In the following year he raced that Japanese manufacturer's 750, and also entered a few events with a 500 cc Suzuki, though the season was a confused one for him with rides on the 350 and 500 cc MV Agusta machines as well, not to mention an uncharacteristic excursion for a mature rider into the 250 cc class on behalf of Morbidelli. Already he was talking of retiring from racing however, and within a year he had virtually done so.

ALDANA, DAVID: Born in Southern California in 1949, Dave Aldana is a flamboyant professional racer who grew up in a family of Mexican extraction in which motorcycling was an established activity, his father being a regular motocross rider.

Dave began his competition career at the age

Dave Aldana in 1979. (Orbis Publishing)
Aldana at Brands Hatch. (Orbis Publishing)

of 14, but it was his victory at the Ascot dirt track near Los Angeles in 1968 that confirmed his ability. In the following year he found support from BSA and won the junior title of the American Motorcycle Association. This led to his being graded as an expert for the following year, and he justified it with a string of victories that earned him third place in the AMA national championship and also the top award for the Rookie of the Year. In 1971 he was selected for the American team taking part in the first Anglo-American match-race series, but his lack of road racing experience told against him. Thereafter he rode a Norton as a privateer and was at some pains to improve his versatility, demonstrating his success during the 1973 Daytona week by racing in a speedway event on a Jawa, winning the main short-track event on a Kawasaki, racing another Kawasaki in a motocross event, and finally running competitively in the major race, the Daytona 200 miles epic, on a Norton. Persevering with Nortons, he was top scorer for the American team in Britain in 1975, by which time he had earned the attention of Suzuki who engaged him to support their leading rider Barry Sheene.

Aldana's colourful ways sometimes interfered with his career, however: an official at Houston had him suspended from racing for 60 days for alleged aggressive riding and for some supposed breach of etiquette in having a skeleton painted on his leathers!

ALLAN, VIC: Born in Aberdeen in 1945, Vic Allen began his motocross career by riding a 200 cc Dot at Tain in the north of Scotland at the age of 14, two years younger than he had to pretend to be in order to compete. He was still riding a 250 Dot as well as a 500 Matchless Metisse when for the first time he became the double Scottish champion in 1965, and he took both the 250 and 500 cc Scottish championships again in the following year. Moving to the south of England in 1967 in order to further his career, he became an extremely popular rider sought successively by Greeves, BSA, Bultaco and CCM, and he succeeded in winning the unified British championship (the 250 and 500 cc categories were combined for championship purposes in 1973) in 1974, 1975 and 1976.

Fergus Anderson, 1954 world champion on the 350 cc Guzzi. (Orbis Publishing)

ANDERSON, FERGUS: Tall, shrewd, and a witty writer (he worked as a journalist in Hamburg before World War II), this Scottish road racer spent his peak years in the 1950s living in Italy and riding for Guzzi. His contract with them began in 1950 — though he had raced before the war on a variety of British and German machines — and when he won the 350 world championship in 1953 it was the first time that the 350 class had been won by a non-British machine. He retained the title in 1954 and then retired from racing to take charge of the factory's competition department. He resigned in 1955 on a point of principle and sought to race again, although by now he was 47 years of age. Offered a BMW for the 1956 season, he crashed at Floreffe in Belgium and was killed.

ANDERSON, HUGH: Four times world champion, this New Zealander specialised in racing small-capacity machines. Born in 1936, he began his European road racing career in the early 1960s riding large-capacity AJS and Norton machines, but was approached by Suzuki in 1962 to ride their ultra-lightweight 2-strokes. In the following year Anderson was supreme in the 50 and 125 cc classes, finishing the season as world champion in both. He retained his invincibility in the smaller class in 1964, lost it in the following year but regained supremacy in the 125 cc category — these swings and roundabouts representing phases in machine development by the rival Suzuki and Honda factories. In 1966 Anderson lost both his titles and his taste for racing, which he declared was getting too dangerous, and he withdrew from the scene.

ANDERSSON, HAKEN: Born in June 1945 at Uddevalla in Sweden, Andersson began his motocross career shortly after his 16th birthday, on a 175 cc Husqvarna. Whether impetuous or unlucky, that career was marked by an unusually profuse succession of accidents and serious injuries, despite which he succeeded in winning the 250 cc world championship in 1973, when he won eleven of the 22 races counting in the series.

ANDERSSON, KENT: Born in August 1942, Kent Andersson is the only Swede to have become a world champion in motorcycle road racing. He began his competition career in 1963 only after a serious road accident hospitalised him with a broken back, and persuaded him that he might be safer riding on tracks than on the public highway. Finishing second on a 125 Bultaco at his first race meeting, he made rapid progress and was able to enter his first international event at Oulton Park in England in 1965, winning his first international victory at Mouscron in Belgium in 1966. By the end of that season he was invited to take part in the Japanese Grand Prix (he finished sixth in the 250 cc race) and he impressed Yamaha enough to secure their support for the following season. Maico added theirs for 1969, by the end of which he ranked second in the 250 cc championship tables. This encouraged Yamaha to bring him into their new factory team, riding in support of Rodney Gould, for the 1970 season, but it was not until 1973 that he won a world title, confirming his grasp of the 125 cc championship by finishing second in the Swedish GP at Anderstorp despite a broken leg sustained in a crash at Assen in the Dutch TT. In 1974 he won the 125 cc championship again and finished eighth in the championship rankings for the 250 cc class. In the following winter he went to Brazil for the international series there and emerged overall victor. In 1975 Andersson could do no better than third in the 125 cc championship table, the Yamahas being forced to defer to the new and significantly faster Morbidellis; and when Yamaha offered him a job as a development engineer, he retired from racing in 1976.

ANDREWS, MICK: Born in Derbyshire in 1944, Mick Andrews has an exceptional history as a trials rider. Twice European champion in the days before the series was elevated to world status, he has a particularly outstanding record in the Scottish Six Days Trial, the most important event in the calendar. He was the first rider to win it on a Japanese machine, the first to win it five times in 6 years, the only one to win it on both Spanish and Japanese motorcycles; and in the course of 15 successive years from 1962 to 1976 he scored five wins, four second places and three thirds, failing on only three occasions to finish in the first three places.

He started riding at the age of 14 on a 125 cc James, began to win awards at 16, and a year later became the youngest member of the AJS factory team, riding a 350 cc 4-stroke for the 1961 season during which he won the Northern Experts title and was the youngest ever rider to win a trade-supported national trial, the Bemrose Trophy event held at Matlock. Persevering

Mick Andrews (350 cc AJS) winning the 1957 Northern Experts Trial. (All Sport/Don Morley)

Mick Andrews, later a trials champion, could be seen (through all that mud?) riding in scrambles back in 1962. (All Sport/Don Morley)

steadily in his attempts to succeed in the Scottish Six Days Trial, Andrews began to show particular promise after becoming the first trials rider to use an Ossa machine from Barcelona. This enabled him to establish a minor record of finishing third on three different makes of machine, which he completed in 1968 — the year when Sammy Miller became the first man to achieve five wins and thus beat the existing records of Gordon Jackson and Hugh Viney — the former being one of Andrew's team mates in the AJS team back in 1961. Andrews could do no better than second in the following year which was the last time that a rider (Bill Wilkinson) won the Scottish on a British machine (a Greeves); but in 1970 he won at last. This may have been because Ossa asked him to concentrate exclusively on trials, abandoning the motocross distractions for which he had shown considerable talent over the past 5 years. Concentrating on trials, Andrews kept his success in the Scottish Six Days event of 1970 by also winning the Spanish round of the European trials championship, to the natural delight of Ossa. He won the Scottish again in 1971. Then in 1972, in the course of a season in which he took the European championship for the second time, he won it for the third time to secure only the second hat trick in the history of the Scottish event, which was then celebrating its 50th anniversary. To trace the previous hat trick, it would be necessary to go back almost halfway through that history to the years 1947 to 1949 inclusive, when Hugh Viney did it for the first time. The reward for Andrews was an approach from Yamaha with a contract that made him the highest-paid trials rider of the time, and riding for them he won the Scottish again in 1974 and 1975. A bid for a second hat-trick was foiled by a foot injury in 1976, but he recovered quickly enough to win the 15th Bemrose trophy with the lowest loss of marks in the history of that event.

ASHBY, MARTIN: Born in Marlborough in Wiltshire, England, Martin Ashby earned the nickname 'Crash' as a result of an accident when making his speedway début at Bristol as a 16-year-old, late in 1960. Within another 16 years he had become one of the most reliable and safe of riders, having appeared on over 70 occasions in teams representing England or Great Britain.

For most of his career he has ridden in the Swindon team, assuming the captaincy of it in 1973 upon the retirement of the New Zealander Barry Briggs; but there was an interim period when he rode for Exeter, beginning in 1968 when he became a full-time speedway rider and continuing until the end of the 1970 season. It was during that period that he made his début in the world final at Gothenburg, Sweden, and rode for Great Britain to take the world team cup championship final at Wembly for the first time since the championship had begun 8 years earlier. Riding for the British Lions against Australia in the 1969–70 Antipodean season, he helped to win back the Ashes; and in 1972 he finished second in the British League Riders Championship final, after having rejoined the Swindon team. Later international feats included helping the English foursome win the world team cup for the second successive year in 1975, and heading the English score charts in an unprecedented 5:0 defeat of Sweden in a test series played away.

AUTREY, SCOTT: Born in Maywood, California, in 1953, Autrey became America's top speedway racer after demonstrating his versatility by first becoming one of California's most outstanding scramblers and then proving successful in road racing. Only in the early 1970s was he pursuaded to concentrate on speedway, and by 1976 he had succeeded so well as to reach the world final — the first time that an American rider had competed in it since the late Ernie Roccio finished 15th in 1951. Before that, Autrey had done a good deal of travelling after coming to England to join the Exeter club and gather experience of other European speedway competition.

He also toured South Africa, Rhodesia, Australia and New Zealand in the middle 1970s, but had to return hurriedly to California in 1976 to take part in the qualifying competitions for the top 32 riders of America to find the man to represent America in the Intercontinental final to be held at Wembley. Autrey won through and thus qualified to ride in the world final at Katowice in Poland. In front of a vast and enthusiastic crowd he scored three second places and a third to take ninth place overall, a most impressive world final début showing promise that an American rider might yet be world champion again, the last time being when Jack Milne took the title in 1937.

Double champion in 1978, Ballington. (All Sport/Don Morley)

BALLINGTON, HUGH NEVILLE: Better known as Korky or more recently Kork, Ballington is a South African rider who began his career in his native country in 1967 at the age of 16. From then until 1972 he won national championships in 50, 175 and 500 cc classes and a local 'rider to Europe' award. During his tenancy of this award he did sufficiently well to impress a number of potential sponsors and entrants leading eventually to a place as factory-entered rider for Kawasaki in 1978, when he was rewarded with two world championships, the 250 and 350 cc titles.

BANKS, JOHN: Born in 1944 at Bury St. Edmunds, Suffolk, this English rider began trials riding at the age of 16 and was immediately successful, promptly turning to motocross to seek a sterner challenge and finding success again almost immediately with a third place in the Swiss Grand Prix in 1961 when he was just 17. He has been British 500 cc champion four times and in 1968 and 1969 was runner up in the world championship.

BICKERS, DAVID: Born on 17th January 1938, this English scrambles rider was European 250 champion in 1961, in the days before the title was upgraded to world status. In 25 years of competitive riding all over the world he was consistently successful, and when he announced his official retirement from world championship racing in 1968 (which was not the same thing as giving up racing for fun) he could look back on 9 years in which he had always finished in the first six of either the 250 or 500 cc class.

BOOCOCK, ERIC AND NIGEL: Brothers with distinguished careers in British speedway, their careers ran parallel for many years — they even rode together in the 1970 World Pairs final, to take third place — although Eric was 6 years younger than Nigel who was born in 1937 in Wakefield, Yorkshire. Nigel's first appearance was in 1954 and he had achieved star rating within 5 years, riding for England for the first time in 1960 and qualifying for the first of his eight world finals in 1963. For the first 5 years of British League racing, which began in 1965, his average never dropped below 10·52 and his total points score in league matches was invariably in the region of 400 in each term. Eric's stardom began in 1965, and for the rest of that decade and the early 1970s the Boocock brothers were virtually automatic selections for any English or British team. Eric retired as British Champion in 1974 when he suffered a serious arm injury, Nigel finishing in 1976.

BRAUN, DIETER: Although he made his name in road racing, Braun began his competition career in motocross, in 1962 at the age of 19. The following year he won the area championship near his home at Ulm, West Germany, but he won his first race on tarmac in the following year at Avus on a 350 Yamaha. In 1965 he was runner-up in the German junior championship; an excursion into Formula 3 car racing distracted him in the following season, and he returned to motocross in 1967; but that, too, was brief, and he confirmed his preference for road racing by taking the German 350 championship on an Aermacchi.

In his first Grand Prix in 1968 Braun finished fourth at the Nürburgring and ended the season in fifth place in the 125 championship, again winning the German national title. He rose to second place in the 125 championship in 1969 and took the German 250 championship, finally winning the 125 title in 1970 on a Suzuki with which he won four of the eleven events of the series including the isle of Man TT. In 1972 he was fourth in the 350 world championship and first private entrant in the lists, and in the following year he took that title with a water-cooled Yamaha while also being runner-up in the 250 and 350 classes in 1974. His career was curtailed by severe injuries resulting from a crash in 1976 during the West German GP.

BRELSFORD, MARK: He was born in 1949. Winner of the American Motor Cycle Association's top junior award in 1968, Brelsford emerged at the top of the expert category in 1973, having scored the highest number of points in the 1972 season; but he only carried the coveted number 1 for three races before an accident at Daytona in March 1973 virtually ended his career in the sport.

BRIGGS, BARRY: Four times world speedway champion, Briggs was born on 30 December 1934 in Christchurch, New Zealand. But he pursued his career to Britain in 1952 and after a controversial beginning qualified to race in the world final in every year from 1955 to 1970, winning in 1957, 1958, 1964 and 1966. Although he looked set for another victory in 1972, he was felled by two Russian riders in his second heat, losing his left index finger in the crash. Despite the fact his career was less energetically pursued thereafter he remained popular and competitive. In 1973 he was the first speedway rider to be honoured in the Queen's Birthday Honours List when he was appointed an MBE.

BROWN, GEORGE: The supreme British sprinter of the 1950s, Brown took several world records in the following decade. His motorcycling career began at the age of 22 when he started work for the Vincent factory, in 1934. He became the factory's chief tester and was responsible for much of the development of the successive series of 1000 cc Vincents: the racing version that he built himself (it was christened Gunga Din) was the prototype of the firm's Black Lightning racer. Brown left Vincents in 1951, shortly before the factory closed down. Having found more success and enjoyment in sprints and hill climbs than on road circuits (in all of which he had been active previously), he began to concentrate on sprints in 1953, building himself a special machine from the remains of a scrapped Vincent twin. Calling it Nero, he rode it to take his first world records in 1961, averaging 180·74 mph (290·87 km/h) over the standing kilometre and, with an outrigger wheel fitted to simulate a sidecar, averaging 98·98 mph (159·29 km/h) over the same distance to take that category's record too. In 1964 he was timed at 172·64 mph (277·84 km/h) over the flying kilometre, and with Nero and other machines he took several class and national records as well, notably the 1300 cc flying kilometre at 189·33 mph (304·7 km/h). Reaching his 55th birthday in 1967, Brown was forced to retire from the sport by the age rules of the FIM: when he did so, it was with seven world and nine national records.

BRYANS, RALPH: Born in 1948 in Northern Ireland, Bryans began to concentrate on road racing in 1962. Riding for Honda from the beginning of the 1964 season, he won the 50 cc world championship in 1965.

CAMPBELL, KEITH: The first Australian to win a road racing world championship, Campbell was the last rider of a Guzzi to do so when he took the 350 cc title in 1957. It was only his second year with the Italian firm: he had come to Europe first in 1951, after beginning as a scrambles rider and later taking part in road racing in Australia; but that initial trip was unsuccessful and he returned to Australia, only coming back to Europe for the 1955 season. At the end of 1957 Guzzi, together with all the other factory teams except MV Agusta, withdrew from racing and Campbell had to revert to being a privateer. He was killed in 1958 while racing at Cadours.

CARRUTHERS, KEL: This Australian rider won the 250 cc world championship in the road racing season of 1969, riding for Benelli. Born in 1938, he was the first rider to make his name on three continents, having won championship events in Australia (where he took up road racing in the late 1950s), Europe, and afterwards in the USA where he moved to in 1971. Retiring from racing in 1974, he took over the management of the Yamaha international race team.

CECOTTO, ALBERTO: Generally known as 'Johnny', Cecotto was born in Caracas, Venezuela, on 25 January 1956. On 24 August 1975, at the age of 19 years 211 days, he clinched the 350 cc road racing world championship and thus became the youngest rider ever to win a world championship in any category.

Roger de Coster. (Christian Lacombe)

COLLINS, PETER: Born in Manchester on 24 March 1954, Collins won his first motorcycle race — a grass-track event — at the age of 16 and a year later won the British 350 cc grass-track championship — the youngest grass champion ever. He won it again in 1972 and took second places in the 250 and 500 championships, progressing to speedway which he had first assayed in 1971. He won the British junior championship in 1973, was European champion in 1974 and was world speedway champion in 1976.

COX, DI: The first woman professional racer on the American mile and $\frac{1}{2}$ mile tracks, beginning her serious riding in the mid-1970s.

CRAVEN, PETER: Twice world champion, this Liverpudlian (born on 21 June 1934) was only the second Englishman to win the speedway title when he captured it for the first time in 1955, only 4 years after his career really got under way. A consistently successful performer thereafter, he gained his second title in 1962, but died in the same year from injuries incurred in avoiding a fallen rider. He was then 29 years old — and it was to be another 14 years before another Englishman was to be a world speedway champion — curiously enough a man with the same initials, Peter Collins.

CROXFORD, DAVID: Sometime British 500 cc champion (in 1968 and 1969) Croxford has had a very varied road racing career in the course of which he claims to have needed nothing more than a few stitches despite suffering a total of 189 crashes.

de COSTER, ROGER: Born in 1945 at Brussels, Belgium, de Coster finished fifth in the world motocross championship three times in a row in 1967, 1968 and 1969 when he was riding in the 500 cc class for CZ. For the 1970 season he was moved into the 250 class by CZ, but at the end of that season he was engaged by Suzuki to ride for them in the larger category, and in 1971 he scored the first of five world motocross championships in that class.

DEGNER, ERNST: Born in Germany in 1931, this road racer was the first 50 cc world champion. His most significant contribution to motorcycling was in the development of the 2-stroke, especially in the disc-valved engine developed by the engineer Walter Kaaden in the East German

Ernst Degner with his 250 cc MZ in 1959. (Orbis Publishing)

factory of MZ. Degner was the team's only regular rider and he was undoubtedly very good; but he was more than merely that, and if he did not have the engineering stature of the creative Kaaden he did at least fully comprehend the new science of 2-stroke tuning and was himself an adept practitioner of it. He was thus very precious to the team, especially towards the end of the 1961 season when he led his nearest rival in the 125 cc championship by two points with only one race to go. That race was the Argentine GP, but Degner was not allowed to take part in it. He had chosen the occasion to seek asylum while out of his native country, and while the politicians and diplomats debated his defection his racing licence was suspended, allowing the title to go by default to Honda rider Tom Phillis. As a confirmed expatriate, Degner went to Japan and sold his science and skills to Suzuki, who rewarded him with a 50 cc machine on which he was able to win his title in the following year. His last Grand Prix win was in 1965 when he won the 125 class at Ulster, beating the MZ machines; his last race in the Isle of Man was in 1966 when he finished fourth in the last 50 cc TT.

DEUBEL, MAX: Only the second sidecar pilot to win the world championship four times (after Eric Oliver), Deubel is the only one to have done it in successive years, taking the title in 1961 for the first time and keeping it until Fritz Scheidegger took it from him in 1955. In 1962 he was the first to achieve a sidecar lap of the Isle of Man circuit at over 90 mph (145 km/h). He retired after the 1966 season, having for a second time finished second in the championship tables, to manage his hotel.

DIXON, FREDDIE W.: Born in Stockton-on-Tees, Durham, in 1892, he was very much a hard man, whether it were a matter of taking knocks or taking drink. This tough and colourful character was the only man to win the TT on two, three and four wheels. Dixon, as well known by the initials FW as by the familiar Freddie, began his motorcycle racing career before the Great War, and was particularly associated with Indian and Harley-Davidson motorcycles in track racing at Brooklands. He also had a great deal to do with the Douglas factory, and scored his first Isle of Man victory (in the 1923 Sidecar TT) driving a Douglas combination equipped with a sidecar of his own design, in which the passenger worked a lever to raise or lower the sidecar wheel for right- or left-handed bends respectively, thus banking the outfit and taking advantage of the camber thrust of the tyres. This was typical of Dixon's ingenuity, which was highly respected: he was a gifted engineer, albeit of the type that could be described as an inspired mechanic rather than an academic theorist, and his services were much in demand by Douglas, Brough Superior and others. He rode all manner of machines, winning the 1927 Senior TT on a HRD, but in the 1930s he switched to car racing, being very successful with Rileys, to which he applied the tuning principles that he had learned during his motorcycling career. He died in 1957.

DUKE, GEOFFREY: Born in 1923 at St Helens, Lancashire, Duke learned to ride a motorcycle during the World War as an army despatch rider and afterwards rode in trials for some time before taking to road racing. His clean and stylish riding was immediately remarked, and led to his being adopted by the world's currently most famous racing teams, to his recognition as unquestionably the greatest rider of his day, to his almost universal adulation, to calumny and victimisation, and to an OBE, in that chronological order. Perhaps the most astonishing thing about his career in retrospect, is that it was fairly brief: his rise was meteoric, his decline slower and obscured by the tremendous changes that were taking place in the world of motorcycling in general and racing in particular.

On emerging from the army in 1947, Duke was employed briefly by BSA in their trials workshop before going to Norton with whom he hoped to develop a career as a trials rider. Advised by the journalist Charles Markham to concentrate on road racing, Duke led the Manx Grand Prix on a borrowed 350 Norton until it split its oil tank — but this alone was enough to draw attention to his immaculate style, so that he was described as the most polished all-rounder in the sport — a comment that might be justified by his victory in the Allan trial and fourth place in the international motocross meeting at Spa. In 1949 Norton provided machines on which he won the Junior Manx GP and the Senior Clubman's TT, and in the following year he was given a place in the factory team which was then supreme in the sport. In his first attempts at the TT, he came second in the Junior and set a new lap record while winning the Senior. In the year 1951 he won virtually everything he entered in the world championship series, including the Junior and Senior TT races, in both of which he set lap records and race records. The year 1952 was more difficult, opposition from the Italian teams (notably Gilera and Guzzi) becoming significantly stronger; nevertheless, it was one of Duke's greatest seasons, in which he won both 350 and 500 cc world championship titles again, not to mention the Sportsman of the Year title, the Seagrave trophy, and the OBE. He also made an experimental foray into car racing, driving for Aston Martin, but the venture was not successful, being marked not only by some clashes of personality in the team but also by a bad accident. Angered by ill-judged press comment, Duke allowed himself to be approached by Gilera, with the result that he transferred to that team for the 1953 season and won for them the 500 cc world championship title 3 years in a row. His performance in the Senior TT in 1955 attracted some comment, because although his new record lap was officially announced as 99·97 mph (160·88 km/h), unofficial timing from a different point on the circuit credited him with

Geoffrey Duke riding in the 1957 Scott Trial. (All Sport/Don Morley)

Geoffrey Duke on Manx Norton. (All Sport/Don Morley)

being the first to average 100 mph (160 km/h) around the Island course.

Possibly the greatest upset to his career came in 1956 when he was suspended by the FIM for supporting a riders' strike at the Dutch TT, something that he did on a matter of principle (the start money being paid to the private entrants and less distinguished riders was woefully inadequate) rather than for any personal need. When he returned to racing late in the season his Gilera broke down, in the next race it crashed, and thus Duke lost his grip on the championship. Injury kept him out of contention for much of the following season, at the end of which the Italian factories withdrew from racing and the best that Duke could find to ride thereafter was a some-

what unsatisfactory BMW. On British short circuits he did surprisingly well with some Nortons, but by 1960 his career as a racing rider was finished. In 1963 he returned as an entrant attempting to revive the Gileras by simply bringing them out of storage and setting Hartle and Minter (and later Read) to ride them; but although they did well, the bikes had enjoyed no development in the 5 years of their absence and could not do well enough. Apart from his impeccably smooth and unspectacular riding style and his contribution to the elevation of the status of motorcycle racing, Duke should also be remembered as the pioneer of close-fitting one piece leathers, which he devised to cut down wind resistance.

Giacomo Agostini. (All Sport/Don Morley)

Barry Briggs. (All Sport/Don Morley)

Mick Andrews riding an Ossa. (All Sport/Don Morley)

Mike Hailwood in April 1979. (Orbis Publishing)

Peter Collins. (All Sport/Don Morley)

Kenny Roberts. (Orbis Publishing)

In a brief and unsuccessful campaign with a 500RS BMW, Geoffrey Duke starts in the 1958 Senior TT. The BMW was very powerful and exceptionally fast in a straight line, but its handling left a lot to be desired. (All Sport/Don Morley)

ENDERS, KLAUS: Born at Giessen in 1937, this German rider began racing in 1960, both in solo and sidecar events, and had reached the level of German junior champion in 1963. In the following year he began to concentrate on his sidecar racing, and he entered his BMW-powered outfit in the world championship series for the first time in 1966, finishing fifth in the lists at the end of the season. The following year he was world champion, and he repeated this success in 1969, 1970, 1972, 1973 and 1974. In 1971 he absented himself from the sport, trying car racing as an alternative. He retired altogether in 1976.

EVERTS, HARRY: Born in Belgium in 1952, Everts was junior national champion at the age of 15, a legal impossibility because the Belgian governing body (the FMB) required riders to have reached the age of 16 before competing. Everts, fired with ambition by the great Belgium tradition of motocross riders, simply lied about his age. His potential was quickly recognised, and by the time he was 20 he was regularly finishing so high in world championship placings that he was contracted by Puch to ride for them in their world championship team for the following season. Injuries marred his performance that year, but he was third in the championship table in 1974 and won the world 250 cc motocross championship in 1975.

FATH, HELMUT: The only road racing world champion ever to win a title with an engine of his own design, this German sidecar racer (born in 1929) finished third in the championship table in his very first international season in 1958; in 1960 he won the Sidecar world championship for the first time riding a BMW-powered machine. Sidelined by injuries sustained in 1961, Fath was unable to obtain a suitable engine from BMW when he wished to make a comeback, and so set about designing and building his own. With the technical assistance of Dr Peter Kuhn, he produced a mechanically intriguing 4-cylinder engine of great power and considerable novelty. Riding it for the first time in 1967, Fath proved its supremacy in the following season: on his URS machine (named after his hometown of Ursenbach) he became world champion for the second time, breaking the 14-year monopoly of BMW. His associate Horst Owesle rode the machine to another world championship in 1971.

FOSTER, ALBERT ROBERT: Born in Gloucestershire, England, Bob Foster was an all rounder with grass-track experience, expert status as trials rider, international status as a motocross rider, and an even higher reputation in road racing both before and after the World War. He won the 350 cc world championship, riding a factory-entered Velocette, in 1950, and retired from racing in the following year.

FOWLER, HARRY REMBRANT: Commonly known as 'Rem', Fowler was the winner of the twin-cylinder class at the very first Isle of Man TT meeting, in 1907. Riding a V-twin Peugeot-engined Norton, he averaged 36·22 mph (58·29 km/h). He was never as successful thereafter, though he carried on racing in the Island up to 1911. By no means a professional, he pursued the trade of a toolmaker, and his racing was a purely private venture. One thing he did however have in common with the greatest of modern-day professionals: he shared the same birthday as Mike Hailwood.

FRIEDRICHS, PAUL: Born in 1940, this East German rider won the 500 cc world motocross championship in 1966, 1967 and 1968. He was not only the first rider to be world champion 3 years in succession but indeed the first to win the same title three times since the championships were instituted by the FIM in 1952.

FRITH, FREDDIE L.: The first motorcyclist to be honoured by Royalty when he was awarded the OBE after winning the road racing world championship in the 350 cc class on a Velocette in 1949, Frith was an exceptionally stylish rider with a distinguished pre-war career, the highlight of which was the first TT lap at over 90 mph (145 km/h) in the 1937 senior event. Born (1910) and raised in Grimsby, where he had worked as a stonemason, Frith returned there when he retired after winning his world title, 19 years after taking part in his first road race in the 1930 Junior Manx Grand Prix.

FUNDIN, OVE: Born in Sweden on 23 May 1933, Fundin is the only speedway rider to have been world champion five times. Beginning his riding career at the age of 19, he was chosen by Sweden to represent his country in the world championships in 1954, and since that time he has appeared in 15 world finals, totalling 173 points; from 1956 to 1967 he was never out of the top three in the final, except for 1966 when he did not compete. He won his first world championship in 1956, after having already won the European and Swedish championships, and he won his tenth Swedish championship in 1971 — also a record. In addition he has been European champion, Nordic champion, and the first International champion, this last success being repeated 3 years in succession. After a career of unparalleled success, he retired from the track in October 1976.

GOULD, RODNEY ARTHUR: (Born in Banbury, Oxfordshire, in 1944). The 250 cc world champion of 1970, this English road-racing rider began his racing career in the early 1960s on traditional large-capacity British 4-stroke machines. In 1967, at the age of 23, he began riding a Yamaha 250 and did sufficiently well in his first full Continental season during the following year to earn the support of the Yamaha factory. He won his title by a large margin, winning six of the twelve Grands Prix of 1970 and being runner-up in two others. At the end of the 1972 season he retired from racing to take a position at Yamaha's European headquarters in Amsterdam where he was responsible for their racing operations and for all aspects of public relations.

GRAHAM, R. LESLIE: This English rider was popularly considered unlucky in his native country where he was best known, mainly because of his misfortunes in the Isle of Man TT races. In fact he was reasonably successful in the early years after the World War (he had been a well-known rider on British circuits in the late 1930s), as is shown by the fact that he was the first 500 cc world champion, when the road racing world championships were introduced in 1949. He won his title riding the twin-cylinder 'porcupine' AJS, and was third in the 500 championship table in the following year, as he was also in the 250 listings. During 1951 he was contracted by MV Agusta to develop and race their 4-cylinder 500, and with it he rose to second place in the championship lists in 1952. In 1953 he was killed in a crash during the Senior TT.

GUTHRIE, A. JIMMY: Born at Hawick, Scotland, in 1897, Guthrie was one of the most distinguished road racing riders of the period between the World Wars. In those days there were no world championships, but he did collect the European championship in 1936, which was the highest distinction then attainable. A year earlier he also embarked on a successful record-breaking attempt when he set a new world 1-hour record of 114·092 miles (183·613 km) at the Montlhéry track in France.

He spent much of his long riding career on Nortons, championing them consistently from 1920 to 1937 apart from a year spent on AJS in 1930. In 1934 he won both the Senior and Junior TT races, but the event for which he will probably be best remembered was the 1935 Senior, when he was generally thought to have won and thus to have brought off the double yet again — only to be disillusioned while actually receiving his plaudits with the news that he had in fact lost by a mere 4 seconds to Stanley Woods on a Guzzi. He came close to winning the German GP of 1937 too — but within a mile of the finish, while well in the lead, he crashed at the last corner and died shortly afterwards. In 1939 a memorial to him was unveiled at a spot between the Gooseneck and the Mountain Mile, at which he had stopped when he retired in his last TT.

HAAS, WERNER: Possibly the most meteoric rise to stardom ever seen in motorcycle racing was that of this young German road racer who, in only two full seasons of Grand Prix racing, won three world championships. He was the first German to win a world title and only the second man of any nationality to achieve a championship double.

He began this career in 1952 by winning the 125 cc German GP on an NSU. His earlier rides that year had been on a Puch, but the NSU factory sought his services to ride their new single-cylinder 123 cc and twin-cylinder 248 cc racing machines, beginning at the end of the 1952 season at Solitude. There was one more championship meeting after that, at Monza, where Haas finished second on the 250. In 1953 he carried off the titles in both classes, by a margin of ten points in the smaller and five (ahead of his NSU team mate Reg Armstrong) in the larger. In 1954 he won five Grands Prix in a row on the 250, setting new record race averages at Solitude and the Isle of Man, where he brought the average speed above 90 mph (145 km/h) for the first time in the class. At the end of the season, with Haas once again 250 world champion, NSU withdrew from racing and Haas did likewise. He was killed in an air accident early the following year.

HAGON, ALF: Scrambler, speedway rider and grass-track racer extraordinary, Hagon reached world class in sprinting in the late 1960s. Born in Essex, 1932, he began riding at the age of 15 but retired from racing in 1965. It was then that he began his sprinting career, culminating with a number of world records, including the standing kilometre at 19·1 seconds, riding the supercharged JAP 1260 cc V-twin which he had built and developed himself over the years.

HAILWOOD, STANLEY MICHAEL BAILEY, GM, MBE: Born in Oxford on 2 April 1940, Mike Hailwood can claim the most distinguished career of any competition motorcyclist in history. In a decade of motorcycle racing that began in 1957 he won twelve TT victories and captured nine world championships; and then in 1978, after another decade of virtual absence from motorcycle racing, he made an unprecedented comeback in which he scored another of each title.

His first race was on a 125 cc MV at Oulton Park, where he finished eleventh. Within weeks he had scored his first win at Blandford, again on the 125 MV; and in the following year, after spending the winter racing in South Africa, he embarked on his first international season. This included entries in all four solo classes of the TT, with replicas being won in each: third in the 250, seventh in the 125, twelfth in the 350 and thirteenth in the 500. In 1961 he became the first rider to win three TT races in a week, failing only in the 350 race because a gudgeon pin broke in his AJS when he was leading comfortably, a dozen miles from the finish. In that same year he won his first world championship, the 250, riding a privately entered Honda. His performance in that year earned him a contract with MV Agusta, for whom he rode in the 350 and 500 world championship series until the end of 1965, during which time he took four world titles in succession and set innumerable records: for example in 1963 he broke every lap and race record but one in the entire world championship series. He also set a new record for 1 hour, riding an MV at Daytona, Florida, in February 1964, covering 144·8 miles (233 km). In the afternoon of the same day he won the United States Grand Prix at record speed, also setting a new lap record of 103·3 mph (166·2 km/h) for the 3·8 miles (6·1 km) road-racing circuit there. After winning the 500 cc world championship four times in succession for

Hailwood (4) is still running to get his Norton started for the 1958 TT, while Surtees (3) is already bumping his MV Agusta into life. Surtees won — it was his fifth year in the Island, but Hailwood's first. (All Sport/Don Morley)

Mike Hailwood in his first race, on an MV Agusta at Scarborough. (All Sport/Don Morley)

MV Agusta, Hailwood then contracted to ride for Honda and captured for them the 1966 and 1967 world championships in the 250 and 350 classes, also earning victories in the 250 and 500 TTs — in the last of which, despite the outrageous mis-behaviour of his machine, he set a new absolute lap record for the Isle of Man circuit which stood at 108·7 mph (174·9 km/h) until 1976, when Mick Grant raised it to 109·82 mph (176·74 km/h) on a 750 Kawasaki.

When Honda withdrew from racing early in 1968, Hailwood did likewise, turning to motor racing; and apart from one or two events of minor importance he was not seen in motorcycle racing again until 1978 when he returned to the Isle of Man to win the Formula 1 TT on a Ducati, a success which also carried with it the Formula 1 world championship for the year.

To make such a come-back seemed super-human at the time, and it was observed that his riding style had grown smoother and more polished in the intervening years: he had even cured himself of the habit of sticking his knee into a corner. In 1979, however, he confirmed his apparent superiority yet again in the Isle of Man: after riding respectably in the F1 TT, in which his Ducati was outpaced by the latest works Hondas, he won the Senior TT on a Suzuki RG500A at a record-breaking 111·75 mph (179·84 km/h). During that race he set a new lap record of 114·02 mph (183·49 km/h) in 19 minutes 51·2 seconds, just 3·2 seconds outside the absolute TT lap record set on a 750 cc machine.

For his parting shot, Hailwood rode the 500 Suzuki again in the Open Classic — and failed by

Winner of the 1978 Formula 1 TT, Hailwood on Ducati. (All Sport/Don Morley)

The Honda RC181 racing 500 cc machine of 1966/7. (Honda Motor Co Ltd)

only 3·4 seconds to win that too, from the 998 cc Honda that set a new race record; but he raised the 500 lap record even higher, to 19 minutes 50 seconds (114·14 mph, 183·65 km/h). A splendid swansong.

HALLMAN, TORSTEN: With four world championships and 37 Grand Prix wins to his credit, this Swedish motocross rider has one of the most distinguished records in the sport. Only two riders have beaten his championship record, but none could rival the degree and extent of his successful involvement in the sport. A graduate in engineering from Gothenburg University, Hallman helped to design and build the Husqvarna which in 1962 became the first 2-stroke-engined machine to win a world championship — which it did in his hands. Fifteen years later he helped to design and build the first 4-stroke machine to win a motocross Grand Prix for 7 years, though this time it was ridden by Bengt Aberg. Hallman began competitive riding in trials at the age of 16 and a year later scored his first major success in an international event, winning a gold medal in the 1959 Tatra trial in Poland. Invited to ride for Husqvarna after he had completed his compulsory military service, he won his world championships in the 250 class in 1962, 1963, 1966 and 1967. He retired the following year but in 1971 he was hired as development rider by Yamaha, working first on their 2-strokes but later developing the 500 cc 4-stroke Yamaha with which the Japanese company scored its first motocross world championship in 1977.

HANDLEY, WALTER: With the distinction of having a corner of the TT course named after him (because he crashed his Rudge there in the 500 cc race of 1932), Handley was an outstandingly fast and successful rider in his day. Beginning road racing at the age of 18, he broke the lap record in his first event, the 1922 Lightweight TT, from a standing start. On the next lap he was forced to retire. His later career was studded with successes, as well as more than a few failures, his most remarkable feat being that he scored the first-ever double TT victory in a single week, riding in 1925 for the Rex-Acme team to which he later acted as team manager. He left motorcycle racing for car racing at the end of the 1934 season, but returned briefly to win a Brooklands Gold Star with a new BSA from which the BSA Gold Star model was (in theory, if not in practice)

developed. Handley was killed in 1941 while on active service in the Air Transport Auxiliary.

HARTLE, JOHN: A very fast and consistent rider, notably of Gilera, MV Agusta and Norton machines, Hartle seemed doomed to be eternal runner-up to the prevailing star, most commonly Surtees. In a curious quirk of his career he was killed while riding at the Oliver's Mount circuit in Scarborough in 1968, 14 years after his first major race meeting at the same track.

HENNEN, PATRICK: Born in Phoenix, Arizona, in 1953, Pat Hennen was the first American to win a Grand Prix motorcycle race, doing so in August 1976 when he won the Finnish GP on an RG 500 Suzuki.

HOCKING, GARY: Generally recognised as a Rhodesian, Hocking was born in South Wales, coming to Europe in his 21st year to ride in the Continental circus where he made an immediate mark, finishing sixth in his first event, the 500 cc Dutch GP of 1958. Again the following year he was given a place in the MV Agusta team, riding as second string to John Surtees. At the end of the 1960 season MV closed down the racing department but allowed Hocking to continue riding with factory support, and in the following year he scored a championship double, winning the 350 and 500 cc titles. In 1962, moved by the death of his friend Tom Phillis, he announced his retirement from motorcycle racing after winning the Senior TT, and he returned to Rhodesia where he had been brought up and where he had made his first forays into motorcycle sport, racing on grass tracks. Later that year he was tempted into car racing, and in December he was killed while driving in practice for the Natal Grand Prix.

IVY, W D 'BILL': Born in Kent on 27 August 1942, this bantam of a man was one of the most proficient and provocative road racing riders of the 1960s. Only 5 ft 3 in tall, he was physically very strong and quite at ease on motorcycles of all sizes: whilst his first race was at Brands Hatch in 1959 on a 50 cc Itom, he won the 125 cc ACU Star in 1964 on a Yamaha, and the following year repeated that and took the 500 cc class honours as well on a G50 Matchless. Whilst he was competitive on anything, his small size gave him an advantage on small machines, and it was in the 125 category that he won his only world

Above: Pat Hennen and his mechanic discuss gear ratios in their Suzuki pit. (All Sport/Don Morley)

Left: Bill Ivy. (Christian Lacombe)

championship, riding for Yamaha in 1967. That was his second year in the Japanese factory's team; in his third year he was detailed to win the 250 championship, while his team mate Phil Read was intended to win the 125 title. Read made sure of his programmed success, but then took the 250 title from under Ivy's nose at the end of the season. Ivy then retired briefly from the sport to try his hand in car racing, but returned at the invitation of Jawa to ride for them in 1969. He was killed while practising at the Sachsenring, his engine seizing up on a wet corner while he was riding one-handed and trying to clear his visor. A trophy is awarded annually in his memory, but many people remember little Bill for the controversy surrounding his apparent feud with Read in 1968.

He is perhaps best remembered for what was surely his greatest achievement, the first 100 mph lap of the Isle of Man course on a 125 cc

Bill Ivy winning at Brands Hatch in 1963. Almost alongside him is David Degens (5), later known as the long-distance racer and builder who put Tritons on the map and went on to manufacture the Dresda. (All Sport/Don Morley)

Takazumi Katayama. (All Sport/Don Morley)

motorcycle, which he achieved at an average speed of 100·32 mph (161·45 km/h) in the course of winning the 1968 TT.

KATAYAMA, TAKAZUMI: He was born in 1951. The first Japanese to win a world championship, Katayama — who also has some reputation as a pop singer in his native country — captured the 350 cc title in 1977 riding a Yamaha. His motorcycle career began in 1971, after an unsuccessful foray in car racing, and in the following year he won the Japanese 250 cc title, taking the 350 title in 1973. His international career began in 1974, when he finished the season fourth in the 250 championship.

KESSEL, HENK van: This Dutch rider started racing in 1967 on 50 cc machines, later adding a 125 and eventually a 250, so that by 1978 he had won nine Dutch championships, mainly in the smallest classes. Making his Grand Prix début in 1972, he did well enough to earn a place in the Van Veen Kreidler factory team, and in 1974 he won the 50 cc world championship for them.

KNIEVEL, ROBERT CRAIG: Better known as Evel (he claims to have changed the spelling of his teenage nickname 'because it was an unnecessary evil') Knievel is the best known and best paid, and probably the most injured, of stunt riders. By 1973 his reputation was such that he was able to earn more than $1 000 000 jumping

Evel Knievel. (Orbis Publishing)

motorcycles over a variety of obstacles including cars and trucks; in the following year he pocketed no less than $6 000 000 for an abortive attempt to cross the Snake River Canyon in Idaho in a jet-propelled 'skycycle', a device bearing some remote resemblance to the land speed record machines used on the salt flats in Utah. Except in its garish display, this was an atypical venture: most of his stunts have been performed on a fairly conventional V-twin Harley-Davidson.

Born in Butte, Montana, USA, on 15 October 1939, Knievel had a chequered and not entirely law-abiding career until he found that stunt riding (which had fascinated him since the age of nine) could be sufficiently lucrative. Between 1966 and 1971 he made a total of almost 200 jumps, crashing eleven times and undergoing nine major operations as a result. One of the most signifi-

cant of his ventures was the attempt made before a crowd of 70 000 in February 1970 to establish a new world record for motorcycle jumps over cars. Nineteen cars were drawn up side by side in a row at the Ontario motor speedway in California, and on an XR 750 Harley-Davidson (a type intended as a flat-track racer) Knievel cleared them in a successful and uneventful jump of 43 yd (39 m), setting up a new world record. After the Snake River Canyon debacle of 8 September 1974, Knievel did not jump again until 26 May 1975 when he attempted to clear 13 single-decker buses side-by-side at Wembley Stadium, London, England: he cleared the buses but crashed on the landing ramp, adding yet another case of a broken pelvis to his record of injuries, itself so extensive that he has himself lost count of how many bone fractures he has suffered.

The largest number of people to ride a single motorcycle is 17. This feat was first accomplished in April 1974, when the Huntingdon Park Elks drill and stunt team of California mounted 17 men on a 1200 cc Harley-Davidson. This performance was equalled on 21 May 1976 in Australia at the Sidney Showground, where Police Sergeant Henry Brennan drove 585 yards (535 m) on a 750 cc Honda carrying 13 other policemen and three policewomen.

LAMPKIN, HAROLD MARTIN: One of a famous trio of Yorkshire brothers, all with distinguished records in competition motorcycling, and all best known for their prowess in trials despite having all been successful motocross riders, Martin Lampkin is the youngest, having been born on 20 December 1950. His special distinction is in being the first world trials champion, in 1975. He had already won the European and British championships in 1973, went on to win the Scottish Six Days Trial in 1976 and successfully defended his crown in 1977.

Three Lampkins — Sid, Arthur and Martin — pose outside Arthur's Yorkshire premises with the Scottish Six Days trophy.
(All Sport/Don Morley)

LEONARD, JOE: This American rider was the youngest ever to be the overall motorcycle racing champion of the USA, in 1954 at the age of 19. In 1976 Jay Springsteen came closest to depriving him of that distinction, missing by a matter of four days.

> Daniel Liske of Nebraska rode a 600 cc BMW R60 from northern Alaska to the tip of South America, 95 000 miles (153 000 km), in 6 months; as a sequel he rode 40 000 miles (64 500 km) to complete a longitudinal transit of the Old World, going from the northernmost point in Scandinavia to the southernmost of Africa.

LUNDIN, STEN: The Swedish motocross rider won the 500 cc world championship in 1959 and 1961, was runner-up in 1960, and also has six third places in the championship listings to his credit in a career that began in the early 1950s and officially ended with his retirement in 1969, although he has ridden occasionally since. Born in 1930, he belonged to an era in which large-capacity 4-stroke singles were dominant in the sport, and he strenuously resisted the trend to lightweight machines and 2-strokes in the mid-1960s, demanding instead that the large category be expanded to admit engines up to 750 cc. The FIM conceded by introducing a 750 cc class in 1966, but it was poorly supported and, although Lundin won it in 1966 and in 1967, it never really caught on.

McINTYRE, ROBERT McG.: (Born on 7 November 1928). Riding a 500 cc factory-entered Gilera in the eight-lap Jubilee TT of 1957, this tremendously respected Glaswegian was the first rider to lap the Isle of Man at over 100 mph (160 km/h). On his second lap he raised Geoffrey Duke's 99·97 mph (160·88 km/h) record, set in 1955, to 101·03 mph (162·59 km/h), and on the fourth lap raised it again to 101·12 mph (162·74 km/h), finally winning with four laps in excess of 100 mph. Although his career lasted 10 years, Bob McIntyre was a works rider in only three seasons — in 1954 for AJS, in 1957 as team leader for Gilera and in 1962 when he enjoyed a contract with Honda after being lent a machine by them in 1961. Once again (as in 1957, when ill health prevented him from taking part in the final Grand Prix of the season, with every probability of winning the world championship) his season ended prematurely. So did his career. At the age of only 33 years, and after a number of successes on Hondas that left him well placed for the 250 cc world championship, McIntyre died in 1962 as a result of a crash at Oulton Park where he was riding an experimental Norton. His name was already on the record books: shortly after the withdrawal of Gilera from racing at the end of 1957, McIntyre rode a 350 Gilera to set an absolute world record for 1 hour at 141 miles (227 kilometres) on the Monza circuit, a record which stood until 1964 when Hailwood slightly improved on it at Daytona riding an MV Agusta.

MAUGER, IVAN, MBE: The only speedway rider ever to win the world championship in three successive years (1968, 1969 and 1970), this New Zealander is also alone in equalling the record number of five world championships first scored by the Swedish rider Ove Fundin (qv). Born on 4 October 1939 in Christchurch, New Zealand, he came to London to ride in 1957 after only one season as a novice in his native land, but he returned home in the following year, and it was not until his return to Britain in 1963 that he began to show his true potential. It was in 1966 that he won the European championship and made his first appearance in the world finals, finishing fourth. After completing his hat-trick, his later world titles were won in 1972 and 1977. He also won the world 1000 m long-track championships in 1971, 1972 and 1976. He was awarded the MBE in the New Year's Honours List of 1975, and was only the second speedway rider to achieve this distinction, following his compatriot Barry Briggs who was similarly honoured in 1963.

MICHANEK, ANDERS: Born in Stockholm on 30 May 1943, this Swedish speedway rider won the 1974 world championship by the largest margin ever — four points. His score was the maximum possible, 15 points, while runner up Mauger scored only eleven.

MIKKOLA, HEIKKI: Born at Sajaniami, Finland, in 1945, Mikkola (his Finnish nickname is 'Hessa') began his motocross career in 1964 riding a Husqvarna, winning 14 out of 15 races in his first season. Scoring his first world

Winning the eight-lap Golden Jubilee Senior TT of 1957, the 4-cylinder Gilera piloted by Bob McIntyre was the first to accomplish a lap of the Mountain circuit at more than 100 mph. (All Sport/Don Morley)

Sammy Miller, on his famous 500 cc Ariel (GOV 132) wins the Travers Trophy trial in 1957. Within 20 years, this incredible rider, perhaps the greatest virtuoso in the history of motorcycling, had a tally of victories exceeding 900. (All Sport/Don Morley)

championship points in 1967, he won the 500 cc championship in 1974, becoming only the second Finn in history to take a world title in motorcycle sport, following the example of the road racer Saarinen in 1972. Mikkola took the 500 world title for the second time in 1977 on a Yamaha, after winning the 250 title for Husqvarna in 1976.

MILLER, SAMUEL HAMILTON: Born in Belfast on 11 November 1933, Sammy Miller became the most accomplished and successful trials rider in history. His early competition career was in road racing, which he began to take seriously in 1954; by 1957 his ability was so highly esteemed that he was invited to ride in works teams and finished third in the 250 cc world championship. Dissatisfaction with his position as a member of a road racing team prompted him to abandon road racing and concentrate on trials after 1957; and in a career of passionately concentrated devotion to perfection, he amassed an incomparable collection of awards in trials. He was for eleven consecutive years the British champion and twice the European champion, and for most of his career he has been associated with only two makes — Ariel first and Bultaco thereafter — before retiring from competition to act as a consultant to Honda. (See also TRIALS.)

MILNE, JACK: Born in New York in 1910, this speedway rider had a very long and successful career in the USA, Australia and Britain, travelling and riding together with his younger brother Cordy. The two brothers' careers were almost equally distinguished, but Jack was the only one to win the world championship, and the only American speedway rider ever to do so. He gained the title in 1937, 4 years after his riding began to be notably successful; he only retired in the 1950s when speedway had virtually died in the USA, whither he and his brother had returned in 1949.

MINTER, DEREK W.: Born in 1932 in Kent, this British rider was perhaps the best short-circuit road racing man of his day, reaching his peak in the early 1960s. Particularly outstanding was his mastery of the Brands Hatch circuit, around which he was the first to lap at more than 90 mph (145 km/h). He was also the first rider to accomplish a 100 mph lap of the Isle of Man TT course on a single-cylinder machine, which he did at 101·5 mph (162·62 km/h) in the 1960 Senior

TT, just seconds before Hailwood (who started after him) also produced a 100 mph Norton lap.

MOISSEEV, GENNADY ANATALIE-VICH: Born in Leningrad, USSR, on 3 February 1948, this motocross rider began his motor-cycling career in 1964, turning professional 3 years later and winning the Soviet championship for the first time in 1968, going on to repeat that success in 1972, 1973 and 1976. He won the world 250 title, riding a KTM, in 1974, and recaptured it in 1977.

MOORE, RONALD: Born in Tasmania on 8 March 1933, Ronnie Moore settled in New Zealand after touring with his parents as a wall-of-death rider. He first rode in a speedway event at Christchurch in New Zealand and won his first major title, the South Island's championship, in 1949. In the following year he made his début in Britain at the age of 17, and he made his first appearance in the world finals in 1950 representing Australia; it was 3 years later that he took New Zealand citizenship. From 1950 onwards he appeared in the world finals 14 times, the last occasion being in 1971, and this total has only been exceeded by Fundin (15) and Briggs (18). In the course of his unusually long career, which ended when he announced his retirement in 1971, Moore was twice world champion, in 1954 and 1959; and he has the unusual distinction of having won both championships while injured. He took his 1954 title with a broken leg, fractured weeks before in Denmark and sup-ported by steel braces so that he could con-tinue to ride; and he took the 1959 title while suf-fering a fractured foot. He also took second place in the 1955 world finals riding with a broken collar bone.

MÜLLER, EGON: Born in Kiel on 26 November 1948, this West German rider has twice been world 1000 m sand-track champion, in 1974 and 1975. He has also dabbled in speedway, although without much evident en-thusiasm — despite which he has twice reached the world finals, the first occasion being in 1976 when he was West Germany's first representative in them since 1960. In 1977 he broke the world record for the fastest lap on a grass track with a speed of 135·11 km/h (83·95 mph) at Cloppen-burg, following this shortly with a new world record in speedway with a lap of 81·25 km/h (50·49 mph).

MÜLLER, HERMAN-PETER: This West German rider, born in 1909, was aged 46 when he won the 250 cc road racing world champion-ship and this made him the oldest rider ever to win a world championship in any category. He died in 1976.

NIETO, ANGEL: Born in 1947 in Madrid, Nieto's racing career got on to a proper footing in 1968, although in fact he had raced a motorcycle when he was only 13 years old. A very small man, only 5 ft 2 in tall, he had the lightweight build appropriate to the smallest machines, and it was in the 50 cc category that he made his name. In 1968 he was working as a mechanic for Bultaco, but the rival Derbi factory (also in Barcelona) offered him a Grand Prix ride on their 50 cc racer. Nieto did well enough to earn a works contract for the following year, when he won the 50 cc world championship, the first for Derbi and indeed the first for Spain. In 9 years he won seven world championships, mostly in the 50 cc category but in 1971 and 1972 also in the 125 cc class. He retained the small-capacity title for Derbi in 1970, took the 125 for Derbi the following year and then took both (again for the same manufacturer) in 1972. Derbi then ceased international racing, but in 1973 the Italian firm Morbidelli approached Nieto to ride for them in 1974. The venture was unsuccessful, and in the

Angel Nieto, 50 cc world champion on this tiny Kreidler. (Christian Lacombe)

following year Nieto became a privateer, riding a Van Veen Kreidler on which he again won the 50 cc championship, though he fared poorly in the 125 class on a Bridgestone-engined machine. In 1976 he found himself riding for Bultaco, who had returned to the arena, and he won the 50 cc world championship for them twice in succession, ending second in the 125 cc championship in 1977 and 1978.

NILSSON, BILL: This Swedish motocross rider was the first world champion of the sport, winning the title in 1957 — the year in which the 500 cc class championship was upgraded from its European status.

O'DELL, GEORGE: The first British sidecar world champion since Eric Oliver's last success in 1953, O'Dell won the title in 1977 without winning a single Grand Prix. However, he never finished lower than fourth in any world championship round and thus amassed enough points to defeat his nearest rival that year, the Swiss rider Rolf Biland. Another distinction he earned in that same year was to achieve the first 100-mph lap of the Isle of Man 'mountain' circuit by a sidecar outfit during the TT races: his speed of 102·8 mph (165·4 km/h) involved reducing the old lap record by no less than 52 seconds.

> The record for riding a motorcycle around the continent of Australia — a coast-hugging route of about 9650 miles (15 500 km) is held by Sydney submariner Terry O'Grady, an Able Seaman in the Royal Australian Navy. In March 1979 O'Grady completed the journey in 8 days, 23 hours 57 minutes. He rode a 750 Honda, as did the previous record-holder whose 1977 time O'Grady reduced by almost a day. In the course of his run, O'Grady (who averaged 23 hours riding each day, at one time covering a 40-hours stretch with only one 30-minutes rest break) had to contend with temperatures of 50°C (122°F) and often rode for as long as 4 hours at over 100 mph (161 km/h). His Honda carried a twin-headlamp fairing of the endurance racing type pioneered by Dresda in the Barcelona 24-hours race, and ran on Avon Roadrunner tyres, the rear tyre being changed at two-thirds distance. The machine consumed 231 gallons (1050 litres) of petrol and 6 gallons (27 litres) of oil.

OLIVER, ERIC S.: One of only three British riders to win the world Sidecar championship, Oliver excelled by winning it four times (in 1949, 1950, 1951, and 1953), a feat which was not equalled until Max Deubel scored four consecutive championships in 1964, nor exceeded until Klaus Enders won his fifth title in 1974.

Born in Crowborough, Sussex, England, Oliver began his competitive career in 1931 as a solo rider on grass tracks, but soon switched to road racing. Sidecars first attracted him in 1936, but only after war service in the RAF as Flight Lieutenant did he begin sidecar racing seriously. He was the first world champion in this class, but having established his superiority on conventional combinations of the time he pioneered a new type of passenger machine, being the first to race a fully-faired integrated-chassis three-wheeler with a kneeling riding position; this machine of Oliver's was later to be the first to use a 10-in (254 mm) diameter sidecar wheel.

He retired from competition in 1955, but made an extremely sporting and frolicsome comeback in 1958, when he rode in the Sidecar TT a perfectly ordinary road-going Norton Dominator 88 machine that had been coupled to a touring Watsonian Monaco sidecar in which the passenger, Mrs Pat Wise, remained normally seated instead of clambering about after the fashion of a racing passenger. It was a demonstration rather than a serious attempt to win, but Oliver nevertheless finished in tenth position at an average speed of nearly 60 mph (96 km/h), compared with 73 mph (117 km/h) average of the winner Walter Schneider.

OLSEN, OLE: Born on 16 November 1946 in Haderslev, Denmark, Olsen first rode in speedway events in 1965, winning the Danish Junior championship and finishing second in the national championship in his first year of competition. Coming to England at the end of his second season to gather experience, he made rapid progress, appearing in the world final in 1970, winning the world speedway championship for the first time the following year — the first Dane to do so. In the same year he won the Danish, Nordic and New South Wales titles as well as the Danish 1000 m sand-track championship. It was not until 1975 that he was able to recapture his world championship, though many lesser titles had come his way, and although the world championship eluded him thereafter he was

Former world champion Eric Oliver drives Mrs Pat Wise in a touring sidecar to a respectable tenth place in the 1958 TT. (All Sport/Don Morley)

reckoned to win more trophies than any other rider in 1976 and 1977.

PARKER, JACK: World champion in 1931, this English speedway rider made his dirt-track début on Whit Saturday 1928, riding a stripped BSA roadster. Employed in the BSA company's experimental department for many years, he had been a brilliant trials rider; but as the new sport of speedway or dirt-track racing became established in Britain, Parker built a BSA dirt-track machine that the factory found sufficiently impressive to put into production — and they even built a private dirt track behind the factory, at the very considerable cost of £2000, for Parker's exclusive use in testing each machine as it was finished. As well as the distinction of his world championship and of being the only rider to have his own private track built for him, Parker had many other claims to fame. When he retired in 1953 at the age of 47, having been racing for 27 years, he was still the highest points scorer (with a total of 460) of all those who had ever competed in the test matches between England and Australia. In the course of 5 years beginning in 1946, he defeated no less than 24 challengers for his Golden Helmet match race championship title. For many years he was the Chairman of the Speedway Riders' Association.

Renzo Pasolini. (Christian Lacombe)

The first coast-to-coast crossing of the United States of America on a motorcycle was accomplished by Cannonball Baker riding an Indian in 1921. By 1939 the record time for the trip on a motorcycle was 76 hours, but this was reduced to 52 hours 11 minutes in 1959 by John Penton, who rode a 600 cc R69 BMW from New York City to Los Angeles. His time was checked by Western Union, and represented an average speed of 58·47 mph (94·08 km/h) for the 3051 miles (4909 km) journey, during which he slept for only 3 hours. The imposition of new speed limits subsequently made it legally impossible to beat the record and socially imprudent to claim to have done so; but Captain Brooks Joseph Breece of the US Marine Corps claims a record of 69 hours 45 minutes on a 125 cc motorcycle, a Yamaha RD125, in 1975.

PHILLIS, TOM: This Australian rider won the world championship in the 125 cc class while leading the Honda team in the road races of 1961. It was in 1958 that he came to Europe, but he made his greatest impression only after signing for Honda in March 1960. He was killed in 1962 while racing a 285 cc Honda in the 350 Manx TT, pushing his machine to its limits in an attempt to challenge the MV Agusta machines of Hailwood and Hocking. On his second lap he hit the wall at Laurel Bank.

PILERI, PAOLO: An enthusiastic amateur rider for more than 10 years, this Italian rider born at Terni was approached by the new Morbidelli team late in the 1974 season, and the following year he rode for them with such success that he won seven Grands Prix in the championship series, taking the title in his first full year of Grand Prix racing.

POMEROY, JIM: The first American motocross rider to win a European Grand Prix, Pomeroy achieved this at his European début when he won the 250 cc Spanish event in 1973. Four years later he was the first American to win a US Grand Prix race as well.

Tarquinio Provini wins the 1957 TT on a 125 cc Mondial. (All Sport/Don Morley)

PROVINI, TARQUINIO: Born in 1930, this Italian rider was outstanding among his contemporaries during the 1950s and the first half of the 1960s. He retired in 1966, having begun his racing career in earnest in 1954, and during that period he won no less than twelve Italian championships, a record which remained his until that total was beaten by Agostini in 1972. His speciality was riding lightweight machines, and his most outstanding achievements were on those of Mondial make, 125 and 250 cc racers designed by Alfonso Drusiani. On these he won the 125 world championship in 1957 and the 250 title in the following year.

RAHIER, GASTON: A motocross rider of diminutive stature, the Belgian Rahier was always very competitive but was unable to attain championship status until the FIM introduced a world championship for the 125 cc category in 1975. For this the Suzuki factory built a new machine, the RM125, and they appointed their teamster Rahier to ride it. He was virtually invincible in the class, amassing a sufficiently large points advantage half-way through the season to assure him of the world championship, and he did the same in 1976 and 1977.

RAYBORN, CALVIN: Prevented by the circumstances of motorcycle sports organisation in the USA and by the terms of his employment by Harley-Davidson, Rayborn was seldom able to demonstrate or properly to exploit his exceptional talent as a road-racing rider of impeccable style and exceptional speed. Nevertheless, he was always very highly respected for his talent, not least in Britain when he represented America in the match races of 1972, winning three events and finishing second in another three. His name belongs in the record books, however, for setting a new figure for the world's fastest motorcycle, achieving a two-way average speed of 265·492 mph (427·268 km/h) piloting a Harley-Davidson streamliner on the Bonneville salt flats in Utah. Rayborn's career was cut untimely short by a crash while riding at Pukekohe in New Zealand in December 1973, causing his death at the age of 33.

READ, PHILIP WILLIAM: He was born in Luton, Bedfordshire, in 1939. A road-racing rider with an uncommonly long career and associated with an exceptional variety of machinery, Read began his racing career at the age of 16 on a BSA 350 cc Gold Star in 1956. He made rapid progress, scoring his first victory early in 1958 on a 350 Norton at Mallory Park. In the same year he rode in the Isle of Man for the first time, but it was 1961 before he was to win a TT, the Junior — and this was the last Grand Prix in the Isle of Man for Norton. Read then became a professional and in 1964 became the leader of the Yamaha team, justifying his position by taking the 250 cc world championship. He repeated this success in 1965, 1968 and 1971, scoring a double in 1968 when he took the 125 championship as well, after a year of notorious rivalry with his team mate Bill Ivy, much of which appeared to be deliberately generated for publicity purposes. After Yamaha disbanded its team, Read became a privateer until he was appointed to the MV Agusta team in 1973. Once again he featured in a clash of personalities, this time with his team leader Agostini: Read took the 500 cc championship in 1973 and 1974. Further championships eluded him until 1977 when he was tempted to the Isle of Man circuit (which he had criticised severely in past years) by an offer from Honda to ride one of their machines in the Formula 1 event. He won this race impressively; and since, by a technicality, it carried with it a new world

Phil Read. (Motor Cycle News)

championship title, Read was able to increase his tally of these titles to eight.

REDMAN, JAMES (JIM), MBE: Born in Hampstead, London, on 8 November 1931, Redman emigrated to Rhodesia and was eventually naturalised there. In the early 1950s he began motorcycle racing, and in 1957 he won the South African 350 cc championship, finishing second in the senior championship by only a few points. The following winter he came to Britain, but it was not until 1960, after a return to Africa, that he really reached the highest level of the sport when he was signed up by Honda, for whom he continued to ride until they retired from racing in 1967, when he did the same. Throughout his period with Honda, he distinguished himself as team leader rather than merely as star rider: his approach was an exceptionally intelligent and reasoned one, and he often played the tactician so as to protect a team mate and allow him to win. Nevertheless, Redman himself won world championships in both the 250 and 350 cc classes in 1962 and 1963, as well as taking second place in the 125 championship in the earlier year. The 350 championship also fell to him in 1964 and 1965.

Joel Robert in 1968. (Press Association)

ROBB, TOMMY H.: On a results basis this Ulster man is probably the most successful road racer ever to come from Northern Ireland. Born in 1935, he won his first race at the age of 16 on a dirt track, switching to road racing at the age of 20. After becoming Irish 500 cc champion in 1961, he reached the high spot of his career when he was engaged to ride for Honda in the following year in four classes — the 50, 125, 250 and 350. Twice third in the world championship tables and twice fourth — the last time as recently as 1970, riding a 500 cc Seeley — he retired at the end of 1973 after at last winning a TT (the 125) after two decades of road racing during which he had collected 29 TT replicas.

ROBERT, JOEL: Born in Belgium on 11 November 1943, Robert was the son of a grass-

track racer and made his first forays into motorcycle sport in that same branch, but was soon banned after punching an official. He then turned to motocross at the age of 16 and made such progress that, 4 years later, he was the world champion in the 250 cc class, the youngest-ever holder of the title at the age of 20 years and 8 months. His second world title, again in the 250 cc class, came in 1968, and this success was repeated in 1969, 1970, 1971 and 1972, the last three as a works rider for Suzuki, with earlier ones while riding for CZ.

ROBERTS, KENNY: Born in California, USA, on 31 December 1951, Roberts first raced motorcycles as a 14-year-old amateur. He was AMA Novice champion in 1970, Junior champion in 1971, and Grand National champion in

Eric Oliver, with passenger Stan Dibben. (All Sport/Don Morley)

Don Vesco in April 1979. (Orbis Publishing)   John Surtees in his MV Agusta days. (All Sport/Don Morley)

Kenny Roberts, the first American to be a road-racing world champion. (All Sport/Don Morley)

1973 and 1974. In 1978 he became the first American to win a world championship in road racing, capturing the 500 cc title while riding a Yamaha. He thus displayed a remarkable versatility, for many kinds of racing are involved in the AMA championship series, and when taking his second such crown in 1974 Roberts excelled in all of them, winning every type of event involved. These included the San José mile on a flat track, the Hinsdale short-track race, the Peoria TT steeplechase, and the road races at Atlanta, Monterey and Talladega. The lack of suitable Yamaha machinery with which to challenge Harley-Davidsons on dirt tracks hampered his progress in the following years, but he was noted for leading the United States team to victory over the British in the 1977 Transatlantic series of road races on English tracks.

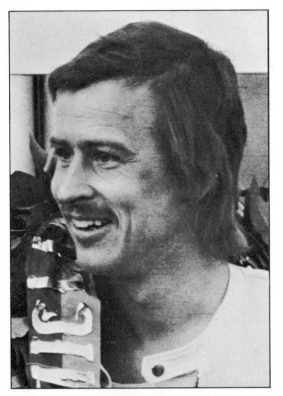

Jarno Saarinen. (Christian Lacombe)

SAARINEN, JARNO: Born on 11 December 1945 at Turku, Finland, Saarinen began his competitive motorcycling career in 1963 in ice racing and later speedway before moving into road racing in 1964. Only in 1967 did he concentrate entirely on road racing, in which his career was brilliant but short. Riding for Yamaha he won the 250 cc world championship in 1972. In the following year he had the distinction of winning the 200 mile Daytona race on a 350 Yamaha against opposition from much larger machines, following this with victory in the 200 mile race at Imola in Italy, where he led for 63 of the 64 laps. The rest of the season followed equally dramatically until he was killed in a crash at Monza, when he had already established substantial points leads in the 250 and 500 cc world championship tables.

SANDFORD, CECIL: A British rider who began his compeition career in grass-track racing late in the 1940s, Sandford rose to fame in road racing after putting in some impressive performances on a 350 AJS in 1950. Offered a place in

the MV team for the 1952 season, Sandford established himself as a highly competitive rider in the 125 category and won the championship in 1952. Not only was he the first British rider to win that title, but he was the first rider ever to win a world championship for MV. He took his second world title in 1957 in the 250 class, riding for Mondial, and this made him also the first Briton to win the title. He then retired from the sport.

SHEENE, BARRY: Born at Holborn, London, on 11 September 1950, Sheene has two or three world championships to his credit: he took the 500 cc road racing title in 1976 and 1977, and in 1973 he won the Formula 750 title, though in those days it was known as the FIM Formula 750 prize, only acquiring championship status in 1977. He also has the unenviable distinction of having survived a crash at about 180 mph (289 km/h): the worst of many such accidents, this happened to him when he suffered a tyre failure on the rear wheel of the Suzuki 750 he was riding at Daytona in 1975. In the widely publicised consequences of this misfortune, Sheene suffered a broken leg, wrist, arm, forearm, collar bone and six ribs as well as compression damage to some spinal vertebrae, a split kidney, and the loss of a lot of skin.

Barry Sheene. (Keystone Press Agency)

Barry Sheene on the RG500A Suzuki. (All Sport/Don Morley)

Cyril Smith with passenger Stan Dibben cornering their Norton in the 1954 TT. (Orbis Publishing)

SMITH, CYRIL: One of only three British riders to win the world Sidecar championship, Smith scored his title in 1952, in what was his first full season of serious competition after starting road racing only 2 years earlier. His previous experience had been in grass-track racing, beginning in 1949, and he retired from racing in 1959, dying 3 years later at the age of 46.

SMITH, JEFF: Born in Lancashire on 14 October 1934, Smith was a motocross rider who was nine times British champion and twice world champion in a career that touched three decades. A motorcyclist from the earliest legal age, he soon became proficient as a cross-country rider, and was contracted to Norton for trials events. After competing in the Scottish Six Days Trial, he

Jeff Smith scrambling his BSA. (All Sport/Don Morley)

Jeff Smith in 1962. (All Sport/Don Morley)

won a gold medal in the 1951 International Six Days Trial at the age of 16. His first British motocross championship was won in 1955, by which time he was riding for BSA, in whose Competitions Department he was employed for 20 years. His first world championship came in 1964, at the age of 29, when he took the title from the Swedish rider Rolf Tibblin in the last round of the season, the Spanish Grand Prix. In the following year he retained the title; his ninth and last British championship was won in 1967, the year in which he finished second in the world championship. In 1970 he was awarded an MBE, the only motocross rider to be thus honoured. In 1972 he emigrated to Canada where he joined the Can-Am Company as development rider. Within 3 years he won a gold medal in the International Six Days Trial on a Can-Am 250.

SPRINGSTEEN, JAY: Born on 15 April 1957 in Michigan, Springsteen began to race professionally at the age of 16 and advanced rapidly through the mandatory years at novice and junior levels so that in 1975 he was qualified to race as an expert, faring so remarkably well that by the end of the year he had reached third place in the AMA championship table. This performance impressed Harley-Davidson sufficiently for them to offer him a full factory contract for the following year. It was an extremely competitive season in which the 28 events produced 15 different winners, but in the course of the year Springsteen won enough events to score the second highest total ever achieved in a single season. This was without contesting the four road races, for which Harley-Davidson were unable to field a competitive machine. He suffered the same limitation in 1977, when he successively defended the AMA title that he had won in the previous year, scoring points in all but three of the 24 events he was able to enter.

STEINHAUSEN, ROLF: Born on 27 July 1943 at Numbrecht in Western Germany, Steinhausen made his motor-cycle racing début on a solo BMW at the age of 18 years, crashing heavily at the Nürburgring and suffering severe facial injuries. A skiing accident later left him with a permanently impaired leg, but his enthusiasm led him to start sidecar racing at the age of 24. Riding a BMW-engined outfit he won the German championship in 1970, the year in which he became a full-time professional. Soon afterwards he began to develop the König 2-stroke engine (made in Berlin for motorboat racing) for sidecar use, and with its aid he won his first Grand Prix at Spa in Belgium in 1974, a year in which he finished fourth in the championship table. The following year he won the world sidecar title (including a win in the Isle of Man TT), and he repeated the success in 1976.

SURTEES, JOHN: The only person ever to become world champion on two wheels and on four, Surtees was born in 1934, the son of Jack Surtees (1901–72), who was well known as a sidecar pilot in British grass-track racing. John had his first solo race at such an event when he was only 15, and although he was worked very hard by his father he enjoyed great encouragement from him. Serving an apprenticeship in engineering with the Vincent Motorcycle Co, Surtees rebuilt and developed a 500 cc Vincent Grey Flash found in scrap condition, and it was on this machine that he won his first road racing event at Brands Hatch in 1951. Thereafter as a privateer on NSU and Norton machinery he had four very

John Surtees aboard a works Norton 500 at Scarborough in 1954. (All Sport/Don Morley)

The MV Agusta ridden in the 1957 Senior TT by John Surtees. (All Sport/Don Morley)

successful seasons on British short circuits, most notably in 1955 when he won 65 races out of the 72 in which he took part. It was in that year that he was invited to join the Norton factory team, but he moved to MV Agusta in 1956 because Norton were winding up their racing programme. He was then 22 years old, and in his first season with the Italian team he won his first world championship. This was in the 500 cc class, and was in spite of a fall which fractured his left arm: the injury and mechanical problems prevented him from repeating the success in the following year, but as he returned to form he became virtually invincible, winning four more world championships and six TTs, and setting numerous records before he retired from motorcycle racing in 1960. In 1958 he was double 350 and 500 cc world champion,

repeating the double in 1959, with the unique achievement of winning every one of the 27 world championship rounds he had contested. In 1960 he set a new record by winning the Isle of Man Senior TT for the third year running. Once again he was double world champion.

In the course of his career he had won 38 world championship events (including seven wins out of seven starts in the senior category in 1959) and he was awarded the MBE for his services to motorcycling. Having been attracted to car racing, which he tried for the first time in 1959, he decided to retire from motorcycling, and he went on to become a world champion driver in Formula 1 car racing, driving for Ferrari, in 1964. In 1969 he formed his own car racing team and only retired from the sport (possibly temporarily) at the end of 1978.

SWAIN, BERYL: The first woman to ride a solo machine in the TT races, Mrs Swain rode a 50 cc Itom in the 1962 event. Not until 1978 was another female soloist seen in the Island, when Mrs Hilary Musson riding a Yamaha finished in the Formula 3 event, immediately behind her husband John riding a Honda.

SZCZAKIEL, JERZY: Born in Grudtzice, Poland, on 28 January 1949, this speedway rider began racing at the age of 18 and won his first national title in 1969. The outstanding achievement of his career was to win the world speedway championship in 1973.

TARABANKO, SERGEI: Born on 25 August 1949 at Novosibirsk, this Russian started ice racing in 1966. He rose to become world champion in this branch of the sport 4 years in succession, the first being 1975.

TAVERI, LUIGI: A Swiss rider with a distinguished record spanning 13 seasons at international level, Taveri was a small man who specialised in the smallest capacity classes but rode larger machines occasionally. In his first international season in 1954 he rode Nortons and a 250 Ducati, as well as acting as passenger to the Swiss sidecar pilot Hans Haldemann. He

Dave Taylor is the most professional and accomplished of stunt riders, and says that doing wheelies (that is riding along on only the rear wheel) for long distances is the most difficult feat in his repertoire. Nevertheless, he has done it all the way round the Isle of Man TT Course; here he is demonstrating the same uncanny skill on the way out of a corner at the Hockenheimring.
(All Sport/Don Morley)

Luigi Taveri, the Swiss rider who scored 30 wins in world championship events in a 12-years career. Of those 30 wins, 22 were in the 125 cc class. (Motor Cycle News)

became a works rider the following year, in the MV team, when he finished the season in second place in the world championship (behind his team mate Ubbiali) in the 125 class and fourth in the 250. He rode consistently for MV and other teams until 1961 when he joined Honda. In the following year he won his first TT and five other events on the new 125 Honda twins to win his first world championship, also finishing third in the first 50 cc championship. In 1964 he took the 125 title again with five wins including the TT (and four second places) on the 4-cylinder 125 Honda. In 1966 Honda produced their 5-cylinder 125 machine and in Taveri's hands it dominated the class, allowing him to take his third title before retiring from the sport.

TIBBLIN, ROLF: This Swede is the only rider to have held both the 250 and 500 cc motocross world titles — though the 250 championship which he won in 1959 riding for Husqvarna was designated European despite the fact that its status was equivalent to a world title. The 500 championship he won in 1962, again on a Husqvarna.

Carlo Ubbiali winning the 1956 Ultra-Lightweight TT on a 125 cc MV Agusta. In that year he also won the 250 cc race on a machine of the same make. (National Motor Museum, Beaulieu)

Carlo Ubbiali aboard the 125 cc MV Agusta in the 1960 Ulster GP. (Orbis Publishing)

UBBIALI, CARLO: Born on 22 September 1929, this Italian rider had one of the most distinguished of road racing careers, with a tally of nine world championships, nine Italian championships, five Isle of Man TT wins and 39 classic Grand Prix victories to his credit in the course of a racing career which lasted from 1947 until 1961. However, he also demonstrated his competence in other branches of motorcycling sport: although he won his first race as a youth on a road circuit, his early enthusiasm was for trials and scrambling, and this versatility enabled him to win a gold medal in the 1949 International Six Days Trial, staged that year in Wales. Ubbiali was offered his first works ride by MV Agusta at the end of 1948, and in the long and respectable career that followed, his efforts were all concentrated on the Lightweight and Ultra-Lightweight classes where his diminutive stature gave him some advantage in riding and was not such a disadvantage on the starting grid. The 125 cc world championships that he won were for the years 1955, 1956 and 1958–60 inclusive; the 250 cc titles were for the years 1956, 1959 and 1960. As well as the MV Agusta, he also rode for Mondial in the seasons 1950, 1951 and 1952.

VESCO, DONALD A.: Born Loma Linda on 8 April 1939, this American rider began road racing at the age of 15 and won his first major road race at Willow Springs, California, in 1959. In the early 1960s he rode in American events for Honda and for Yamaha, but later became more active as a tuner than as a rider. His skills found their greatest realisation in the preparation of machines for record-breaking attempts on the Bonneville salt flats in Utah, attendance at the annual speed week having been a tradition in the Vesco family since 1949. Don's father was a car driver, and Don himself drove frequently there before switching to motorcycles. By 1978 he had captured ten of the 20 streamliner records in categories from 250 to 2000 cc. His principal concern was, however, with the world motorcycle land speed record, the pursuit of which he began in 1969. He realised his ambition for the first time in 1970 after recording an average two-way speed of 251·9 mph (405·4 km/h). This record was taken from him 4 weeks later by the late Cal Rayborn, but Vesco returned in August 1964 with a stretched version of his streamliner now accommodating two 750 cc 4-cylinder Yamaha racing engines, and recaptured the record at an average 281·7 mph (453·3 km/h). In October 1975 he became the first man to exceed 300 mph on a motorcycle, and possibly the first to crash twice at 250 mph. In September 1978 he produced a new Kawasaki with which he raised the record speed to 318·598 mph (512·734 km/h).

VESTERINEN, YRJO: Born near Helsinki, Vesty began to compete seriously in 1969 when he became Junior Trials champion of Finland. By 1975 he had progressed so much that he was able to gain more points than anyone else in the world championship, although he did not receive the title (it went to Martin Lampkin, similarly mounted on a Bultaco) because of the rules which allowed only the seven best scores of the season to count. Vesterinen was undisputed world champion in the following year, and he took the title again in 1977.

VILLA, WALTER: Born in 1943 at Modena, this Italian rider won the 250 cc world championship in the road racing seasons of 1974, 1975 and 1976, the first and only rider to achieve this hat trick in that category. In 1976 he also captured the 350 cc world title.

Walter Villa — one of the handful of world champion racing riders who are also competent engineering designers. (L J K Setright)

Henk Vink, most successful and internationally famous of Dutch riders, an all rounder best known for his drag racing exploits. (Kawasaki)

VINK, HENK: Born on 24 July 1939, he is the holder of an impressive number of sprint or drag-racing records and is generally considered the fastest rider in this branch of the sport outside the USA. Vink is in fact an all-rounder with eleven Dutch national trials championship wins to his credit as well as a record of participation in road racing, motocross and speedway. The son of a trials rider who was likewise a road racer (having won the Dutch TT in his day), Henk started sprint riding in his native Holland in 1969, making his first foray into Britain — where he has competed consistently ever since — in 1972. His mounts have always been powered by Kawasaki engines, simply because he is the importer of that make for Belgium and the Netherlands, and by 1978 his was the fastest single-engined Kawasaki in the world. The year earlier Vink set new FIM records in the 1000 and 1300 cc classes for the standing start $\frac{1}{4}$ mile and kilometre at Elvington in England.

The fastest single Kawasaki-engined drag racer in the world, that of Henk Vink during a visit to Britain. (Kawasaki)

WADE, BRYAN: This motocross rider is the only man ever to win national titles in 3 classes (125, 250 and 500 cc) and is likely to remain so since the ACU, the governing body of the sport in Britain, abandoned the separate capacity classes in 1975. He began riding in scrambles at the age of 16 and so impressed the Greeves competition manager that he was invited to join the factory team as soon as he left school, riding with Dave Bickers, then the European champion. In 1969 he won his first British title in the 250 class, 6 years after joining Greeves; but when they withdrew from racing he switched to Husqvarna on whose machines he won the 250 title in 1971, the 500

in 1972, and the newly created 125 championship in 1973 and again (this time on a Suzuki) in 1974.

WOODS, STANLEY: In the days before world championships, this Dublin-born rider was popularly considered the greatest all-rounder of them all, a winner in speedway, hill climbs, scrambles, trials, sand racing, grass-track and long-distance record attempts. His greatest claim to fame was as a road racer, however, winning nearly 40 international events in the 9 years from 1930 until the outbreak of war. His record of racing on the Isle of Man for 18 consecutive

Not to be confused with Stanley Woods of the same period (nor, for that matter, with the Stan Woods of the 1970s), Stan Wood who rode this Rudge into ninth place in the 1939 Lightweight TT was generally known as Ginger. (Orbis Publishing)

years remains unbeaten, and his ten TT victories have only been equalled much more recently by Agostini and exceeded by Hailwood. He competed in this first TT as a works rider for Cotton in 1922 at the age of 17, when he finished fifth despite a fire and mechanical troubles; his first win came the following year, and thereafter he rode for many different teams. In the four seasons from 1932 to 1935 inclusive, riding first for Norton and later for Guzzi, he scored three TT doubles in the senior and junior races and set five out of a possible six fastest laps. Eighteen years after the war forced his premature retirement he rode a Guzzi around the TT course at 86 mph (138 km/h) in 1957 when the Island was celebrating the Jubilee of the Tourist Trophy.

YOUNG, JACK: This Australian started speedway racing in the mid-1940s, travelling to Britain a decade later and enjoying a scintillating career throughout the 1950s before retiring early in the following decade. Amongst the records he set was that for a record transfer fee (£3750 to move him from the captaincy of the Edinburgh team to West Ham) which was not exceeded for more than 20 years. More noteworthy were the facts that he was the first and only second-division rider to win the world speedway championship, and also the first rider to win it 2 years in succession, in 1951 and 1952.

The longest time during which a motorcycle has been kept in continuous motion is 500 hours. During this time Owen Fitzgerald, Richard Kennett and Don Mitchell covered 8432 miles (13 570 km) in Western Australia between 10 and 31 July 1977.

SECTION III

BRAND MARKS

A Honda 1047 cc CBX ridden by the author.

Ewald Kluge winning the 1938 Lightweight TT on a supercharged 2-stroke DKW. (National Motor Museum, Beaulieu)

Since motorcycling began, there have been more than 2000 different makes of motorcycles (including mopeds and motorised bicycles) put into production, not to mention a fairly large but indeterminable number of one-off specials. Those that went into production on any scale worthy of the word are listed on these pages, in alphabetical order.

The letters alongside each entry are the international code symbols for their country of origin. The nation with the greatest number of makes to its credit is Great Britain, with more than 600; Germany follows next with 445. There are 262 French entries, 249 Italian. In view of the complete domination of the world markets in recent times by the four great Japanese manufacturers, it may be interesting to note that a total of 55 makes are produced in Japan.

Selected and described in greater detail here are some of those firms which have made the most significant contributions to the development of the motorcycle.

Whatever their other claims to fame, this firm deserves credit in these pages for having produced what was probably the noisiest motorcycle of all time. Their supercharged split-single 2-stroke 250 cc racing machine of the late 1930s was so loud, after it had been equipped with a megaphone exhaust system in 1935, that it could be heard all the way around the Mountain Circuit used in the Isle of Man Tourist Trophy races, and could even occasionally be heard as far distant as the coast of Lancashire.

That machine was fast as well as noisy, and once it had also become reliable, by 1938, it was very successful. The new European championships fell to the DKW rider Ewald Kluge in 1938 and 1939, and he also won the title of champion of champions in both years for amassing the greatest number of points in any of the various categories. Thirdly, the machine was also uncommonly thirsty: its fuel consumption averaged as little as 15 mpg — the same as was achieved in 1978 by the larger, much faster, and (with 121 bhp at its disposal, compared with the 30 of the little DKW) vastly more powerful RG500A Suzuki.

The first DKW of 1920. (National Motor Museum, Beaulieu)

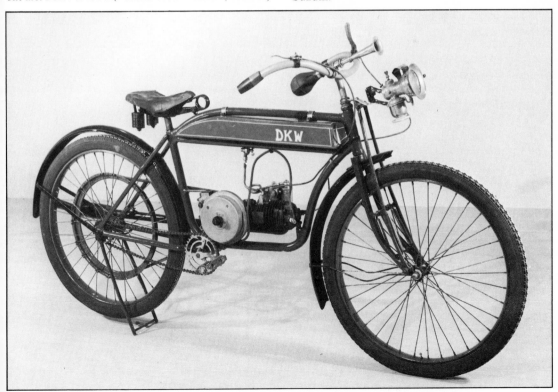

The 3-cylinder 350 cc racing DKW of the mid-1950s developed 45 bhp at 10 500 rpm. It was a very light machine and had outstanding acceleration; interesting features include huge duplex front brakes in leading-link forks. (National Motor Museum, Beaulieu)

The fame and origins of DKW grew from much humbler beginnings. The company was founded in Saxony in 1920 by a Dane named Jorgen Skafte Rasmussen, who in the following year introduced a 122 cc auxiliary engine designed by Hugo Ruppe. This engine could be attached to an ordinary pedal cycle, driving the rear wheel by a leather belt, and it quickly achieved enormous popularity. Within a year 25 000 examples had been sold, and an adoring public nicknamed the device 'Das Kleine Wunder' (the little marvel), from which Rasmussen took the initials DKW as his company's future trade mark. (It is said these initials were originally intended to represent the words Deutscher Kraft Wagen (German Motorcar).)

Established in the town of Zschopau and known formerly as the Zschopauer Motorenwerke, the factory was less successful with its next ventures, but struck a more profitable vein when pioneering a pressed-steel motorcycle frame in 1953. The first piece of outstanding technical pioneering came in 1929 when DKW revolutionised 2-stroke engine design practice by introducing the loop scavenge system that had

been devised by Dr Schnuerle. Characterised by its flat-topped pistons and carefully angled inlet ports in the cylinder walls, the loop scavenge engine was much more powerful, more flexible, and more consistent in its behaviour, than the earlier 2-strokes which relied upon clumsy deflectors on the piston crowns to control the flow of incoming charge. The Schnuerle patents have long since expired, but it has recently been suggested that they were never valid originally — though they were never legally challenged.

At about this time DKW had diversified into car manufacture, and this led to their becoming part of the new Auto-Union group in 1932. A year earlier they adopted the split-single cylinder layout for their racing motorcycle engines, and with the aid of a supplementary supercharging cylinder they became highly competitive. By the late 1930s the factory-entered racers were water-cooled and — as already noted — exceptionally thirsty, noisy and successful.

The ban on supercharging that took effect when racing was resumed after the World War put a stop to further DKW developments on these lines. In any case their wartime activities had been rather different: although regularly bombed, the Zschopau factory built large numbers of simple 2-stroke motorcycles for the German Army. Afterwards Zschopau fell into the Russian sector of Germany, and the factory there was reorganised under Russian control as Motorradwerk Zschopau. This gave the initials MZ under which the firm continued to pioneer new technical developments in 2-stroke engines, introducing with outstanding conviction if relatively little success (the machines were exceptionally fast but seldom sufficiently reliable) the rotary disc inlet valve that had been invented by Dr Zimmerman and was developed at Zschopau by engineer Walter Kaaden and rider Ernst Degner. By 1961 Kaaden had achieved the first unsupercharged engine to yield 200 bhp per litre, in a single-cylinder motorcycle that was the fastest 125 in existence.

Meanwhile the DKW title had been taken westwards to Ingolstadt, where the company was freshly constituted. Despite some valiant racing efforts, notably with a 3-cylinder 350 cc machine capable (with full permitted streamlining) of reaching 140 mph (225 km/h) in the mid-1950s, DKW was not very successful. In 1966 the Auto-Union Group, of which it still formed part, was taken over by Volkswagen the car manufacturers, and the motorcycle division of DKW was severed and disposed of to another company, Zweirad Union, which at that time was producing Express, Hercules and Victoria motorcycles and mopeds. Although this firm is now the largest manufacturer of motorcycles in Germany, its products have seldom attracted much attention, but an exception must be made for a new model that appeared in the spring of 1974. This was the W2000, known either as a Hercules or as a DKW according to the market in which it was sold. What was significant about it was its Wankel engine, the first to be put into production for a motorcycle. This power unit was based on an industrial engine built by Sachs under licence from NSU (also now part of the Volkswagen group) and from a displacement of 294 cc it gave in motorcycle trim 25·4 bhp. Although a very pleasant and well-behaved machine, the W2000 was not a commercial success. Although for its size it was reasonably fast and somewhat thirsty, it was not particularly noisy . . .

The DKW-Hercules W 2000 was a well behaved, but commercially not well received, roadster distinguished by its air-cooled Wankel engine. Although the crankshaft was longitudinal beneath the frame, a conventional transmission incorporating a six-speed gearbox provided for a final drive by chain. (M Decet)

The Ducati 900 Super Sport. (Orbis Publishing)

DUCATI

Although established as a make earning the utmost respect of enthusiastic riders all over the world, Ducati is a comparatively young company that did not embark on motorcycle manufacture until 1950. Their factory at Bologna, Italy, initially built mopeds and ultra-lightweight motorcycles, and in 1951 made a name for themselves by keeping one of their 48 cc machines running on the track at Monza for 40 hours, averaging 39·3 mph (63·2 km/h). Although the company, Ducati Meccanica SPA, prospered steadily, it achieved nothing of note until it engaged the brilliant engineer Fabio Taglioni as chief designer in 1954. Soon they began to produce small-capacity road-going motorcycles of distinctly racy appearance and character, which greatly endeared themselves to Italian riders and by no means disgraced themselves in domestic competition. It was in 1956, however, that Ducati first achieved international fame in racing when the new 125 cc road racing model appeared in the Swedish Grand Prix. It won on its first outing, and this drew attention to a mechanical feature that has since become Ducati's outstanding technical characteristic. The engine had desmodromic (or positively-activated) valves, capable of operation at much greater cyclic rates and with much greater reliability than conventional spring-returned valves. The idea was not a new one, having been toyed with by various motorcycle and car manufacturers since the early 1900s, but although the idea had been proved to work admirably in racing car engines by Mercedes-Benz in 1954, the Ducati was the first successful application of the principle to motorcycles. Such was the speed and reliability of Taglioni's new machine that later in 1956 it took first place in the 24-hour race at Barcelona.

Thereafter the company and its products developed steadily along fairly conventional lines, the machines gradually growing larger and more powerful. By 1960, however, Ducati had to cut back on their racing and concentrate on marketing, which they did very successfully in Britain and the USA as well as at home, but their model programme seemed confused by a plethora of variants and a distinct lack of continuity. The most remarkably atypical Ducati of all appeared in 1966 in the form of a vast and bloated device known as the Apollo: this was a heavyweight high-powered bruiser intended generally for the American market and specifically for the American police, and it was most remarkable for its 100 bhp 1260 cc 90° V4 engine. Perhaps not surprisingly, this 5 cwt machine did not go into production, but it was the source of what has since become the definitive modern Ducati, the high-powered 90° V-twin.

It was in 1970 that the first of this new series was announced, its engine looking like two displaced single-cylinder barrels and heads mounted on a common crankcase, but being also tantamount to half of the Apollo. This original version had a 750 cc engine with valve springs, but before long a desmodromic version appeared, able to run at an engine speed of 9500 rpm and a road speed of 140 mph (225 km/h). It became, not unexpectedly, quite successful in racing, for its handling was of the most distinguished quality, and most of the enlargements and other variants that have appeared since have inherited those qualities. Small-capacity desmodromic single-cylinder engines have also been produced in fair quantities, and even some 2-strokes, but throughout the 1970s it has been the big V-twins that have attracted attention and praise, notably in

endurance racing: in 1973 an 860 cc Ducati ridden by Salvatore Cannellas and Benjamin Grau broke the record for the 24-hours race at Barcelona by no less than 31 laps. A year later, after a very successful season, they won the event again, and continued to do very well up to the end of 1975. Commercially the company had been faring less satisfactorily, however, and it was offered for sale to Count de Tomaso. The technical trends that Ducati pursued in the 1970s looked likely to be continued; such was the remarkable success of a semi-privately prepared and entered Desmo Ducati in 1978, in the hands of SMB Hailwood, that it would seem to be tempting providence to embark on anything else.

Although in existence as motorcycle manufacturers since 1909 under the direction of Count Giuseppe Gilera, this Italian firm's real claim to fame lies in having, in the 1930s and 1950s, acquired and developed and finally proved a design which was the archetype for the modern high-performance motorcycle with a transverse in-line 4-cylinder engine.

When this design first appeared in 1934 it was as the Rondine, but Gilera acquired the rights in it in 1936 and rapidly developed it into a race winner. Its engine was a 500 cc 4-cylinder machine, water-cooled and supercharged and really elegant in its layout, especially in the disposition of the two overhead camshafts. By 1939 it was competent enough to win the Senior European road-racing championship, having already established some redoubtable world records.

The first of these was captured on 21 October 1937 when the Gilera, totally enclosed in a streamlined fairing which also enveloped the rider Piero Taruffi, took the world speed record from BMW, raising it to 170·37 mph (274·18 km/h). Six months later the same rider and machine set a

The flying pillar box — Piero Trauffi's record-breaking supercharged Gilera, timed at 274·181 km/h (170·27 mph) in 1937. (Orbis Publishing)

new distance record for 1 hour, bettering the previous figure by 7 miles to leave it at 121·23 miles (195·10 km). An even more remarkable 1-hour run was undertaken in the spring of 1939 when Taruffi rode the Gilera up and down the Autostrada between the towns of Brescia and Bergamo, 28 miles apart. At each end of the route, the machine was manhandled around to face in the opposite direction (turning it in the road would have been too slow, so unwieldy was the streamliner at very low speeds) and then he set off again. On one run his fuel tank ran dry and he had to coast for the last two miles, but despite all these handicaps the 1-hour distance was raised to 127 miles (204 km).

After the World War, supercharging was proscribed in racing, and the Gilera had to be redesigned. This work was done by the engineer Pietro Remor (later responsible for the very similar MV Agusta), and when it reappeared in 1950 he had made it into an air-cooled engine, its cylinders more upright than before, each with its own carburettor and exhaust pipe and altogether developing 55 bhp at 10 000 rpm. With a five-speed gearbox (most rivals made do with four) the Gilera was immediately competitive on the high-speed circuits, but its handling was not yet as good as that of the popular single-cylinder Norton; development rapidly overcame this deficiency, and at the same time the performance of the engine was steadily increased until by 1956 it was developing 70 bhp at 10 400 rpm and, given competent riding, was virtually invincible. Suitably competent riders were easily found, the most outstanding of all being the Englishman Geoffrey Duke, who joined the team in 1953. Gilera had already captured the 500 cc world championship in 1950 and in 1952 (Duke on the Norton frustrated them in the intervening year when the Gilera riders Milani and Masetti split their team's successes between them) and thereafter Gilera retained the championship until they retired from racing at the end of 1957. During this period they scored many notable triumphs. At Assen in 1952 Masetti's Gilera recorded the first 100-mph lap of the circuit while winning the Dutch TT; by 1954 Duke had raised this further to 105·42 mph (195·24 km/h), a figure which still stands due to changes subsequently made to the circuit. In 1957 Bob McIntyre recorded the first 100-mph lap of the Isle of Man mountain circuit and repeated the feat three more times in winning the Senior TT. Later that same year, McIntyre raised the world record for 1 hour to 141·37 miles (261·82 km) at Monza, riding the 350 cc version of the Gilera.

Thereafter with the firm's withdrawal from racing, the championships that had been its preserve began to fall in steady succession to MV Agusta, machines which inherited the design and the designer of the Gilera and confirmed the essential rightness of the concept. When Honda entered the arena in the 1960s, they did so with machines that conformed to the same basic pattern, which is today the accepted one for any high-performance machine of fairly large capacity.

Today the Gilera company contents itself with the manufacture of mopeds and ultra-lightweight economy and pseudo-sporting motorcycles, but the glories of the racing fours remain untarnished. Indeed, the 1957 team racers were taken out of the factory at Arcore in 1963, after having been in storage for 6 years, and with virtually no development or modification proved to be still highly competitive in racing. It was then that John Hartle put in a lap of the TT circuit which, 12 years later, still ranked as the 12th fastest ever.

500 cc GP Gilera in 1954 trim; tank and front brake were varied according to the circuit. (Christian Lacombe)

R. McIntyre in the course of winning the 1957 Jubilee Senior TT at record speed on the 500 cc 4-cylinder Gilera. (National Motor Museum, Beaulieu)

MOTO GUZZI

No firm in the motorcycle industry has such a long record of making unusual machines and successfully proving their worth, whether in racing or on the road. Like all other manufacturers, they have had their bad times: during the 1960s when a slump hit hard at every manufacturer outside Japan, Guzzi were barely kept in business by dint of their contracts with the Italian army and police, but even then they never allowed their products to lose the inimitable individuality that has always been a mark of almost every Guzzi motorcycle.

The company was founded in 1921 by a former aviator, Giorgio Parodi, and a motorcycling enthusiast called Carlo Guzzi. The Parodi family were rich shipowners as well as keen riders, and put up the necessary capital as well as providing the managerial skills. Guzzi was active primarily as designer until the 1960s, but the most brilliant design work was done by engineer Carcano, who was later succeeded by Tonti.

Seventeen motorcycles were built in the company's first year, in workshops at Mandello del Lario on the eastern shores of lake Como where the company still has its factories today. Those first machines were impressive by contemporary standards and were successful. Known as the Falcone, the design embodied a 500 cc engine with a single cylinder horizontal and facing forwards so that all the heavy components of the bicycle were carried as low as possible, with a three-speed gearbox behind the crankcase. The frame was more rigid than most, and the mechanical integrity of the design combined with the good performance and handling it gave, made the Falcone good enough in its class to win the 1921 Targa Florio race in Sicily. Three years later, when the design was modernised with an overhead camshaft operating four valves (its power output was 22 bhp at 5500 rpm), the

Falcone was the most successful 500 cc racer in Europe.

Guzzi remained active and consistently successful in 500 and 250 cc road races from then until 1940. The smaller machine (of similar layout) made a very impressive Isle of Man début in 1926, though disqualified for a technical infringement of a minor nature; nevertheless, it was credited with the fastest lap. Nine years later the Lightweight TT was won by a single-cylinder Guzzi ridden by Stanley Woods, who broke the lap record despite poor visibility. This was the first TT win by a spring-framed motorcycle (Guzzi had produced an elegantly triangulated trailing fork suspension before 1930) and the first win by a foreign machine since an Indian captured the Senior title in 1911. The very next day the Senior race was again won by Woods, this time on a 2-cylinder Guzzi.

This V-twin was called the Gambalunga (long legged), and first appeared in 1933, being kept competitive by successive developments right up to 1951. Its 2 cylinders were set at an included angle of 120°, the front one horizontal as in the single cylinder 250. In 1933 this engine gave 44 bhp at 7000 rpm, but by the time of Woods's victory it was giving more than 50 and this was the first time that the supposedly magic level of 100 bhp per litre had been reached by an unsupercharged engine — some time before Norton achieved it, though they claimed to be the first and were widely believed.

As supercharging came into fashion for racing in the late 1930s, Guzzi applied it successfully to the 250 Albatros racer, obtaining 40 bhp, and they began work on a supercharged 3-cylinder 500, desisting on the outbreak of war. It was the second time they were unlucky with a 3-cylinder engine: the previous occasion had been in 1933 when they offered a 500 cc triple on the touring market. All 3 cylinders lay horizontal, facing forwards in the Guzzi tradition, but it was an essentially touring design intended to challenge multi-cylinder tourers that appealed to British and American luxury markets: an economic crisis in 1934–35 doomed what had been meant as a fairly costly mount.

After the World War, Guzzi returned promptly to racing with a modified version of the old 250 Albatros in 1948, and when world championships were introduced it took the first of them in the

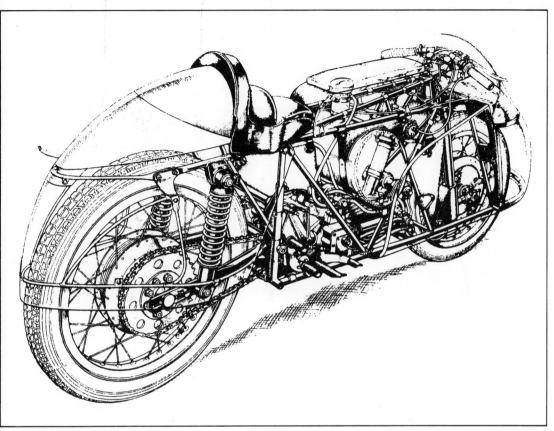

Guzzi Bialbero (twin-camshaft) 350 racer of 1954; note the trellis frame, designed for integration with the fairing. The cylindrical fuel tank was slung beneath the top tubes and steadied in wood blocks. (Christian Lacombe)

In 1953 the Guzzi 500 cc in-line 4-cylinder racer looked like this . . . (Orbis Publishing)

... and a year later it was faired like this. (Orbis Publishing)

250 class in 1949. It was still champion in 1952, and further brilliant engineering development by Giulio Cesare Carcano, spurred on by the shrewd team rider Fergus Anderson, saw the 250 enlarged to a 350 that would capture world championships for Guzzi from 1953 to 1957 inclusive. In its later forms, with the twin-overhead-camshaft engine slung low in a trellis-like space frame designed to exploit the interior of the full fairing, and with the utmost engineering expertise applied to keeping the weight both quantitatively and positionally low, the Guzzi 350 was, despite its antecedents, perhaps the most modern motorcycle ever seen. The whole motorcycle weighed only 216 lb (98 kg), could exceed 140 mph (225 km/h), and was so free-running — the fairing was designed in the firm's own full-scale wind tunnel — that at racing speeds its fuel consumption was no less than 35 miles per gallon (8 litres/100 km).

Its brilliant racing career came to an end with the 1957 season, after which Guzzi retired from racing. This move also put an end to developments of some equally unusual 500 cc machines. The first was an in-line 4, water-cooled and with fuel injection into the inlet ports. Other impressive features were the shaft final drive integrated with the trailing fork rear suspension, and a multi-tubular space frame in which the engine assembly was a stressed part of the structure. The engine lay-out was an impediment to good handling at racing speeds, however, though the bike was fast enough to win the 1953 Hockenheim race at a record 107 mph (198 km/h), and to set a new lap record of 113·27 mph (209·77 km/h). Thereafter the Straight 4 was a failure, but by 1956 Carcarno had created something even more remarkable, a 500 cc V8 engine. No motorcycle engine has ever had more cylinders than this. The eight tiny pistons of the Guzzi had a stroke of 44 mm in bores of 41 mm, with eight 20 mm carburettors criss-crossed in the angle between the two banks of cylinders. There were two batteries, two distributors, four coils, four camshafts (two above each cylinder head), four contact-breakers, and eight separate constant-bore exhaust pipes. In its original form this water-cooled engine was conservatively rated at 62 bhp at 12 000 rpm, sufficient to propel it at over 160 mph; but it proved more flexible than expected, able to exploit a power band beginning as low as 7000 rpm, so the original six-speed gearbox was simplified to contain fewer ratios. The engine was full of niceties: the big-end bearings were plain, the main bearings of rolling-element type, a very

The 500 cc V8 Guzzi racer in 1957 trim. (Orbis Publishing)

rare combination of the two ideal applications. Particularly audacious was the absence of valve seat inserts in the cylinder heads, where the valves seated directly in the aluminium alloy of the castings, evidently without harm — a tribute to the excellence of the cam design. By the end of 1956, this engine was doing 75 bhp at 13 500 rpm and the machine had been timed at 168 mph (270 km/h). Better reliability came in 1957 with a few victories and world records to suggest that it had a great future. Its power output already exceeded 79 bhp at the rear wheel when the 1957 season reached its end, but then Guzzi gave up racing.

Not all its progress was made on the race tracks anyway. Other claims to fame were the sprung frame of the little 65 cc Cardellino in 1936, or the rotary disc valve (anticipating MZ) of the post-war 2-stroke 98 or 110 cc Zigolo. There was even a flywheel on the 175 Lodola camshaft in 1954 to ensure smooth running; and perhaps the most impressive civilian machine of the 1950s was a scooter, the Galletto, which represented one of the most nearly perfect of compromises between the conflicting ideals of a motorcycle and of a two-wheeled car. Built up around a true stressed-skin monocoque housing a single-cylinder 4-stroke engine of 160 cc, it

housed its engine in the horizontal Guzzi tradition that dated from 1921. Successively enlarged to 175, 192 and finally 200 cc, it even ended its career with a dyno-starter, typical of attention throughout the design of the machine to the requirements of the most discriminating and civilised scooter customers.

As times grew hard in the 1960s, Guzzi almost capitulated with a range of dull and conventional-looking machines for the commuter trade and trail riding, about which the most charitable thing to say might be that they were intended for the American market. At home, a quite different class of customers provided the firm's eventual salvation. As early as 1947 Guzzi had been commissioned to design an ultra-lightweight military vehicle, a kind of miniature jeep that could be carried easily by air. Carcarno had designed the engine for this as a lightweight 90° air-cooled V-twin; and when there seemed to be scope for a large motorcycle of touring character and perhaps with military applications, it was found that this engine could readily be installed in a shaft-drive motorcycle frame. Thus the 703 cc Guzzi V7 was brought into being very late in the 1960s; it was soon enlarged to 757 cc, and in 1971 to 850, by which time the engine gave 64

External damper and spring units were a logical and sensible feature of the 1957 Guzzi 500 cc racer; but nobody paid them much attention, so bemused were they all by the brilliant water-cooled V8 engine.

bhp and the bike weighed 510 lb (231 kg). Later it was enlarged even further to 1000 cc and fitted with a semi-automatic transmission consisting of a two-speed gearbox and hydrokinetic converter coupling. Sporting versions were meanwhile developed in 748 and 850 cc forms; this was being done by the designer Lino Tonti, who had been responsible for the Linto racers when he was working on his own. These modern Guzzi machines have been quite effective if never dominant in production and endurance racing; their principal technical distinction is in embodying something which had been done before but had long been forgotten, the coupling of front and rear brakes for simultaneous but balanced operation by one pedal. In the Guzzi system, hydraulic circuitry provides for one of the front discs to be applied in concert with the rear brake, the other front disc being operated by the handlebar lever. Yet, while the Guzzi traditions of idiosyncracy and performance are maintained, the dictates of good commercial management are not being forgotten any more than the history of bad times past: the latest additions to the Guzzi range are smaller V-twins, intended for military or more modest use.

HARLEY-
DAVIDSON

The longest surviving make of motorcycles, and the most characteristically American of motorcycles, the Harley-Davidson name is associated with an enviable list of achievements. In racing of every kind, in stunt riding, in military and public service, and in folk mythology, the make acquired a tremendous reputation; and if its sheer age is its most outstanding achievement, there is also much to be said for the fact that the firm remained a family company for most of its life, which began with the century.

William Harley was a draughtsman in 1901, and Arthur Davidson was a pattern maker. They wanted to motorise a pedal cycle, and enlisted the help of two of Davidson's brothers and a friend named Ole Evinrude who was later to achieve fame as a manufacturer of outboard motors. Borrowing a workshop, they made themselves an engine (according to legend the carburettor was based on a tomato juice can), fitted it to the bicycle, and found that it was just about powerful enough to maintain motion along a level road. Enlarging it to 25 in^3 (400 cc) displacement, they found that it was now adequately powerful but that the bicycle frame was too flimsy to support it; their third prototype had a new frame of their own design, the main tube looping in a cradle beneath the engine's crank case. Carried away by their enthusiasm, Harley and Davidson decided to set themselves up as full-time motorcycle manufacturers. Buying a simple wooden shed measuring 10 ft × 15 ft (3 m × 5 m) they launched themselves as the Harley-Davidson Motor Company — and today those crudely painted words may still be read on the door of that shed, which has been preserved in the grounds of the huge factory in Milwaukee, Wisconsin.

After the first few machines had been made in 1903, the engine was enlarged to 29 in^3 (450 cc),

and by 1906 fifty had been built. Another 100 followed in the next year, during which time Harley took an engineering course at Wisconsin University and the company was formally granted incorporated status. The following year Davidson brought the make its first competition success, by winning the FAM endurance run. Later that same year in an economy trial over a hilly route, the machine he rode averaged no less than 188·23 mpg (1·25 litres per 100 km).

In 1909 came the first V-twin, which set some lasting Harley-Davidson fashions. To this day the make is associated with big V-twins, but for many years it was also respected for its parallelogram-action front forks, which gave leading-link geometry, and which were good enough to be enthusiastically pirated by Brough-Superior and others in Britain in the 1920s and 1930s. Another innovation in the 1909 V-twin specification was the twist grip throttle control — but the years before America's joining in the Great War were years in which considerable progress was made by American motorcycle manufacturers in general in modernising their products, and the twist grip was only one example of this. A spring loaded telescopic seat pillar and a rear hub clutch appeared in 1913, chain drive in 1914 along with optional two-speed transmission; automatic lubrication and a step-starter followed in 1914, a year in which the company set up its own competitions department. Private owners had already been doing well on Harley-Davidsons in the dirt-track and board-track races that were proliferating in the USA, so much so that the firm was able to advertise no less than 23 victories gained in various states on Independence Day, 4 July 1914. A works-supported Harley won the national 1-hour championship, and among 26 victories in 1915 the winning of the 300 miles race at Dodge City was perhaps the most significant. Even more

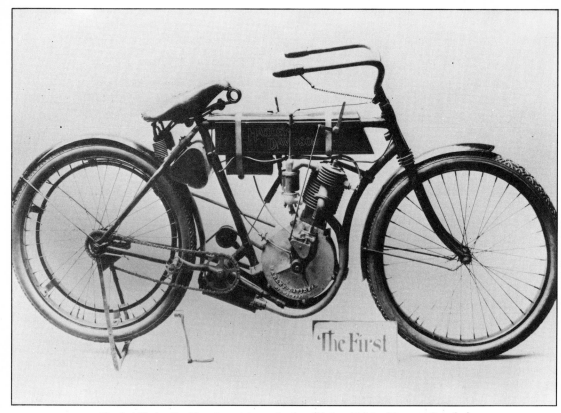

The first Harley-Davidson to go into production. (National Motor Museum, Beaulieu)

outstanding was the setting of a new world 1-hour dirt-track record in 1916, when Floyd Clymer riding a factory-entered Harley-Davidson set the figure at 83 mph (154 km/h) on the Dodge City track and continued to cover 100 miles in 71 minutes. The machine on which he did so was technically very important indeed, a V-twin with four valves in each cylinder head, two exhaust pipes emerging from each pot. Added to a new three-speed gearbox, it made the established 61 in³ (1000 cc) V-twin outstandingly effective by contemporary standards — and indeed for some time afterwards, seeing that eight-valve Harley-Davidsons were very successful in Britain in the 1920s, especially in the hands of Freddie Dixon.

Meanwhile America had entered the war in 1917, and in 2 years Harley-Davidson had provided its army with 20 000 machines as well as some training schools which survived the war for the education of dealers' mechanics. Many of these motorcycles did yeoman service on the western front, and the first American soldier to enter Germany, Corporal Roy Holtz, did so on 12 November 1918 driving a Harley-Davidson with sidecar.

In the first year of peace the firm brought out a new and atypical twin, a 35 in³ (600 cc) horizontally opposed twin with the cylinders arranged longitudinally, a three-speed gearbox built in unit with the engine, and a totally enclosed chain final drive. Electric lighting was standard, and this must have helped one Hap Scherer to set up a new record of 64 hours 58 minutes for the so called Three Flags run, a journey of 1685 miles from Canada across the USA to Mexico. This new little Harley, the model W of 1919, was the smallest to have figured in the Three Flags run at that time, and was only capable of about 55 mph (100 km/h); its record was beaten within a month, but within another month Harley-Davidson had it back with a 1000 cc V-twin ridden by Walter Hadfield, his time being 51 hours 22 minutes. Incidentally, the Three Flags run survives to this day, but because of speed limits and other political or social restrictions it is no longer a high-speed event, being run as a 3 days touring event in which large numbers of motorcyclists take part.

For a while Harley-Davidson continued on their competition programme. An eight-valve 1198 cc twin was sent to England for F W Dixon to race very successfully at Brooklands, where on 28 April 1921 another Harley, ridden by one Douglas Davidson (no relation to the manufacturer), was the first to lap the track at over 100 mph (180 km/h). Dixon captured the world speed record in September 1923 at a speed of 106·5 mph (197·2 km/h) with his eight-valver, but a less officially authenticated record of 112·61 mph (208·55 km/h) had been set up earlier by a works Harley on Daytona Beach.

By 1921 the firm felt that it was devoting too much time and money to racing, and it withdrew from direct participation. It also stopped making pedal cycles and reorganised the factory to give it an annual production capacity of 35 000 motorcycles. These were all V-twins, of either 61 or 74 in³ (1000 or 1200 cc) displacement, and these two

F W Dixon with his special 998 cc Harley-Davidson at Brooklands in 1923. (National Motor Museum, Beaulieu)

Brooklands star, D H Davidson, with a rare flat twin Harley-Davidson. He was no relation to the manufacturers. (National Motor Museum, Beaulieu)

remained their stock-in-trade until 1926 when a little 350 cc side-valve single was added to the range.

It was a timely introduction, for the American authorities began to discourage large-capacity racing machines due to the high incidence of fatal accidents in track racing. Harley-Davidson were able to go with the fashion by evolving an overhead-valve track-racing version of the single, a machine which was to enjoy lasting fame as the Peashooter.

Within a couple of years the Peashooter was supreme in short-track racing, not only in America but also in Australia and New Zealand; and when shale-track speedway was brought from those Antipodes to Britain, the little Harley Davidson was the design that was almost universally followed, with its skimpy telescopic front forks (wheel movement was only about an inch), stub exhaust, single-speed countershaft transmission and complete lack of brakes.

There was not a great deal of refinement in subsequent production models. Most important of these was the 45 in³ (750 cc) side-valve V-twin of 1929, the engine of which has survived with surprisingly little evolutionary development as an

industrial unit almost half a century later. Technical advance was checked as much by hard times as by paralysing conservatism: after the Wall Street slump, virtually the whole of the once extensive and thriving motorcycle industry had disappeared, leaving only Harley-Davidson and Indian in business. Technical advances became slight and superficial, interchangeable wheels in 1936 being the only worthwhile development when new, bigger engines came along from Harley-Davidson, greater size being easier for them to arrange than greater efficiency. The new models of that year were the ohv 61 in³ (1000 cc) V-twin — known as the 'Knucklehead' from the shape of the rocker-box covers — and the 80 in³ (1350 cc) side-valve V-twin. The eight-valvers were long gone, and the new monsters were rough and vibratory horrors, but in isolationist America there was no fear of foreign competition nor indeed much enthusiasm for motorcycles. As to so many other industrialists, salvation came to Harley-Davidson with the war, when the US army chose the 45 in³ Harley side-valver as its standard motorcycle. The factory built 90 000 between 1942 and 1946, together with enough spares for another 30 000. They also designed a 750 transverse flat twin with shaft drive and plunger-sprung rear wheel, on BMW lines,

The 1200 Harley-Davidson FLH, a 772 lb (350 kg) cruiser of which it has been said . . .

William J Harley, Walter C Davidson and William H Davidson pose with the first shipment of 1961 Aermacchi Sprint motor-cycles made in Italy to be marketed as Harley-Davidsons in the USA. (Orbis Publishing)

specifically for the army, but built only 1000 before returning to peacetime construction. This took as its basis a 74 in³ (1208 cc) ohv twin originally designed in 1941, and was supplemented by a 125 cc lightweight 2-stroke which, like the BSA Bantam, was pirated from DKW. It was not a good time for a motorcycle manufacturer in the USA: the car industry was booming, but demand for motorcycles was slight, and such as there was tended to veer towards the more responsive and more manageable products of the British industry. Harley-Davidson kept the threat of imported machines at bay by all available means, procuring for example a revision of AMA competition rules that favoured the domestic product: 750 cc side-valve engines were allowed to compete with pushrod ohv 500 cc machines, and any engine sporting an overhead camshaft was banned altogether. With such artificial aids, Harley-Davidson contrived to remain dominant in national competitions for a few years until they could produce their own

light-alloy overhead-valve 750, which thereafter continued to prosper in competitions that seemed to have been devised expressly to favour it. At the same time the firm continued with its lightweight 2-strokes (they even built a 165 cc scooter), but in 1960 they amalgamated with the Italian firm Aeronautica Macchi, originally aircraft manufacturers, who had been very successful in Europe with their 250 and 350 cc sporting and racing Aermacchi singles. The new firm became Aermacchi-Harley-Davidson, and the Italian bikes were marketed under the American name in the USA.

It was a desperate effort to stay in business at a time when the traditional lumbering American was attracting fewer and fewer customers. The police were the only consistent buyers of the big V-twins, which had taken a long time to acquire such things as hydraulically damped rear suspension. Acquiring bulk was easier, and by the time that the bloated big twin had been given an electric starter in 1965, it had been necessary for the Harley-Davidson Company to become a public corporation, putting an end to the long years of control by the Harley and the numerically greater Davidson family. More defensive measures were necessary, however, and in 1969 the corporation was taken over by AMF (the American Machine and Foundry Group) and production in America and Italy was severely rationalised. Apart from the 750 Sportster, the big V-twins grew more grotesque than ever, while the Italian 4-strokes were dropped finally in 1974. In place of the latter came a new generation of 2-strokes designed by the brothers Villa, one of whom (Walter) was a particularly brilliant rider. From their base in Varese, Italy, their water-cooled 250 cc 2-stroke twin emerged as an im-

mediately successful racer on which Walter Villa secured Harley-Davidson's first road racing world championship in 1974. He repeated this feat in the following year, and then in 1976 he not only did it again but won the 350 title too. Meanwhile in the USA, with motorcycling enjoying a momentous boom in popularity, Harley-Davidson machines continued to dominate most national sporting events (which were still in the main kept incompatible with European or Japanese concepts of motorcycle competition) and with regular attention to drag racing and record-breaking they kept their name sufficiently current to ensure a steady demand for the hulking great Milwaukee monstrosities that seemed destined to go chugging along the straighter roads of America for ever.

Unquestionably the greatest motorcycle manufacturer of all, Honda has a history so richly studded with facts and feats that to deal with them all would require an entire book, and to deal with a few would only give the faintest impression of the greatness that is the truth. The achievements have been noteworthy in every branch of motorcycle sport that the firm has seriously entered, particularly in Grand Prix road racing, endurance racing and, more recently, in off-road events. Their record of innovative engineering is unrivalled in its richness and variety, in everything from engine configuration to production processes. Their record of commercial achievement is so astonishing as to be barely credible, involving a climb from a tiny hut in 1946 to an organisation operating at a sales level in the region of 2 million motorcycles a year together with large quantities of internationally respected cars, industrial engines, cultivators, generators and other petrol-engined products. In all these things Honda have been exceptional and

have deserved the utmost praise; yet their greatest achievement may prove to have been that they repopularised the motorcycle, restoring it to respectability at a time when it looked as though social ostracism was doomed to become permanent.

The story of this phenomenon began in war-shattered Japan in 1946 when Soichiro Honda, an engineer and inventor who had sold a wartime piston ring business, was 40 years old. He came across a consignment of 500 war-surplus 2-stroke engines designed to power communications generators, bought them cheaply and adapted them for fitting to bicycles. The work was done in a little shed, measuring only 12 ft × 18 ft (3 m × 5 m), containing a couple of aged machine tools, but the demand was so lively that, when the war-surplus engines had all been used, Honda decided to continue the business and to make his own engines. The venture prospered enough to justify him setting up the Honda Motor Company Ltd in

Mr Soichiro Honda. (Honda Motor Co Ltd)

September 1948. A year later Honda became the first Japanese manufacturer after the war to produce his own engine and frame in the first of the models called Dream.

The next Dream, the 150 cc E type, was Honda's first 4-stroke 'bike, and it appeared in 1951. By that time he had opened an office in Tokyo and established a factory at Itabashi. Another factory was to follow at Shirako in 1952, the year in which the Honda Cub clip-on power unit was launched, suitable for fixing to the rear wheel of a pedal bicycle. By October 1953, Cub output had risen to 6500 a month, giving Honda 70 per cent of the Japanese market for clip-on power units. The following winter was almost disastrous: having borrowed more than a million dollars to buy new machine tools, Honda was relying on the continued buoyancy of a market that in fact was shrinking because of the end of the Korean war and of the American boost to the Japanese economy that it had prompted.

The company survived, established yet another factory at Hamamatsu, and set about producing more new models. Already it had begun to export: in 1957 two machines had been sent to

Okinawa! In 1958 the export record was even better: two to the USA, two to Holland and one each to England and to Australia. Far more important that year was the introduction of the 50 cc Super Cub, a small and economical lightweight that was easy to ride and attractive to look at. Much more advanced than the crude scooters then being made in Japan, and making no attempt to appeal to traditional motorcycling enthusiasts, the Super Cub created a whole new buying public for the motorcycle, and with it Honda not only prospered but also created a situation in which other manufacturers could do likewise. This little step-through runabout attracted a demand for more than 167 000 in just one year. In less than a decade the total production of Super Cubs had reached 5 million and, by 1974, 10 million.

Meanwhile, Honda had been looking ahead to further developments and further methods of attracting favourable publicity. In 1954 he had visted the Isle of Man TT races as an observer; in 1959 Honda entered those races for the first time, and although the 125 cc twins were hardly competitive on that occasion, they won the manufacturers' team prize.

The Honda racing team returned to Europe in 1960 with an improved 125 cc twin and the first of the classical 250 cc fours. The first really significant result was for Bob Brown to finish fourth in the 250 TT, and that was barely the beginning. In 1961 Honda dominated the world championships in the 125 and 250 classes, mounting the world champions in each class. In another year the 350 champion was a Honda rider too, and so it went on. In just 7 years of international racing, Honda collected 16 world championships and 137 Grand Prix wins, a record without precedent. It included the first Honda 100 mph laps on the Isle of Man in 1964, the 50 cc world championship in 1965, and in the following year truly complete domination of road racing with all five solo classes contested and the manufacturers' titles being won in each of the five, while the individual world champion riders rode Hondas in the 125, 250 and 350 classes.

In the following year, having achieved what they set out to do and won everything worth their winning, Honda very simply and professionally withdrew from racing. They had done it in the grand manner, their investment being enormous, but they had also produced machinery that was

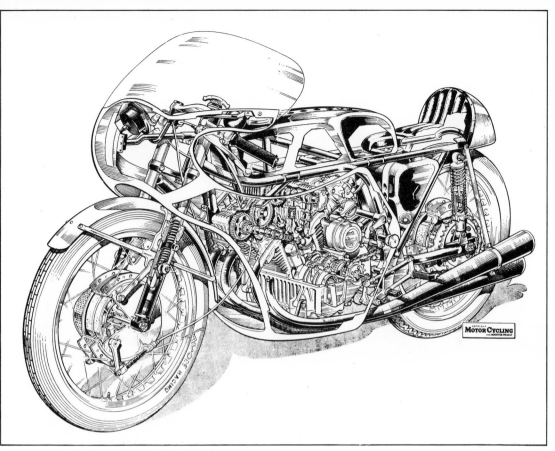

1962 Honda 250 cc 4-cylinder racer. (Christian Lacombe)

Honda's racing 50 cc twin, with caliper/rim front brake. (Honda Motor Co Ltd)

The only in-line 5-cylinder motorcycle, Honda's 125 cc GP racer was safe at 24,000 rpm. (Honda Motor Co Ltd)

to prove immensely significant in the technical development of motorcycles generally. Most noteworthy was their cultivation of the four-valve cylinder head, in pursuit not only of very high rates of revolution but also very high levels of combustion efficiency, combining the two to the greatest extent in the twin-cylinder 50 cc and 5-cylinder 125 cc racers of the mid-1960s. These ran up to 22 000 and 24 000 rpm respectively, and proved to be astonishingly insensitive to fuel quality despite prodigious specific power outputs. The engines were the subject of remarkable papers presented by Honda engineers to various learned societies, in which they demonstrated a level of expertise in engine design and development that had not previously been imagined.

The devotion of similarly cultivated production and commercial skills had by 1963 made Honda the largest motorcycle company in the world, with an annual production running at $1\frac{1}{4}$ million. Their exports were more than 330 000 machines, of which more than 114 000 had been sold in the

USA, where a subsidiary company had been established at Los Angeles in 1959. Now in 1963 another satellite was established in Belgium. Nor was their cleverness devoted entirely to marketing: as early as 1959 the Honda Research and Development Company Limited had been established as a largely autonomous firm deriving its income from a guaranteed $2\frac{1}{2}$ per cent of the parent company's annual turnover.

Even then, Honda motorcycles were technically advanced: when the Dream was exhibited in Europe for the first time at the Amsterdam show of 1959, it introduced the idea that such refinements as overhead-camshaft multi-cylinder engines, built-in electric starters, very efficient silencing systems, and easily-cleaned superstructures, were such as might reasonably be incorporated in quite ordinary everyday machines — and it did not take long for the customers to be convinced. Thus, when total production passed the 10 million mark in 1968, and 1 million motorcycles had been sold in the USA, new

The 1960 Honda 250 cc Dream C72. (Honda Motor Co Ltd)

The Honda CB450 was distinguished by torsion-bar valve springs in the heavy but efficient twin-overhead-camshaft engine.
(Honda Motor Co Ltd)

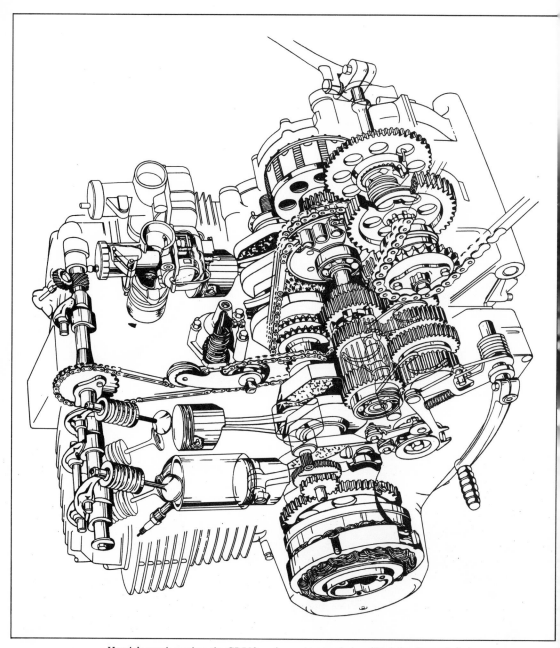

Honda's epoch-marker, the CB750 engine and transmission. (Christian Lacombe)

technical achievements had been ratified in production, such as the torsion-bar valve springs of the powerful CB 450 twin (444 cc) that had been introduced in the mid-1960s as the largest production Honda yet. Little did people know what was coming; but in 1969, a year in which Honda turned out more than $1\frac{1}{2}$ million machines, there appeared for the first time the CB750, the big four that inaugurated the new era of what became known as superbikes, and which set an engineering fashion that became an almost stultifying convention in the 1970s as every other

Archetype of the modern superbike, the CB750 Honda. (Honda Motor Co Ltd)

motorcycle manufacturer wishing to compete with Honda produced machines of essentially the same type.

Those rivals have never yet succeeded in making them in quite the same way. Honda cultivated automated production in a way that no motorcycle manufacturer ever matched. Machines did most of the work, and the uniform of white overalls and peaked cap (the racing team mechanics used also to wear white cotton gloves) worn by all the workers emphasized the clean, clinical and scientifically business-like attitude to the making of machinery. A measure of Honda's achievement in this respect was the unrivalled productivity of their Japanese factories, which produced over 300 motorcycles per man-year, approximately twice as many as any of their rivals in the industry.

Having made motorcycling a clean and sanitary, even smart and fashionable activity at every level from the factory floor to the High Street, Honda deserved to profit from the boom in the popularity of motorcycling in the 1970s. It needed only a little effort in sporting competition to remind the public of the past glories of Honda in this regard, and the magnificent CB750 provided the vehicle for the task. A specially prepared one was the winner of the 1970 Daytona 200 miles race, one of the world's most important in terms of commercial and sporting prestige. In Europe, another 750 won the 24-hours race for the Bol d'Or, the French event that was by far the most important of the long-distance races that were slowly beginning to attract enthusiastic interest throughout Europe. Postponing a return to Grand Prix road racing until late 1979, Honda chose instead to improve their representation in off-road events, mainly because of the vast market that they influenced in the USA. Thus in motocross and trials their activities increased rapidly in the mid-1970s so that in 1975 the American National Trials Championship was won for Honda by the young American rider Marland Whaley, and another US national title was won in motocross. Back in Europe, modified

The Honda GL1000 Gold Wing. (Honda Motor Co Ltd)

4-cylinder production Hondas took the first six places in the 500 cc Production TT in that same year, while in the two previous years a 750 had won the 24-hours race on the Spa circuit near Liège, the fastest pure road-racing course in the world. Honda's success was more truly worldwide than ever, so extensive that new subsidiaries were established in Switzerland and Peru. In less than three decades, the name had become globally famous — but it was time for Mr Honda himself to rest a little from his perpetual exertions, and so in 1973 he took office as Supreme Adviser to the company, leaving the day-to-day administration to others, just as he had long been content to share the commercial direction of the company with the brilliant salesman Takeo Fujisawa.

Supposedly conceived as a tribute to him, the Honda GL 1000 Gold Wing appeared as the new flagship of the Honda motorcycle range in 1974, and attained a level of engineering elegance beyond any that had ever previously been displayed. Essentially a heavyweight high-speed tourer, the Gold Wing was built around a unique water-cooled overhead-camshaft flat four engine of exquisite detail design, uncanny quietness and utterly convincing power. Allied to shaft drive and a new large-section 17-in (nearly 432 mm) rear tyre upon which alone a prodigious sum of money had been spent in development, this driveline was installed in a lavishly braked and comprehensively furnished chassis in which the distribution of masses was so carefully studied that the petrol tank was moved from its conventional location (where a dummy remained to contain electrical equipment and storage space) to a better site under the seat. Nevertheless, the most important feature of the whole Gold Wing was the counter-rotating alternator, carefully arranged to balance out all the gyroscopic precessions and torque reactions that otherwise result from an engine with a longitudinal crankshaft and impair the handling and stability of the bicycle as was the case in rival designs with their engines thus disposed.

It was the first of a whole new series of technically adventurous motorcycles, which appeared in a spate of 18 models in as many months in the late 1970s, introducing advanced new counterbalancing systems, ingenious and effective electronic ignition, three- and four-valve cylinder heads, water-cooled V-twin engines, constant-depression carburettors, tubeless tyres, and lightweight composite-construction wheels. Many of these developments were proved in endurance racing, a branch of motorcycle sport into which Honda flung themselves with enthusiasm in 1976, utterly dominating it in that and the following two seasons with 4-cylinder 1000 cc machines. They had a fairly conventional layout but incorporated twin overhead camshafts and four valves per cylinder, not to mention some subtly perfected suspension and steering geometries and some admirably effective exhaust and silencing systems. These RCB racers evidently acted as test beds for ideas that were incorporated in the new range of 750 and 900 cc 4-cylinder Hondas which appeared in 1978; but although they were enthusiastically received they made nothing like the same impact as the dramatically handsome, expansive, expensive and exquisite 6-cylinder 1047 Honda CBX which made its appearance at the beginning of that same year and immediately ranked as the fastest and most refined in behaviour of all the world's production motorcycles. Rival manufacturers (notably Suzuki) have contrived to claim higher speeds for production motorcycles, by arranging for an outside customising and tuning specialist to market on their behalf specially prepared large-capacity machines that in tuned form can outstrip the standard CBX; and if Honda choose to do the same, no doubt the title of the world's fastest production motorcycle will move again.

Stan Woods aboard a Honda RCB endurance racer. (All Sport/Don Morley)

The author aboard the 6-cylinder Honda CBX.

This 5 hp Indian featured a sliding-pinion gearbox in 1909. (National Motor Museum, Beaulieu)

In the first decades of the century the American motorcycle industry was thriving, and in many respects more advanced in its engineering than were the majority of European manufacturers. Outstanding among them at this time was the firm which was known by its Indian trade mark, although the company's original title was the Hendee Manufacturing Company. Famous around the world for their big V-twin motorcycles, this Massachusetts firm enjoyed a half-century of international popularity before succumbing to financial distress after World War II. They began as cycle manufacturers until the proprietor George M. Hendee, who had been impressed by a De Dion-engined pacing motorcycle at the Madison Square cycle track in 1900, approached its builder and invited him to motorise one of his Indian pedal cycles. The builder's name was Oscar Hedstrom, and as time went by he played an increasingly important part in the design of the motorcycles that Hendee set about producing. His first adaptation of an Indian bicycle was a great success, the sales rising from three in 1901 to 546 machines 3 years later. In 1905 Hedstrom produced the first Indian V-twin, and 5 years later a new two-speed gearbox was adopted, together with the red finish that was thereafter the standard Indian colour. In 1911 a team of 585 cc two-speeders were sent to Europe, scoring an historic 1-2-3 victory in the Isle of Man TT race — the first and for a long time the only foreign success in the Island. In 1913 Indian went further with a spring frame, and in 1914 led the world with the installation of electric lighting and the world's first electric starter (which also doubled as a generator charging two batteries) in their big 61 in^3 (998 cc) twin-cylinder motorcycle variously called the Hendee or the Electric Special. It was the pride of their catalogue, the full range of their machines accounting for an output approaching 60 000 a year.

Further developments took place during the Great War after which a famous and long-lived new model, the 596 cc Scout, was introduced, designed by an Irishman called C B Franklyn. Later models were widely used by the American police, and Indians also enjoyed tremendous successes in domestic racing. In Europe, Herbert Le Vack won the Brooklands 500 miles race in 1921 on an Indian, the road race from Milan to Naples was won by Indian-mounted Italian riders in 1920 and 1921, and F W Dixon on a 500 cc Indian single won the Belgian Grand Prix of 1923. In record breaking, the Indian saga began with the American E. Walker claiming the world's motorcycle speed record in 1920 at 104·12 mph (167·56 km/h) on Daytona Beach, riding a 994 cc V-twin. In 1925 the Australian P. Anderson reached 125 mph (201 km/h) and a year later J. Seymour was timed at 132 mph (212 km/h) at Daytona.

Between 1927 and 1941 the design of Indians stagnated, and although the purchase of the Ace company and the revival of the once famous Ace 4-cylinder 1265 cc motorcycle was hoped to maintain the company's commercial stability, their fortunes waned. Various efforts to adopt sundry inept designs from other sources in the years after the World War did the ailing Indian company no good at all, and the last true Indian motorcycle was completed in 1953. Thereafter the name was merely a property that passed from hand to hand with very little hardware or reputation to accompany it.

The American rider T K (Teddy) Hastings with his 4 Indian twin taking part in the 1907 Auto Cycle Club 1(Miles Trial, which started from Hatfield. He is here check in at Whitchurch, near Ross-on-Wye: on the left is ti keeper A G Reynolds, next to him ACC timekeeper J W Brooker, and on the right is W H Wells who was compet on a Viridec but was to become the British importer Indian motor cycles and make them the most success foreign make on the British market in the early part of century. (National Motor Museum, Beaulieu)

Kawasaki

The history of Kawasaki bears little resemblance to that of any other current major motorcycle manufacturer, and contrasts strongly with those of the other great Japanese firms. The Honda story is a classic rags-to-riches romance, that of Suzuki a matter of urgently finding something profitable to do, that of Yamaha being one of steady evolutionary diversification. Kawasaki, however, making its first motorcycle to carry the name exclusively as late as 1962, and not creating its largely autonomous motorcycle division until 1968, had been a big and powerful organisation for a very long time. Their origins go back to 1878 when Shozo Kawasaki founded a dockyard in Tokyo. Rapid expansion made Kawasaki Heavy Industries wealthy and successful, versed in the technology of locomotives, supertankers, aircraft and steel. It was only with the decline in aviation business after World War II that they turned to the making of motorcycle engines, small ones that were supplied to many of the then numerous Japanese motorcycle manufacturers

— one of whom, Meihatsu, was in fact a Kawasaki subsidiary. In 1961 the Kawasaki name was substituted for that of Meihatsu, while Japan's oldest motorcycle manufacturer, Meguro, was taken over in order to secure its marketing outlets. It was a move that was typical of Kawasaki's attitude to motorcycle production ever since: the emphasis has always been on commercially stern and aggressive marketing, with few concessions to motorcycling enthusiasts within the organisation and every possible advantage taken of enthusiasts without. The number of records broken, of races won and events dominated by the name of Kawasaki may be found on examination to consist largely of cases where the engine and gearbox were all that the Japanese factory made, the rest being produced by individuals or small specialist manufacturers. From the very beginning, engines have been Kawasaki's strong point.

Sometimes they were almost too strong: the machine that really brought the name into focus

The 3-cylinder 2-stroke Kawasaki 500 H1D. (Kawasaki)

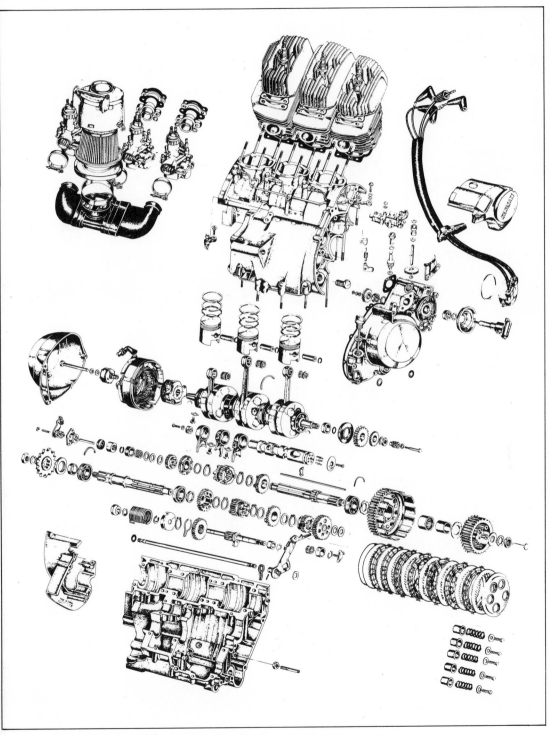

Kawasaki's flying bomb, the 3-cylinder 500 cc two-stroke. (Christian Lacombe)

Refuelling a 650 Kawasaki during a 750 cc class world record run at Daytona in 1977.

in motorcycling was the 3-cylinder 2-stroke 500 cc Kawasaki H1, a 1969 model that has been described as 'a more or less dirigible firecracker with a perpetually short fuse, an incorrigible and intemperate half-litre 2-stroke that instilled respect among onlookers and put the fear of God into its riders'. It was sensationally fast and powerful and very difficult to keep under control, very different from the 125 cc 2-stroke street machine that in 1962 was the first motorcycle to be marketed purely as a Kawasaki. However, the firm had set its sights initially on the vast USA market, where performance mattered more than handling, and as they gradually found their feet their machines grew in size and power. By 1965 they were going racing, though not with any success; but by 1969 they had won their first world championship, in the 125 cc class. By that time they had already developed a 750 cc machine for the American market, only to be beaten to the post by the appearance of the Honda 750 — so they redesigned it as a 900, and introduced it in 1973 to a motorcycle world that was flabbergasted by its size, power and flexibility. Within a couple of years Kawasaki were exporting motorcycles to 90 different countries from their factory at Akashi near Kobe in Japan, where what had originally been built as an aircraft parts plant employed 1700 workers in producing $\frac{1}{4}$ million motorcycles each year. On 22 January 1975 they began motorcycle manufacture actually within the USA, selling 150 000 machines from there in the following year to take 17 per cent of the market, and going on in 1977 to become the largest American motorcycle manufacturer. Second only to the USA in importance is the European market, which Kawasaki have been cultivating with similar intensity, their business acumen so great that they succeed in exporting 80 per cent of their total production. Considerable though that is, the firm's motorcycle production remains only a small part of its overall output, which today includes jet, turbine and diesel engines, locomotives, rolling stock, buses, generators, helicopters, aircraft, industrial and chemical plant, antipollution systems, bridges and nuclear engineering apparatus.

This may explain why the activities of the firm in motorcycle competition do not always follow the conventional pattern. They have been conspicuously absent, for example, from the 500 cc

The winner's rostrum after the 1978 Czechoslovakian GP: Kork Ballington 1, Greg Hansford 2, Andre Baldet 3. (All Sport/Don Morley)

road racing championships, although active in the smaller categories and in the 750 class, and very active in motocross (because of its importance to popularity in America) and indirectly in endurance racing because of its importance in France and other parts of Europe.

Stunts and demonstrations have played an important part in Kawasaki's image-building. Shortly after the 903 cc Z1 machine was announced in 1973, a more-or-less standard model, admittedly very carefully prepared but modified only in the handlebars and riding position, the removal of indicators and the replacement of the rear suspension units, ran for 24 hours around the Daytona Speed Bowl at an average speed of 109·64 mph (176·45 km/h), including fuel stops and maintenance checks. What could be done when the engine was modified was demonstrated at the same track: with the Z1 engine tuned to deliver more than 100 bhp, a much less standard motorcycle set a new 160·28 mph (257·94 km/h) record. In 1976 three Australian riders took a stock standard Kawasaki Z900 (the then current version of the original Z1) from Sidney and rode it around a track for 114 hours to set a new world endurance record. A year later, after the introduction of the similar but smaller 4-cylinder Kawasaki 650, mixed teams of American journalists and racing men

rode a batch of mildly modified production machines to set several new long-distance records in the 750 cc class, again at Daytona. Meanwhile the Dutch distributor of Kawasaki motorcycles, Henk Vink, brought out a new drag racing special built around two 980 cc Kawasaki engines and was timed at 208 mph (334 km/h) from a standing start, becoming the fastest man in the world over 1 km. A pair of similar engines, turbocharged and installed in a long low streamlined chassis, more recently took a Californian rider, Don Vesco, to a new world speed record for motorcycles on the Bonneville Salt Flats in Utah. Already the next likely engine for such feats is in production: late in 1978 Kawasaki unveiled their biggest machine yet, a water-cooled transverse 6-cylinder overhead-camshaft engine of 1300 cc in an exceptionally large and heavy touring chassis that is nevertheless capable of immense performance. Only a few months earlier in the year, what Kawasaki could do with a mere 750 cc was vividly demonstrated by the rider Mick Grant, who set a new absolute lap record for the Mountain Circuit in the Isle of Man while winning the Open Classic TT. Finally, at the end of that same 1978 season, what Kawasaki could do with even fewer and smaller cylinders was confirmed by their rider HN (Kork) Ballington winning the road racing world championships in the 350 and 250 classes.

Carlo Ubbiali on a lightweight MV Agusta in 1956.
(All Sport/Don Morley)

With 37 world championship titles in racing and
over 4000 individual victories, MV Agusta
motorcycles are the most successful in the
worldwide history of competition. Yet the company did not begin to make motorcycles until
1945, when production began in a little factory in
the Italian village of Verghera, from which the
firm took its name — Meccanica Verghera. In
charge was the wealthy Agusta family (mostly
Count Domenico Agusta) who ran the motorcycling enterprise more as a hobby than as a
serious commercial venture, the firm's real money
coming from the licensed manufacture of Bell
helicopters.

The time and place of the firm's beginning in-
dicates that it started by catering for the post-war
demand for cheap utility 2-stroke machines.

John Surtees riding for MV Agusta in the 1957 TT. (All Sport/Don Morley)

Within a couple of years, however, Ing. Pietro Remor was invited to join the company and, as the designer of the already famous and successful Gilera 4-cylinder racer, it was expected of him that he would produce something similar for MV. He did so in 1950, and the machines were scheduled to make their début in the Isle of Man for the Senior TT, but in fact they were not ready to appear until the Belgian Grand Prix. It was not until the end of the 1951 season that it achieved any success, and the single cylinder overhead-camshaft 125 cc racer that Remor had also produced in 1950 was just as fraught with trouble. The 125 was quicker to become competitive, however, and with the aid of some outstandingly good riders, MV Agusta began to dominate the class, collecting their first world championship in 1952 when the title was gained by Cecil Sandford. The 4-cylinder 500 took much longer to be made race-worthy, many of the good ideas in its initial design being rather badly carried out (notably in the suspension and transmission); but eventually it became a winner in the hands of Les Graham, very late in the 1951 season. He was killed in 1953 and the team was demoralised by the accident, although in the 125 class (especially thanks to the inspired riding of Carlo Ubbiali) the MV remained dominant, collecting the constructors' titles for a total of seven seasons in the years from 1952 to 1960 inclusive, during which Ubbiali himself won the rider's title five times. It was not until 1956 that the 500 was similarly successful, by which time MV had become the dominant constructor in the 250 class, their lightweight machine being based on two of the 125 singles on a common crankcase. The year 1956, however, really began a new era for the company in racing, marked as it was by the adoption of John Surtees as their leading rider.

Surtees quickly put his abilities as a development rider/engineer to good use, and by the end of the season emerged as world champion in the 500 cc class. The following season was a poor one for MV, edged out by their rivals in all classes: a 4-cylinder 350 had been built but was not yet competitive, and the 500 was so clearly outclassed by Gilera that MV tried a 6-cylinder engine late in the season. At the end of that year, as MV's luck would have it, Gilera, Guzzi and Mondial all withdrew from racing — as did Norton — and since these were the rivals against

whom MV had not been able to contend successfully, it looked as though the championships might now be delivered on a plate. Simple examination of the records confirms that by remaining in racing, MV Agusta won their reputation with perhaps unmerited ease: the 125 championships was theirs for 3 years, the 250 for 3 years, the 350 for 4 years and the 500 for no less than 8 years in succession.

It was not as easy as that record suggests. In the first place, the decision to remain in racing could only be taken with difficulty because the Agusta family was faced, as had been all the other factories which withdrew from the sport, by the prohibitive costs of building and developing machines sufficiently competitive to bring honour to their reputations. As for the riders, especially Surtees and, from the end of 1961, Hailwood, they had to ride as hard as possible in order to avoid being taunted with gaining easy victories, since their machines were so clearly very much faster than the obsolescent British machinery privately entered by most of their rivals. The result was a string of record laps and record race averages, and of successes that were only checked in the 1960s when the major Japanese manufacturers, headed by Honda, invaded the international racing scene.

The 500 cc class was the last to be dominated by Honda, who were the most successful constructors in that category in 1966 — despite which the individual championship still went to a rider of an MV Agusta, this being the factory team's new acquisition, Giacomo Agostini, who was to continue carrying the MV Agusta banner until 1974. His arrival in the team coincided with the introduction of new 3-cylinder racers, the first starting as a 420 cc machine that was eventually enlarged to 500, and followed by the 350 version. For a couple of years it was only the larger machine that was successful; but then Honda, having achieved all they set out to do, withdrew from racing and once again MV Agusta could capitalise on the absence of effective opposition. Riding the 3-cylinder 350 and the 500 racers, Agostini dominated both classes for the next 5 years, but things began to grow difficult again in 1973. He once again carried off the 350 championship, but Yamaha emerged as the most successful constructor in that class. In the 500 category, it was MV's new rider Phil Read who became champion in 1973 and again in 1974 —

The 1978 expression of MV Agusta racing experience in road-going terms was this 850 Monza, possibly the most glamorous machine on the market and certainly one of the most expensive. (Orbis Publishing)

but in the latter year Yamaha were the most successful constructors in that class too. The 1975 season showed that the Japanese were now in complete charge, and thereafter the distinctive 4-stroke roar of the MV Agusta (the racers had acquired 4-cylinder engines again, in 1971 for the 350 class and 1973 for the 500) was heard no more amidst the shrill trumpeting of 2-strokes.

The sound continued to be made on the public highway. Although MV Agusta production motorcycles were for many years comparatively humdrum, and still designed for the utility and scooter market into which the firm made its first commercial forays, more sporting machines had been offered to the public in the 1960s, even to the extent of a touring 600 cc version of the famous racing 'four'. In the 1970s, when motorcycles were once again fashionable, this theme was further developed in a range of fast and extremely glamorous shaft-drive 4-cylinder super-sports machine (crowning a catalogue of simpler lightweights) that have consistently been among the fastest and almost without exception the most expensive road-going motorcycles on the market.

James Lansdowne Norton, who was apprenticed to a Birmingham jeweller, founded an engineering firm in 1898, built his first motorcycle in 1902, and died aged 56 on 21 April 1925, was a man of sincere and simple faith. It was indeed faith, simple almost to the point of *naïveté*, insular and blindly patriotic, that was largely responsible for the long-lasting popularity of Norton motorcycles — but not his faith, which was religious, so much as that of the British motorcycling public, which was uncritically enthusiastic. There was in fact seldom much technical merit in the production motorcycles that bore the Norton name for three-quarters of a century; the reputation of the make was based almost entirely on its success in racing, and even then it was not so much racing in general as the Isle of Man TT races in particular, in which Nortons achieved unparalleled successes. So long as mechanical simplicity remained the general rule in racing motorcycles, Norton were able to maintain a complete domestic and respectable international supremacy, if only because they were at pains to ensure the generous production of replicas of the works racing machines for sale to private entrants and thus usually to be the most numerous in the field. When advancing technology began to invade motorcycle racing, as it did in the late 1930s and in the mid-1950s, and conclusively after 1960, then the classically simple Norton racer was outclassed: the outbreak of war saved it in 1939, and the aftermath of war allowed it to revive in the late 1940s, but no such costly salvation was available for it in the 1960s. Thereafter the make ran steadily downhill, finally expiring in a bout of ignominious dealings in the late 1970s.

Only two technical features were particularly creditable in the Norton racers. One was the architecturally simple single-cylinder overhead-camshaft engine, progressively developed from the late 1920s to become in many ways a model of efficiency. The other was the quite exemplary roadholding that was a feature of the racing

Norton chassis from 1950 onwards. Nevertheless, the firm's first racing success, which did much to establish the name on the market, was achieved without either type of advantage: the Norton that was ridden by private owner Rem Fowler to win the twin-cylinder class of the very first Isle of Man motorcycle TT in 1907 had a quite undistinguished chassis and was powered by a V-twin Peugeot engine. In the firm's early days, proprietary engines were the rule, for the original tiny factory could do little more than assembly work, relying on the purchase of as many components as possible from outside suppliers.

James Norton was prompted by the sporting — and consequently commercial — success of Fowler's race winner to embark on the production of his own engines, the first being a 633 cc single-cylinder affair called the Big Four because of its nominal rating of 4 hp. This was exhibited in 1907; 4 years later he had a new 490 cc machine (raced unsuccessfully in the TT) that was to endure with modifications for more than 40 years as the touring 16 H model. James (called 'Pa') Norton caught an illness in the Isle of Man in that year, and it took him a long time to recover his health. During this time the business deteriorated so badly that liquidation was threatened, but a takeover rescue was undertaken by an engineering company run by RT Shelley, who thereafter shared with James Norton the managing directorship. This new company, Norton Motors Limited (the original 1898 foundation was the Norton Manufacturing Company) saw that sales of the Big Four could be sharpened by some attention to the high-performance market; and, with the tuning services of D R O'Donovan (an established Brooklands rider with many records to his credit), two sporting models were marketed in limited quantities, each example certified to have covered the measured kilometre at Brooklands at a speed of at least 70 mph (112 km/h) for the BRS model or 75 mph (120 km/h) for the BS. The machine

Boy Scouts have traditionally played a busy part in the Isle of Man TT, recognised here by their inclusion in a formal picture of J L 'Pa' Norton with the Tourist Trophy and the Junior replica. (National Motor Museum, Beaulieu)

ridden by O'Donovan himself, now in the British National Motor Museum at Beaulieu, set 112 British and world records before the outbreak of the Great War. Considering that it was a single-gear belt-driven machine, it was perhaps entitled to be nicknamed 'Old Miracle'.

During that war, Norton supplied motorcycles to the Russian Government and later to the Allied Forces, the boost to production dictating a move to larger premises in 1916 when the firm's most famous factory in Bracebridge Street, Birmingham, was opened. After the war Norton brought out an overhead-valve 500 which, ridden by O'Donovan's apprentice Rex Judd, raised the 500 cc kilometer record to nearly 90 mph (145 km/h) and the mile record to over 88 mph (141 km/h) at Brooklands in 1922. Another year was to pass before this new model could finish a TT race, when the manufacturers' team prize was earned with second, fourth and fifth Senior

places, and in the same year a production version broke the 12-hour record at Brooklands and captured 18 world records in the process.

At last in 1924 Norton won the senior TT, ridden by Alec Bennett, and another piloted by George Tucker won the sidecar race. His passenger on that occasion was Walter Moore, who had until recently been the chief motorcycle designer for Douglas: soon afterwards he took office with Norton Motors, and it was he who created the overhead-camshaft engine that appeared in 1927 to mark the beginning of a new era for Nortons. Thus powered, a Norton won the Senior TT yet again and another raised the lap record to over 70 mph (112 km/h). Following this, the Norton team embarked on a successful campaign on the European continent, collecting victories in several Grands Prix, as they were to do regularly thereafter. Nor was record-breaking forgotten: a Norton became the first 500

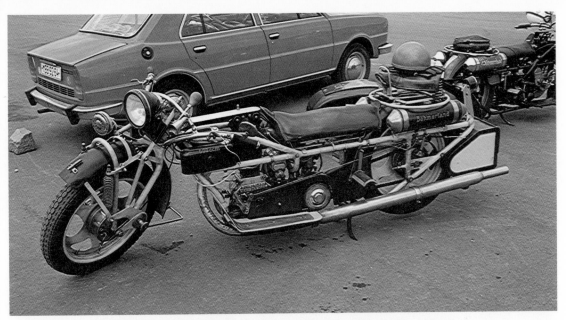

Probably the longest motorcycle, the Böhmerland. (All Sport/Don Morley)

Hailwood aboard a desmodromic Ducati, winning the 1978 Formula 1 TT. (All Sport/Don Morley)

1937 DKW 250 racer. (All Sport/Don Morley)

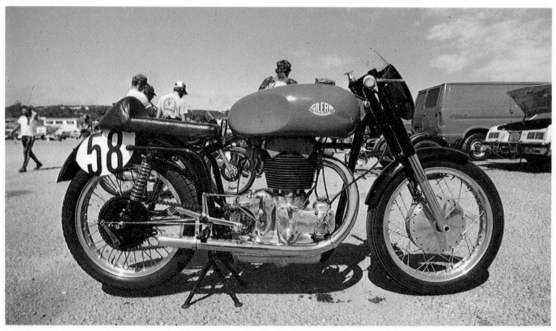

Gilera earned worldwide fame with their 4-cylinder racers, but in the immediate post-war years they built a single-cylinder 500 as a stop-gap. Later it was the mount of many a privateer; this example of the Saturno dates from 1954. (All Sport/Don Morley)

1928 Indian Scout. (All Sport/Photographic Ltd)

Agostini racing the MV Agusta. (Tony Duffy)

A serious and very competent member of the MV Agusta racing team, John Hartle. (All Sport/Don Morley)

The Münch Mammut was built around the modified air-cooled engine of an NSU car. (All Sport/Photographic Ltd)

1955 Manx Norton. (All Sport/Don Morley)

Geoffrey Duke riding the 1912 Norton known as Old Miracle, once the pride of Brooklands and rider D R O'Donovan, and now in the National Motor Museum at Beaulieu. (National Motor Museum, Beaulieu)

Alec Bennett after winning the 1924 Senior TT on the Norton designed by Walter Moore, who is standing behind him.
(National Motor Museum, Beaulieu)

cc motorcycle to cover 100 miles (160·9 km) in an hour.

All this competition success served to encourage sales of the much more humdrum touring Nortons, which were produced in a profusion of different models. The firm was thus strong enough to survive the slump which undermined so much of the British motorcycle industry in 1930. Perhaps its greatest loss was of Walter Moore, who left to work for NSU: development and design were thereafter the provinces of Joe Craig and Arthur Carroll, who progressively developed the original Moore engine concept, converting it to twin overhead camshafts in 1937 and tuning it to give as much as 52 bhp by 1939. Throughout the 1930s, racing successes were numerous and convincing, though the conviction began to fade as continental successes became fewer and received a nasty shock when a BMW won the 1939 Senior TT and finally brought home to the insular British motorcycling public

how rapidly their national idol was falling behind the times.

The production Nortons that they bought were no better in this respect. Not until 1938 was the valve gear of the pushrod engines fully enclosed, not until 1939 was a plunger-sprung frame made available — and then only for three models, two of which were the highly esteemed 350 and 500 International super-sports machines built in the image of the Manx racers. Admittedly some of the genuine works racers of 1939 had got as far as having telescopic front forks, something that BMW had done in 1935 and others much earlier — but the Norton forks were undamped!

After the 1939–45 war, spent in churning out the ancient 16H for the army, Nortons became the racing favourites again, favoured by new regulations banning some of the technical features (such as supercharging) that had made rival German and Italian racing machinery so much more effective in the late pre-war years.

Les Archer has his Norton checked by scrutineers after winning the 1957 British Experts Grand National scramble. (All Sport/Don Morley)

The last Norton to matter, the 850 cc Commando. (M Decet)

While the vanquished struggled to re-establish themselves, Norton got away to a flying start, but what strengthened their position enormously was their adoption of the so-called 'feather-bed' frame, incorporating the trailing pivoted-fork rear suspension that has since become standard for virtually all motorcycles and that had been originally devised by the brothers McCandless in Belfast. The firm's almost simultaneous adoption of Geoffrey Duke as a rider for the factory was the only other thing that remained necessary to give them an incredible run of successes, with numerous world championships (not forgetting the Sidecar class with Eric Oliver at the helm), innumerable Grand Prix and other victories, and even three successive wins at Daytona. Thus was restored their fading glory.

Alas, their imagination and initiative continued to fade, and Nortons seemed to be incapable of making any further progress in design. The best they could do was the Dominator vertical twin, originally introduced late in 1948 but little more than a latter-day version of the Ariel and BSA twins that had already been designed by their new staffman Bert Hopwood. Only with the later improvement of this engine and the adaptation of the feather-bed frame did Norton at last produce a road-going machine that was a credit to its racing siblings; but as the engine was made bigger and bigger to appeal to American customers, it passed the point of maximum attraction at about 600 cc and thereafter became merely a bloated banger, more and more vibratory as it grew larger. It ended its life at a nominal 850 cc (actually 828) in a new chassis called the Isolastic which made the Norton Commando (originally a 750) notorious for the variability of its handling. When it was good it was very good, and certainly by the standards of the early 1970s it was fairly fast; but while it sometimes went well, it seldom went for long without trouble, and despite the intelligent development work done by Peter Williams all Norton progress in the late 1960s and throughout the 1970s was towards the grave. The firm had been taken over by AMC in 1962, and 4 years later the AMC group itself collapsed, the new firm of Norton Villiers being raked out of the ashes by the Manganese Bronze Holdings group of companies enlisting Government aid. That is scarcely the way to make good motorcycles, and nowadays — despite the presence of a moped in their catalogues — Norton Villiers can hardly be said to do so, despite a modest if interesting attempt at a Wankel-engined motorcycle of which there were plans in early 1979 to produce a mere two dozen examples.

Although the origins of this company can be traced back to 1873, they only began building motorcycles — or at least motorised pedal bicycles — in 1900. By this time, the factory was established at Neckarsulm, from which the letters NSU were taken as a trade mark. However, their principal claims to motorcycling fame were laid in the 1950s. Prior to that their machines were merely respectable, their only contribution to technical progress being a two-speed epicyclic gear incorporated in the engine pulley for belt final drive early in the century, when most motorcycles still had fixed-ratio transmissions.

In 1951, however, NSU staked a claim to fame with a supercharged 500 cc twin on which Wilhelm Herz took the absolute world speed record for motorcycles at 180 mph. There followed a couple of years of dramatically successful road-racing in 1953 and 1954 in the 125 and 250 cc classes, the latter remaining an NSU province in 1955. Exquisitely engineered twin-overhead-camshaft twin-cylindered machines were responsible for these successes, which included four world championships collected by a very competent team of riders including Haas, Hollaus and Müller. Virtually unbeatable, the 250 NSU was significantly faster than its rivals: when Haas set the first Lightweight TT average of over 90 mph (144 km/h) in 1954, his new record for the distance was no less than $7\frac{1}{4}$ per cent faster than the 1953 record speed set by Fergus Anderson riding a Guzzi. Complex and heavy compared with that Italian, the NSU featured an elaborate built-up Hirth crankshaft, a six-speed gearbox, complicated valve gear and surprisingly small carburettors, and the factory claimed a power output of 42 bhp. The 125 NSU was less highly developed, giving only 16·8 bhp, but apart from its racing successes it deserves remembering as the source of technical inspiration for the

The name on the tank reveals the origin of the letters NSU. (National Motor Museum, Beaulieu)

A very early NSU motorised bicycle. (National Motor Museum, Beaulieu)

Honda CB92, perhaps the first really good roadgoing motorcycle built by the Japanese firm.

NSU pulled out of motorcycle racing in 1956 shortly after their team leader, Werner Haas, was killed in a flying accident. Thereafter they became best known for mopeds, the NSU Quickly enjoying an enormous vogue. Accordingly they embarked on a series of record-breaking sessions with a machine that employed what purported to be a Quickly engine, a machine nevertheless that was perhaps the most extraordinary and efficient motorcycle yet seen. It was a low-slung projectile

fondly known as Gustav Baumm's Flying Hammock.

Baumm was a bearded but youthful scientist who pursued the twin (and not wholly compatible) aerodynamic ideals of minimal frontal area and minimal drag coefficient to the point of logical extremity. He rode his creation himself, lying on his back between the wheels, the handlebars between his knees (the only available place) being linked to hub-centre steering. At his back was the tiny NSU engine which somehow sufficed to propel this extraordinary aerodyne at

The 1953 NSU 250 cc Rennmax. The engine of this championship-winning racer was in its day the most efficient unsupercharged automotive engine in terms of specific performance, as measured in bhp per litre. (National Motor Museum, Beaulieu)

incredible speeds. The most fantastic result of all was with the smallest engine: on the Bonneville Salt Flats in Utah, the Hammock shattered the 50 cc world speed record with a speed of 121·9 mph (196·2 km/h).

Perhaps to maintain some sense of proportion, NSU produced a less unconventional motorcycle to take the absolute two-wheeler record which had meanwhile fallen to rivals, their 500 becoming the world's fastest motorcycle again at 210·8 mph (339·2 km/h). Very little was said about the inconspicuous supercharge that both these machines relied upon for their outstanding performances. Of course much of the credit belonged to Baumm's aerodynamics, for the 50 cc record was taken with a power of only 12·8 bhp — but that was equivalent to 256 bhp per litre for what was tantamount to a well-made moped engine! The secret was in the tiny belt-driven compressor which achieved efficiencies and pressures rivalling the best aero-engine superchargers: it was an early pump version of what was to become the Wankel engine. A year later, NSU's brilliant engineer Walter Froede had accomplished the intellectual feat of turning the relative motions of the rotating inner and outer members of this Wankel compressor inside out, to create the simple definitive Wankel engine that has been so attractively interesting and distressingly controversial ever since. Not that the Wankel engine has been the only noteworthy tragedy of NSU's history: Gustav Baumm crashed and killed himself trying to go faster.

Peugeot

In business for nearly 170 years, the Peugeot firm played an impressively active part in motorcycling from the earliest days of petrol-engined vehicles. By 1904 the Peugeot motorcycle, which featured swinging-arm suspension of Truffault pattern, was one of the most modern in the world. In another 2 years Peugeot were making their own engines instead of buying proprietary ones, starting with a large V-twin which proved considerably more powerful than the engines of other makes. This made it very attractive for other manufacturers wanting to indulge in racing or record-breaking or simply to market high-performance motorcycles, and two firms in particular — Norton and NLG (the initials stood for North London Garage) — were able to make considerable impacts on the racing scene and profitably to impress customers, with the racing successes they were enabled to score with the aid of Peugeot power. It was a Peugeot-engined Norton, for example, that won the multi-cylinder class in the first Isle of Man Tourist Trophy motorcycle event in 1907, and in 1908 two NLG machines powered by even larger Peugeot engines, each a 994 cc V-twin, completely dominated the occasion of the first motorcycle race meeting held at the Brooklands track.

Peugeot themselves were encouraged by these vicarious triumphs to embark on their own racing programme, and in 1919 they fielded a factory team for the first time. Their riders were mounted on machines designed by Jean Antoinescu, a man of considerable gifts both in terms of imagination and of technical ability. His first racing Peugeot motorcycle deserves special mention, not only because it was a 500 cc vertical twin-cylinder 4-stroke of a layout that was to become enormously popular decades later, but more particularly because its valves were operated by twin overhead camshafts. Peugeot had imposed twin overhead camshafts on the engines of racing cars in 1912, setting an engineering fashion that has lasted to this day. It was natural that they should extend their pioneering work into the world of the two-wheeler, and it is more than probable that

this 1913 racing Peugeot was the first motorcycle in the world to have this form of layout for its valve apparatus, the form which has ever since been accepted as the most desirable for a high-speed or high-efficiency engine. In the 1920s Peugeot pulled out of racing and concentrated their work on a new range of road motorcycles. Since then, and with due interruptions for the World War, powered two-wheelers have remained in production as the speciality of a separate company, Cycles Peugeot, which was established to deal with them.

The first motorcycle to be powered by a parallel-twin 2-stroke engine, the first to be based on a properly triangulated straight-tube frame, the first to have a kick-starter, the first 2-stroke with rotary valve control of the induction tract, the early two-speed, 2-cylinder, 2-stroke Scott was a motorcycle of rare distinction and great character, fondly remembered after its heyday and greatly respected during it — and even feared by rivals in competition. As a result of prodigious performances in hill climbs when the Scott made its first public appearance, the make was the first to suffer from discriminatory regulations deliberately contrived to handicap it; but within a few years it was still demonstrating an ineffable superiority, being the first make to win the Senior TT in the Isle of Man 2 years in succession and

George Silk developed a vintage Scott for amateur racing of vintage machines until it was so good that he was prompted to put a road-going version of it into production. The engine is now almost entirely Silk, and the chassis owes nothing to Scott — but the character of the machine remains essentially what that of the Scott always was. This is the larger of the two Silk models — the 700. (Orbis Publishing)

the first to set the fastest lap in that event in four successive years.

All these things were the fruit of one of the most fertile brains in the early days of motorcycling, that of Alfred Angas Scott. Born in Yorkshire in 1874, he became an unusually complete and well-rounded man by the standards of the rude mechanicals who made up so much of the early motorcycle industry. For a keen practical motorcyclist to be on the one hand a trained marine engineer and on the other a talented artist and musician — he even kept a grand piano alongside his drawing board for recreation — was exceptional enough in those or any other days; add to that a good practical mechanical ability, a lusty enthusiasm for potholing, and a measure of native stubborness, and you have not only some picture of an exceptional man but also the essential ingredients of his death at the age of 48. Coming home wet after a potholing session, he caught a cold, refused medical attention, allowed the cold to develop into pneumonia, and died.

By that time he had long abandoned his concern with his brilliant motorcycles, selling out his interest in the Scott Engineering Company in 1919 to form the Scott Auto-Car Company where he would concentrate on development and manufacture of his intriguing three-wheeler, the Scott Sociable.

It will always be by his early motorcycles that he will be remembered. Their basic design endured for over 60 years, successive developments keeping the Scott motorcycle in more-or-less continuous production until 1950, except for a break during the World War years. New versions were promised when the rights were acquired by the enthusiastic Mr Matt Holder of the Aero Jig and Tool Company in Birmingham in 1954; but although a pleasantly updated Scott went into production during 1956, demand had faded until eventually the machines were only made to special order. Nevertheless, the Scott principles endure in the modern Silk, which grew out of development work done on a vintage Scott used for club racing in the late 1960s.

⮂ SUZUKI

One of the most impressive records in the history of the motorcycle industry is that of Suzuki, though they did not make their first motorcycle until 1952. Theirs was not simply a tale of fame earned through competition successes although, after entering classic racing in 1960, they collected eight world championship titles (mostly in the 50 cc class which they almost completely dominated) in their first 7 years of international competition. Industrially and commercially they have an equally impressive record.

The Suzuki business was founded as a textile engineering firm by Michio Suzuki in 1909. After the World War, recession forced the company into diversification, and in 1952 they built a motorised bicycle which was so successful that they were prompted within 2 years to reform the company as the Suzuki Motor Co Ltd. Textile engineering was soon forgotten as the new company blossomed, and soon it was building a big range of 2-stroke motorcycles: by the late 1960s Suzuki was the biggest manufacturer of 2-strokes in the world. The engines were not confined to motorcycles, as they also went in for small cars, vans, motor boats, bicycles and outboard engines. Production soared, with 20 per cent of the Japanese annual output of $4\frac{1}{2}$ million motorcycles a year being Suzuki's by the mid-1970s, and half those Suzukis being exported. The production lines were capable of turning out a new motorcycle every 12 seconds, and the newest motorcycle plant alone (completed in 1972 at Toyokawa) had a monthly capacity of 40 000 machines, 90 per cent of which were expected to be sold overseas. All the engines, however, were built in the main plant in Japan's 'motorcycle city', Hamamatsu. These figures make a fascinating contrast with the output back in 1953, the first full year of Suzuki motorcycle production, when the factory produced 4400 light-weight machines.

Suzuki have offered their fair share of innovative engineering, having been among the early pioneers of separately controlled lubrication systems and disc-valve induction for 2-stroke engines, and being the first to put a Wankel-engined motorcycle into large-scale production. They have seldom been the originators of anything, however, preferring to concentrate on the profitable development of ideas that have already been proved worthwhile. This was the case, for example, with disc valve induction, which they employed first in their racing motorcycles when Ernst Degner defected from East Germany and brought the skills and knowledge he had acquired with MZ to Japan. Their racing programme was immensely successful in the small-capacity classes, but after withdrawing temporarily from official participation in racing at the end of 1967 Suzuki encouraged private entrants to continue, at the same time making a very successful incursion into motocross. This move was aimed at the lucrative North American market, where the demand for off-road and enduro motorcycles was tremendous: Suzuki was the first Japanese factory to compete in motocross, and has been consistently the most successful with the majority of the world championships to its credit.

In the 1970s they returned to road racing in the large-capacity classes, at first with machines derived from standard models but after 1974 with a new 4-cylinder 500 in which the cylinders were arranged in square formation, just as they had been in the 1964 250 cc racer. Known as the RG500, this Suzuki became very successful and was put into production, proving to be the fastest machine ever offered for sale in its class. A developed version, the RG500A, was produced in 1976 for Barry Sheene to ride, and with it he won his first world championship as well as Suzuki's first in the 500 cc class, securing the title for the second year running in 1977.

Among their production machines, Suzuki have three notable 2-stroke machines to their credit. The first was the six-speed 250 cc Super Six, an air-cooled twin that was exceptionally fast by the standards of the late 1960s. Next came the T500 Cobra, a 2-stroke twin that emerged in 1967 and, duly modified, was still in production 10 years later, having in the meantime acted as the basis for a number of quite successful racing machines. The third was the GT 750, which was Suzuki's answer to the new challenge set by the Honda 750 of 1969 and the Kawasaki 900 which followed it. A water-cooled 3-cylinder 2-stroke of lively performance and good manners, it was amenable to (and received) considerable development, growing faster and crisper in behaviour with the passing years — and a racing version proved capable of more than 170 mph (270 km/h) with 100 bhp at its disposal.

Suzuki's next venture was with the Wankel engine, the RE5 motorcycle being the only one to have an engine of this type specifically designed for it rather than being merely adapted from some industrial or automobile engine already in production elsewhere. Its appearance was untimely, coinciding with a time when the world had suddenly become acutely conscious of energy conservation and environmental pollution, while the still young Wankel engine antagonised both interests with its heavy fuel consumption and immoderate emmissions. Suzuki then moved on to 4-stroke production, introducing a very well engineered range of conventional transverse twins and fours, the first being a twin-overhead-camshaft 750 in 1976, accompanied soon afterwards by a 400 and a 1000 cc machine. A developed version of the latter, the Dunstall Suzuki GS1000CS, was in March 1979 the fastest production motorcycle in the world, having been tested on the road by the author at 154·2 mph (248·2 km/h). Not that Suzukis are all big and fast: as one of the world's top four motorcycle manufacturers, the company offers for sale a range of more than 40 different machines, including shaft-drive tourers, off-road trail, trials, and motocross bikes, lightweight commuter machines, and miniature scooters. According to their motto, they 'make only valuable products'.

Manufacturers of some of the world's finest musical instruments (which explains their emblem of crossed tuning forks), Yamaha went into the motor vehicle business in 1955 with a capital of about £30 000. Within 10 years their capital was more like a million and they were building over 13 000 motorcycles a month. After another 10 years their reputation on road and track had become too great for assessment by mere accountants. In addition to their tremendous commercial success all around the globe, they have an enviable record in racing, their parallel-twin 2-stroke 250 and 350 cc motorcycles dominating their classes, whether in results or sheer numbers, for more than 10 years. What made this a particularly notable achievement was that the racing 2-strokes were based so frankly on the road-going motorcycles that anyone could buy. International racing began for Yamaha as long ago as 1958 when an air-cooled 250 twin was sent to America and finished sixth in the Catalina race; but it was the over-the-counter road-racing 250, the air-cooled 2-stroke TDI twin that was the real epoch-marker in Yamaha history. With the exception of a couple of years when Yamaha fielded prodigiously powerful water-cooled V4 racers for Bill Ivy and Phil Read to ride in the 125 and 250 cc Grand Prix, the traditional Yamaha twin has been the classical giant killer. Those V4s were incredible machines, complex to maintain and tune and extremely demanding to ride, water-cooled, disc-valved, twin-crankshaft 2-strokes mustering about 300 bhp per litre. On the 125, Bill Ivy accomplished one of the most astonishing feats of his career (perhaps one of the most outstanding in the history of motorcycle racing) when he completed a lap of the Isle of Man in 1968 at an average speed of 100·32 mph (161·45 km/h). How difficult this must have been may be imagined from his need to keep changing gear frequently enough to keep the engine running as nearly as possible between 17 000 and

The four-cylinder Yamaha racer, ridden by Kenny Roberts in 1978. (All Sport/Don Morley)

18 000 rpm, so narrow was the power band of this hypersensitive engine. The 250 was nearly as difficult, with a power band that stretched from 14 000 to 15 000 rpm, and with the 73 bhp available within that region Ivy lapped the Island in that same week at an average speed of 105·51 mph (169·80 km/h) from a standing start.

Bearing in mind that Yamaha's modern 2-strokes, racing or road-going, rely on simple piston-controlled porting, it is doubly interesting that Yamaha was the first to incorporate the rotary disc valve (invented by Zimmerman, developed for MZ by Kaaden, and employed even earlier in scooters by Guzzi) in production motorcycles in Japan; it was with the aid of disc valves and the new technology of 2-stroke tuning that they were able to impose themselves so successfully on international racing. They were also the first to devise a fully automatic oil injection system (the Yamaha Autolube) to overcome

the incomprehension of South Asian and United States customers faced with the implausible requirement of mixing oil with the petrol in the fuel tank of conventional 2-stroke motorcycles. They were also first with sundry other features, such as reed valves in the induction system and 5- and 7-port flow systems.

What started them on 2-strokes was their programme for entering motorcycle manufacture, established in 1954 before the old-established main company, Nippon Gakki, established its Yamaha Motor Company subsidiary. The prototype, the YA1, was a 125 cc 2-stroke roadster which was virtually a copy of the BSA Bantam, though Yamaha with commendable honesty admitted its similarity to the German DKW which BSA had copied. It was a success soon after it went into production in 1955, when the Yamaha Motor Company had less than a hundred employees and the total

Katayama in the Isle of Man in 1978. (All Sport/Don Morley)

output was only 300 machines a month. Particularly interesting technically were such later models as the 250 cc YD1 which earned a big design award in 1958 and the 173 cc SC1 scooter of 1960, commendable for its monocoque plastics body, its two-speed converter-coupling transmission, and its asymmetric suspension of wheels on stub axles. The year of its birth was one in which the price of Yamaha shares rocketed to heights never previously experienced in the Japanese stock market. Troubles followed with subsequent models which cost the company a million dollars, but by then Yamaha were strong enough to survive their troubles and so big that expansion had prompted them to form the Yamaha International Corporation in California in 1960 and also to form a racing division — the avowed object of which was to encourage engineering development rather than to be commercially profitable. In the 18 following years Yamaha built more than 8000 racing machines, but the racing division still claims to make no profit. The extent to which the company profits from the favourable publicity

earned in racing may be estimated from Yamaha's racing track record: in 1964 and 1965 they took the 250 world championship; in 1967 the 125; in 1968 the 125 and 250; in 1970, 1971 and 1972 the 250; in 1973 the 125 and 250; in 1974 the 125 and 350; in 1975 the 350 and 500; in 1977 the 350 and the newly instituted 750 titles, and in 1978 the 500.

Nor are they limited to 2-stroke machines; however, their reputation may have been acquired with their aid. Recognising the possible proscription of 2-stroke engines in due course, either by environmentalists or by conservationists, they introduced a substantial range of 4-stroke production machines beginning in 1972 with a 650 twin and gradually extending the range in both directions to cover the whole market. Not that they have forgotten what to do with 2-strokes: in 1978 a 500 Yamaha carried Kenny Roberts to the world championship, the first American ever to win a road-racing world title.

Nimbus specialised in heavyweight machines intended for sidecar propulsion; this is a 1935 4-cylinder 750 super sport model.
(C. Gorman)

List of makes

(For international abbreviations see p. 175)

A

ABACO (D)
ABBOTSFORD (GB)
ABC (GB)
ABENDSONNE (D)
ABERDALE (GB)
ABE-STAR (JAP)
ABINGDON (GB)
ABJ (GB)
ACE (US)
ACHILLES (D)
ACMA (F)
ACME (GB)
ADER (F)
ADLER (D)
ADONIS (F)
ADRIA (D)
ADS (B)
ADVANCE (GB)
AEL (GB)
AEOLUS (GB)
AER (GB)
AER-CAPRONI (I)
AER-MACCHI (I)
AEROS (CS)
AGF (F)
AGON (D)
AGRATI (I)
AIGLON (F)
AIROLITE (GB)
AJAX (B)
AJAX (GB)
AJR (GB)
AJS (GB)
AJW (GB)
AKD (GB)
AKKENS (GB)
ALATO (I)
ALBA (D)
ALBERT (D)
ALBERTUS (D)
ALCYON (F)
ALDBERT (I)
ALECTO (GB)
ALERT (GB)

ALEU (E)
ALFA (I)
ALFA-GNOM (A)
ALGE (D)
ALIPRANDI (I)
ALLDAYS (GB)
ALLEGRO (CH)
ALLON (GB)
ALLRIGHT (D)
ALMA (F)
ALMORA (D)
ALP (GB)
ALPINO (I)
ALTEA (I)
ALTER (F)
AMBASSADOR (GB)
AMC (GB)
AMC (US)
AMERICAN (US)
AMERICAN EAGLE (US)
AMERICAN X (US)
AMI (CH)
AMO (D)
AMS (E)
ANCORA (I)
ANDREES (D)
ANGLIAN (GB)
ANGLO-DANE (DK)
ANKER (D)
ANTOINE (B)
APACHE (US)
APEX (D)
APOLLO (S)
AQUILA (I)
ARAB (GB)
ARC (E)
ARCO (D)
ARDEA (I)
ARDEN (GB)
ARDENT (F)
ARDIE (D)
ARDITO (I)
ARGENTRE (F)
ARGEO (D)
ARIEL (GB)
ARLIGUIE (F)
ARMIS (GB)

ARMOR (F)
ARMSTRONG (GB)
ARNO (GB)
ARROW (GB)
ARROW (US)
ASAHI (JAP)
ASCOT (GB)
ASCOT-PULLIN (GB)
ASHFORD (GB)
ASL (GB)
ASPES (I)
ASSO (I)
ASSOCIATED MOTOR CYCLES (GB)
ASTER (F)
ASTON (GB)
ASTORIA (I)
ASTRA (D)
ASTRA (I)
ASTRAL (F)
ATALA (I)
ATLANTIK (D)
ATLANTIS (D)
ATLAS (GB)
ATLAS (D)
AGUSTA (I)
AURORA (GB)
AURORA (GBM)
AUSTEN (GB)
AUSTIN (GB)
AUSTRAL (F)
AUSTRIA (A)
AUSTRO-ALPHA (A)
AUSTRO-MOTORETTE (A)
AUSTRO-OMEGA (A)
AUTINAG (D)
AUTO-BI (US)
AUTO-BIT (JAP)
AUTOFLUG (D)
AUTOGLIDER (GB)
AUTOMOTO (F)
AUTOPED (US)
AUTOSCO (GB)
AVADA (NL)
AVAROS (NL)
AVIS-CELER (D)
AVON (GB)
AWD (D)

AWO (DDR)
AYRES-HAYMAN (GB)
AZA (CS)
AZZARTI (I)

B

BAC (GB)
BADGER (US)
BAF (CS)
BAIER (D)
BAILLEUL (F)
BAKER (GB)
BALALUWA (D)
BALKAN (BG)
BAM (D)
BANSHEE (GB)
BARNES (GB)
BARON (GB)
BARRY (CS)
BARTALI (I)
BARTER (GB)
BASTERT (D)
BAT (GB)
BATAVUS (NL)
BAUDO (I)
BAUER (D)
BAUGHAN (GB)

BAYERLAND (D)
BAYLEY-FLYER (US)
BCR (F)
BD (CS)
B & D JUNIOR (GB)
BEARDMORE-PRECISION (GB)
BEAUFORT (GB)
BEAU-IDEAL (GB)
BEAUMONT (GB)
BECCARIA (I)
BEESTON (GB)
BEFAG (D)
BEHAG (D)
BEKAMO (CS)
BEKAMO (D)
BENELLI (I)
BENOTTO (I)
BERCLEY (B)
BERESA (D)
BERGFEX (D)
BERINI (NL)
BERLIN (DDR)
BERNARDET (F)
BERNEG (I)
BERTIN (F)
BERWICK (GB)
BETA (I)
BEUKER (D)
BFW (D)
BH (E)
BIANCHI (I)

BICHRONE (F)
BIM (JAP)
BIMA (F)
BIMOFA (D)
BIMOTA (I)
BINKS (GB)
BIRCH (GB)
BINZ (D)
BIRMA (F)
BISMARCK (D)
BISON (A)
BITRI (NL)
BJR (E)
BLACKBURNE (GB)
BLACKFORD (GB)
BLACK-PRINCE (GB)
BLANCHE-HERMINE (F)
BLEHA (D)
BLERIOT (F)
BLOTTO (I)
BLUMFIELD (GB)
BM (I)
BMW (D)
BOCK & HOLLANDER (A)
BODO (D)
BOEHME (D)
BOEHMERLAND (CS)
BOGE (D)
BOLIDE (F)
BOMBARDIER (CAN)
BOND (GB)

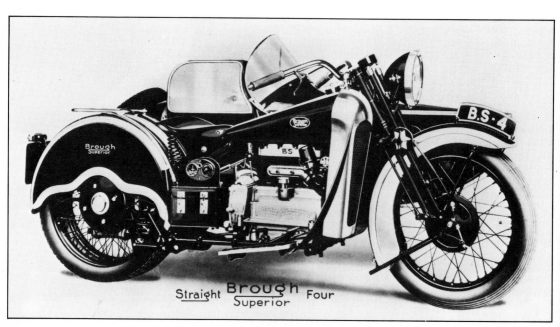

The Brough Superior Straight 4 was designed for sidecar use only, and was accordingly fitted with twin rear wheels driven by shaft from a cosmetically adapted Austin 7 engine. A few examples were made in and about 1933. (National Motor Museum, Beaulieu)

BOOTH (GB)
BORD (GB)
BORDONE (I)
BORGHI (I)
BORGO (I)
BOUCHET (F)
BOUGERY (F)
BOUNDS-JAP (GB)
BOVY (B)
BOWDEN (GB)
BOWN (GB)
BPS (F)
BRADBURY (GB)
BRAND (D)
BRAVIS (D)
BREDA (I)
BREE (A)
BRENNABOR (D)
BREUIL (F)
BRIDGESTONE (JAP)
BRILLIANT (F)
BRITAX (GB)
BRITISH-RADIAL (GB)
BRITISH-STANDARD (GB)
BRM (I)
BRONDOIT (B)
BROUGH (GB)
BROUGH SUPERIOR (GB)
BROWN (GB)
BROWN-BICAR (GB)
BRUNEAU (F)
BSA (GB)
BSM (D)
BUCHER (I)
BUCHET (F)
BÜCKER (D)
BULLDOG (GB)
BULTACO (E)
BURFORD (GB)
BURGERS-ENR (NL)
BURKHARDTIA (D)
BURNEY (GB)
BUSI (I)
BUSSE (D)
BUYDENS (B)
BV (CS)

C

CABTON (JAP)
CAGIVA (I)
CALCOTT (GB)
CALTHORPE (GB)
CALVERT (GB)
CAMBER (GB)
CAMILLE-FACAUX (F)
CAMPION (GB)

CAN-AM (CAN)
CAPPONI (I)
CAPRIOLO (I)
CAPRONI-VIZZOLA (I)
CARABELA (MEX)
CARDAN (F)
CARFIELD (GB)
CARINELLI (I)
CARLEY (F)
CARLTON (GB)
CARPATI (R)
CARPIO (F)
CARREAU (F)
CAS(CS)
CASAL (P)
CASALINI (I)
CASOLI (I)
CASTADOT (B)
CASTELL (GB)
CASWELL (GB)
CAT (S)
CAYENNE (GB)
CAZALEX (F)
CAZANAVE (F)
CC (GB)
CCM (GB)
CECCATO (I)
CECHIE (CS)
CEDOS (GB)
CEMEC (F)
CENTAUR (GB)
CENTER (JAP)
CENTURY (GB)
CF (I)
CFC (F)
CHAISE (F)
CHAMPION (JAP)
CHAMPION (US)
CHAPIUS (F)
CHARLETT (D)
CHARLTON (GB)
CHASE (GB)
CHATER (GB)
CHATER LEA (GB)
CHAT YAMAHA (GB)
CHELL (GB)
CHENEY-TRIUMPH (GB)
CHIORDA (I)
CHRISTOPHE (F)
CIE (B)
CIE (GB)
CIMATTI (I)
CITA (B)
CITYFIX (D)
CLARENDON (GB)
CLAUDE DELAGE (F)
CLEMENT (F)
CLEMENT-GARRARD (GB)
CLEMENT-GLADIATOR (F)
CLESS & PLESSING (A)
CLEVELAND (GB)

CLEVELAND (US)
CLUA (E)
CLYDE (GB)
CLYNO (GB)
CM (I)
CMM (GB)
CMP (I)
COCKERELL (D)
CODRIDEX (F)
COFFERSA (E)
COLOMB (F)
COLONIAL (GB)
COLUMBIA (F)
COLUMBIA (US)
COLUMBUS (D)
COMERFORD-WALLIS (GB)
COMERY (GB)
COMET (GB)
COMET (I)
COMMANDER (GB)
CONDOR (CH)
CONDOR (D)
CONDOR (GB)
CONNAUGHT (GB)
CONSUL (GB)
CORAH (GB)
CORGI (GB)
CORONA (D)
CORONA (GB)
CORONA-JUNIOR (GB)
CORRE (F)
COSSACK (USSR)
COTTEREAU (F)
COTTON (GB)
COULSON-B (GB)
COVENTRY ALERT (GB)
COVENTRY-B & D (GB)
COVENTRY-CHALLENGE (GB)
COVENTRY-EAGLE (GB)
COVENTRY-MASCOT (GB)
COVENTRY-VICTOR (GB)
CPC (F)
CP-ROLEO (F)
CRESCENT (S)
CREST (GB)
CROCKER (US)
CROFT-CAMERON (GB)
CROWNFIELD (GB)
CRT (I)
CRYPTO (GB)
CSEPEL (HU)
CURTISS (US)
CURWY (D)
CUSHMAN (US)
CYC-AUTO (GB)
CYCLE-SCOOT(US)
CYCLONE (US)
CYCLONETTE (B)
CYKELAID (GB)
CYRUS (NL)
CZ (CS)

D

DAIMLER (D)
DALTON (GB)
DANE (GB)
DARDO (I)
DARLAN (E)
DARLING (CH)
DART (GB)
DAVENTRY (B)
DAVISON (GB)
DAW (D)
DAW (GB)
DAX (F)
DAY-LEEDS (GB)
DAYTON (GB)
DAYTON (US)
DE-CA (I)
DE-DE (F)
DE DION BOUTON (F)
DEFY-ALL (GB)
DE HAVILLAND (GB)
DEI (I)
DELAPLACE (F)
DELIN (B)
DELLA FERRAR (I)

DELTA GNOM (A)
DE LUXE (GB)
DE LUXE (US)
DEMM (I)
DENNELL (GB)
DERBI (E)
DERBY (GB)
DERNY (F)
DERONZIERE (F)
DESPATCH RIDER (GB)
DEVIL (I)
DFR (F)
DGW (D)
DIAG (D)
DIAMANT (D)
DIAMOND (GB)
DIEHL (D)
DIETERLE-DESSAU (D)
DIFAZIO (GB)
DILECTA (F)
DIMENSION FOUR (GB)
DISSELHOF (NL)
DIXOR (F)
DJOUNN (D)
DKR (GB)
DKW (D)
DMF (B)

DMF (NL)
DMG (D)
DMW (GB)
DNB (JAP)
DOBRO-MOTORIST (D)
DOGLIOLI & CIVARDI (I)
DOLF (D)
DOLLAR (F)
DOMINISSIMI (I)
DORION (F)
DOT (GB)
DOUE (F)
DOUGLAS (GB)
D-RAD (D)
DREADNOUGHT (GB)
DRESCH (F)
DRESDA (UK)
DREVON (F)
DS (S)
DSH (A)
DSK (JAP)
DS-MALTERRE (F)
DUCATI (E)
DUCATI (I)
DUCSON (E)
DUNELT (GB)
DUNKLEY (GB)

The fastest production racing motorcycle in Britain in the 1978 season was the 888 cc Honda-engined Dresda, seen here at Snetterton ridden by Fred Huggett. (Vic Barnes)

DUNSTALL (GB)
DURAND (F)
DURANDAL (F)
DURKOPP (D)
DUVAL (B)
DUX (GB)
DUZMO (GB)
DYSON-MOTORETTE (GB)

E

EADIE (GB)
EAGLE (US)
EAGLE-TANDEM (GB)
EBE (S)
EBER (D)
EBO (GB)
EBS (D)
EBU-STAR (JAP)
ECA (D)
ECHO (JAP)
ECKL (D)
ECONOMIC (GB)
EDETA (E)
EDMONTON (GB)
EDMUND (GB)
EGLI (CH)
EICHLER (D)
EISENHAMMER (D)
EISLER (CS)
ELAND (NL)
ELFA (D)
ELF-KING (GB)
ELFSON (GB)
ELI (GB)
ELIE-HUIN (F)
ELIG (E)
ELITE (D)
ELLEHAM (DK)
ELMDON (GB)
ELSTER (D)
ELSWICK (GB)
ELVE (B)
EM (A)
EMA (D)
EMBLEM (US)
EMC (GB)
EMH (D)
EMPO (NL)
EMURO (JAP)
EMW (DDR)
ENDRICK (GB)
ENDURANCE (GB)
ENERGETTE (GB)
EO (D)
EOLE (B)
ERCOLI-CAVALLONE (I)
ERIE (US)

ERIOL (F)
ERMAG (D)
ERNST EICHLER (D)
ERNST-MAG (D)
ESCH-REKORD (D)
ESCOL (B)
ESO (CS)
ETA (GB)
ETOILE (F)
EUROPA (D)
EVANS (US)
EVART-HALL (GB)
EVEREST (D)
EVO (D)
EVYCSA (E)
EWABRA (D)
EXCELSIOR (D)
EXCELSION (F)
EXCELSIOR (GB)
EXCELSIOR (US)
EXPRESS (D)
EYSINK (NL)

F

FABULA (D)
FAFNIR (D)
FAGAN (EIR)
FAINI (I)
FAIRFIELD (GB)
FAKA (D)
FALCO (I)
FALTER (D)
FAMA (NL)
FAMAG (D)
FANTIC (I)
FAR (A)
FARNELL (GB)
FATH (D)
FAVOR (F)
FAVORIT (D)
FB (D)
FB (GB)
FB-MONDIAL (I)
FEBO (E)
FECHTEL (D)
FEDERATION (GB)
FEE (GB)
FEILBACH LIMITED (US)
FEMINIA (F)
FERBEDO (D)
FERRARI (I)
FERRARIS (I)
FERT (I)
FEW-PARAMOUNT (GB)
FIAMC (I)
FIDUCIA (CH)
FIGINI (I)

FINZI (I)
FIORELLI (I)
FIX (D)
FKS (D)
FLANDERS (US)
FLANDRIA (B)
FLINK (D)
FLM (GB)
FLOTTWEG (D)
FLYING-MERKEL (US)
FM (I)
FN (B)
FOCESI (I)
FOLLIS (F)
FONGRI (I)
FONLUPT (F)
FORCE (A)
FORELLE (D)
FORSTER (CH)
FORTUNA (D)
FORWARD (GB)
FOX (F)
FRANCE (F)
FRANCIS-BARNETT (GB)
FRANCHI (I)
FRANKONIA (D)
FRANZANI (D)
FRECO (D)
FREJUS (I)
FRERA (I)
FREYER & MILLER (US)
FREYLER (A)
FRISCHAUF (D)
FUJI (JAP)
FULGOR (F)
FUSI (I)
FVL (I)

G

GABBIANO (I)
GABY (GB)
GADABOUT (GB)
GAIA (I)
GALBUSERA (I)
GALLONI (I)
GAMAGE (GB)
GANNA (I)
GARABELLO (I)
GARANZINI (I)
GARELLI (I)
GARIN (F)
GARLASCHELLI (I)
GASUDEN (JAP)
GATTI (I)
GAZDA (A)
GAZELLE (NL)
GAZZI (I)

GB (GB)
GD (I)
GECO-HERSTAL (F)
GEER (US)
GEIER (D)
GE-MA-HI (D)
GENERAL-LUCIFER (F)
GENTIL (F)
GEORGES RICHARD (F)
GEPPERT (D)
GERALD (F)
GERBI (I)
GERMAAN (NL)
GERMANIA (D)
GEROSA (I)
GERRARD (GB)
GIACOMASSO (I)
GIGANT (A)
GIGUET (F)
GILERA (I)
GILLET-HERSTAL (B)
GIMA (F)
GIMSON (E)
GIRARDENGO (I)
GITAN (I)
GITANE (F)
GIULIETTA (I)
GIVAUDAN (GB)
GL (F)
GLENDALE (GB)
GLOBE (GB)
GLOCKNER (A)
GLORIA (GB & F)
GLORIA (I)
GNÄDIG (D)
GNOME-RHONE (F)
GOEBEL (D)
GOGGO (D)
GOLD-RAD (D)
GOLEM (D)
GORI (I)
GORICKE (D)
GORRION (E)
GOUGH (GB)
GRADE (D)
GRANDEX (GB)
GRAPHIC (GB)
GRATIEUX (F)
GRAVES (GB)
GREEN (GB)
GREEVES (GB)
GREYHOUND (GB)
GREYHOUND (US)
GRI (GB)
GRIFF (GB)
GRIFFON (F)
GRINDLAY-PEERLESS (GB)
GRITZNER (D)
GRIZZLY (CS)
GROSE-SPUR (GB)
GROTE (D)

GRUHN (D)
GRUTZENA (D)
GSD (GB)
GUARALDI (I)
GUAZZONI (I)
GUELDNER (D)
GUIA (I)
GUIGNARD (F)
GUILLER (F)
GUIZZARDI (I)
GUIZZO (I)
GUSTLOFF (D)
G & W (GB)

H

HACK (GB)
HADEN (GB)
HAGON (GB)
HAI (A)
HAMPTON (GB)
HANFLAND (D)
HANSA (D)
HARDING-JAP (F)
HAREWOOD (GB)
HARLETTE (F)
HARLEY-DAVIDSON (US)
HARPER (GB)
HARRAS (D)
HASCHO (D)
HASCHUET (D)
HASTY (F)
HAWEKA (D)
HAWKER (GB)
HAXEL JAP (GB)
HAZEL (GB)
HAZLEWOOD (GB)
HB (GB)
HDG (D)
HEALEY (GB)
HEC (GB)
HECKER (D)
HEIDEMANN (D)
HEINKEL (D)
HEJIRA (GB)
HELO (D)
HELYETT (F)
HENDERSON (US)
HERBI (D)
HERCULES (D)
HERCULES (GB)
HERDTLE-BRUNEAU (F)
HERKO (D)
HERMA (D)
HEROS (D)
HESS (D)
HEXE (D)

HIEKEL (D)
HILAMAN (US)
HILDEBRAND & WOLFMÜLLER (D)
HIRANO (JAP)
HIRONDELLE (F)
HIRSCH (D)
HIRTH (D)
HJ (GB)
HJH (GB)
HMK (A)
HMW (A)
HOBART (GB)
HOCKLEY (GB)
HOCO (D)
HODAKA
HOFFMANN (D)
HOLDEN (GB)
HOLLEY (US)
HOLROYD (GB)
HONDA (JAP)
HOREX (D)
HORSY (F)
HOSK (JAP)
HOSKISON (GB)
HOWARD (GB)
H & R (GB)
HRD (GB)
HT (GB)
HULBERT-BRAMLEY (GB)
HULLA (D)
HULSMANN (NL)
HUMBER (GB)
HUMMEL (D)
HUNDRED (SU)
HUNTER (F)
HURIKAN (CS)
HURRICANE (JAP)
HURTU (F)
HUSAR (D)
HUSOVARNA (S)
HUY (D)

I

IBIS (I)
IDROFLEX (I)
IFA (DDR)
IMC (JAP)
IMHOLZ (CH)
IMME (D)
IMN (I)
IMPERIA (D)
IMPERIAL (GB)
IMPERIAL (US)
INDIAN (GB)
INDUS (D)
INTERNATIONAL (JAP)
INVICTA (GB)

INVICTA (I)
IRESA (E)
IRIS (GB)
IRIS (I)
IRUNA (E)
ISCH (SU)
ISO (I)
ITALA (I)
ITALEMMEZETA (I)
ITALJET (I)
ITALMOTO (I)
ITAR (CS)
ITOM (I)
IVEL (GB)
IVER-JOHNSON (US)
IVO LOLA RIBAR (YU)
IVY (GB)
IXION (GB)

J

JAC (CS)
JACKSON-ROTRAX (GB)
JACK SPORT (F)
JALE (D)
JAMES (GB)

JAP (GB)
JAPAUTO (F)
JAVON (D)
JAWA (CS)
J-BE (US)
JB-LOUVET (F)
JD (GB)
JEAN THOMANN (F)
JEECY-VEA (B)
JEFFERSON (US)
JEHU (GB)
JELINEK (CS)
JES (GB)
JEUNET (F)
JFK (CS)
JH (GB)
JNU (GB)
JNZ (NZ)
JOERNS (US)
JONGHI (F)
JOUCLARD (F)
JOYBIKE (GB)
JSL (D)
JUCKES (GB)
JUERGENSEN (DK)
JUERY (F)
JUHOE (D)
JUNAK (PL)
JUNCKER (F)

JUNIOR (I)
JUNO (GB)
JUPP (GB)

K

KADI (D)
KANTO (JAP)
KAPTEN (NL)
KARUE (D)
KATAKURA (JAP)
KAWASAKI (JAP)
KC (D)
KEMPTON (GB)
KENI (D)
KENILWORTH (GB)
KENZLER-WAVERLEY (US)
KERRY (GB)
KESTREL (GB)
KG (D)
KIEFT (GB)
KILEAR (CS)
KING (GB)
KING-FRAM (S)
KING-JAP (D)
KINGSBURY (GB)

This 1969 Kreidler had a 50 cc engine developing 5·3 bhp. (Orbis Publishing)

KINGSWAY (GB)
K & K (D)
KLOTZ (D)
KMB (D)
KOEHLER-ESCOFFIER (F)
KOHOUT (CS)
KONIG (S)
KOSTER (D)
KOVORETZ (SU)
KR (D)
KRAMMER (A)
KRASNYJ-OKTABR (SU)
KREIDLER (D)
KROBOTH (D)
KRS (D)
KRUPP (D)
KTM (A)
KUMFURT (GB)
KURIER (D)
KYNOCH (GB)
KZ (I)

L

LABOR (F)
LADETTO (I)
LADIES-PACER (GB)
LADY (B)
LAFOUR & NOUGIER (F)
LA FRANCAISE-DIAMANT (F)
LAG (A)
LAGONDA (GB)
LA LORRAINE (F)
LAMAUDIERE (F)
LAMBRETTA (I)
LA MONDIALE (B)
LANCER (GB)
LANCER (JAP)
LANCO (A)
LANDI (I)
LA PANTHERRE (F)
LAPIERRE (F)
LATSCHA (F)
LAURIN & KLEMENT (A)
L'AVENIER (B)
LAVERDA (I)
L & C (GB)
LEA FRANCIS (GB)
LEGNANO (I)
LE GRIMPEUR (F)
LELIOR (F)
LEONARD (GB)
LEONARD FRERA (I)
LEOPARD (D)
LEPROTTO (I)
LETBRIDGE (GB)
LETO (D)

LE VACK (GB)
LEVIS (GB)
LEVRON (F)
LGC (GB)
LIAUDOIS (F)
LIBELLE (D)
LIBERATOR (F)
LIBERIA (F)
LILAC (JAP)
LILY (GB)
LINCOLN-ELK (GB)
LINDSTROM (S)
LINER (JAP)
LINSER (A)
LINX (I)
LION-RAPIDE (B)
LITO (S)
LITTLE GIANT (GB)
LLOYD (D)
LLOYD (LMC) (GB)
LMP (F)
LOCOMOTIEF (NL)
LOHNER (A)
LOMOS (D)
LONDON (GB)
LORD (D)
LORIOT (F)
LOT (PL)
LOUIS CLEMENT (F)
LOUIS JANITOR (F)
L-300 (SU)
LUBE (E)
LUCIFER (F)
LUDOLPH (D)
LUGTON (GB)
LUPUS (D)
LUTECE (F)
LUTRAU (D)
LUTZ (D)
LUWE (D)
LUX (A)
LVOVJANKA (SU)
LWD (D)

M

MABECO (D)
MABON (GB)
McENVOY (GB)
McKECHNIE (GB)
McKENZIE (GB)
MACQUET (F)
MADC (CH)
MAFA (D)
MAFALDA (I)
MAFFEIS (I)
MAGATY (F)

MAGDA (F)
MAGNAT-DEBON (F)
MAGNAT-MOSER (F)
MAGNEET (NL)
MAGNET (D)
MAICO (D)
MAINO (I)
MAJESTIC (F)
MAJESTIC (GB)
MAJOR (I)
MALAGUTI (I)
MALANCA (I)
MAMMUT (D)
MANET (CS)
MANON (F)
MANTOVANI (I)
MANUFRANCE (F)
MANURHIN (F)
MANX (F)
MARATHON (US)
MARC (F)
MARCK (B)
MARIANI (I)
MARINI (I)
MARLOE (GB)
MARLOW (GB)
MARMONNIER (F)
MARS (D)
MARS (GB)
MARSEEL (GB)
MARSH (US)
MARTIN (GB)
MARTIN (JAP)
MARTIN-JAP (GB)
MARTINSHAW (GB)
MARTINSYDE (GB)
MARVEL (US)
MAS (I)
MASCOTTE (F)
MASERATI (I)
MASON & BROWN (GB)
MASSEY (GB)
MASSEY-ARRAN (GB)
MAT (CS)
MATADOR (GB)
MATCHLESS (GB)
MATRA (HU)
MAURER (D)
MAUSER (D)
MAVISA (E)
MAWI (D)
MAXIM (GB)
MAXWELL (NL)
MAY BROS (GB)
MB (CS)
MBR (I)
MC (CS)
MCC (GB)
MEB (DDR)
MDS (I)
MEAD (GB)

MEGOLA (D)
MEGURO (JAP)
MEIHATSU (JAP)
MEISTER (D)
MEMINI (I)
MENON (I)
MENOS (D)
MERAY (HU)
MERCIER (F)
MERCO (D)
MERCURY (GB)
MERKEL (US)
MERLONGHI (I)
MESSNER (A)
METEOR (A)
METEORA (I)
METISSE (GB)
METRO (GB)
METROPOLE (F)
METRO-TYLER (GB)
MEXICO (B)
MEYBEIN (D)
MF (D)
MFB (I)
MFZ (D)
MGC (F)
MGF (D)
MG-TAURUS (I)
MIAMI (US)
MICHAELSON (US)
MICHL ORION (CZ)
MICROMOTEUR (F)
MIDGET-BICAR (GB)
MIELE (D)
MIGNON (I)
MILITAIRE (US)
MILITOR (US)
MILLER-BALSAMO (I)
MILLIONMOBILE (GB)
MIMOA (D)
MINERVA (B)
MINETTI (I)
MINEUR (B)
MINISCOOT (F)
MINNEAPOLIS (US)
MINSK (SU)
MIRANDA (D)
MISTRAL (F)
MITCHELL (US)
MIVAL (I)
MIYAPET (JAP)
M & M (GB)
MM (I)
MM (US)
MOBYLETTE (F)
MOCHET (F)
MOHAWK (GB)
MOLARONI (I)
MONACO-BOUDO (I)
MONARCH (GB)
MONARCH (JAP)

MONARCH (S)
MONARCH (US)
MONARD (GB)
MONARK (S)
MONET-GOYDON (F)
MONFORT (E)
MONNERET (F)
MONOPOLE (GB)
MONOTRACK (USA)
MONTEROSA (I)
MONTESA (E)
MONTGOMERY (GB)
MONVISO (I)
MOONBEAM (GB)
MORBIDELLI (I)
MORETTI (I)
MORINI (I)
MORRIS (GB)
MORRIS-WARNE (GB)
MORS (F)
MORSE-BEAUREGARD (US)
MORTON-ADAM (GB)
MOSER (CH)
MOSKVA (SU)
MOTAG (D)
MOTEURCYCLE (F)
MOTOBECANE (F)
MOTOBI (I)
MOTOBIC (E)
MOTOBLOC (F)
MOTO BORGO (I)
MOTOCLETTE (CH)
MOTOCONFORT (F)
MOTOFLASH (I)
MOTO GUZZI (I)
MOTO-LUX (F)
MOTOM (I)
MOTO MONTE (F)
MOTOPEDALE (F)
MOTOPIANA (I)
MOTO-REVE (CH)
MOTORMEYER (NL)
MOTORPED (GB)
MOTOSACOCHE (CH)
MOTOSACOCHE (F)
MOTOSACOCHE (I)
MOTO-WIESEL (D)
MOTTE (D)
MOUNTAINEER (GB)
MOVESA (E)
MOY (PL)
M & P (F)
MP (I)
MPH (GB)
MR (F)
MR (I)
MR (PL)
MT (A)
MT (I)
MUELLER (I)
MUNCH (D)

MUSTANG (S)
MUSTANG (US)
MV-AGUSTA (I)
MVB (I)
MW (D)
MYMSA (E)
MYSTER (F)
MZ (DDR)

N

NARCISSE (F)
NARCLA (E)
NASSETTI (I)
NAZZARO (I)
NEALL (GB)
NEANDER (D)
NECCHI (I)
NEGAS & RAY (I)
NEGRINI (I)
NEKO (HU)
NERACAR (GB)
NERVOR (F)
NESTOR (GB)
NESTORIA (D)
NETTUNIA (I)
NEVE (D)
NEW COMET (GB)
NEW COULSON (GB)
NEW ERA (GB)
NEW ERA (US)
NEW GERRARD (GB)
NEW HENLEY (HENLEY) (GB)
NEW HUDSON (GB)
NEW IMPERIAL (GB)
NEW KNIGHT (GB)
NEW MAP (F)
NEW MOTORCYCLE (F)
NEWMOUNT (GB)
NEW PARAGON (GB)
NEW RAPID (NL)
NEW RYDER (GB)
NEW SCALE (GB)
NEWTON (GB)
NICHOLAS (GB)
NICKSON (GB)
NIESNER (A)
NIMBUS (DK)
NINON (F)
NISSAN (JAP)
NLG (GB)
NMC (JAP)
NOBLE (GB)
NORBRECK (GB)
NORMAN (GB)
NORTON (GB)
NOVICUM (CS)

NOVY (B)
NSH (D)
NSU (D)
NUT (GB)
NV (S)

O

OASA (I)
OBERLE (D)
OD (D)
OEC (GB)
OFFENSTADT (F)
OGAR (CS)
OGSTON (GB)
OK (GB)
OLIVA (I)
OLIVERIO (I)
OLIVOS (GB)
OLLEARO (I)
OLMO (I)
OLYMPIC (GB)
OLYMPIQUE (F)
OLYMPUS-KING (JAP)
OM (D)
OMB (I)
OMC (GB)
OMEA (I)
OMEGA (GB)
OMN (I)
OMT (I)
ONAWAY (GB)
ONOTO (F)
OPEL (D)
OPRA (I)
ORBIT (GB)
OREOL (F)
ORI (D)
ORIAL (D)
ORIAL (F)
ORIENT (US)
ORIGAN (F)
ORION (CS)
ORIONE (I)
ORIONETTE (D)
ORIX (I)
ORMONDE (GB)
ORTLOFF (D)
ORTONA (GB)
OSA (PL)
OSA-LIBERTY (F)
OSCAR (GB)
OSCHA (D)
OSMOND (GB)
OSSA (E)
OTTOLENGHI (I)
OVERDALE (GB)
OVERSEAS (GB)

P

PA (B)
PACER (GB)
PAGLIANTI (I)
PALOMA (F)
PAMAG (D)
PANDRA (JAP)
PANNI (HU)
PANNONIA (HU)
PANTHER (D)
PANTHER (GB)
PAQUE (D)
PARILLA (I)
PARIS-FRANCE (F)
PASCO (AUS)
PASQUET (F)
PASSONI (I)
PATRIA (D)
PATRIARCA (I)
PATZNER (D)
PAUVERT (F)
PAWI (F)
PAX (GB)
PAZ & SILVA (F)
PDC (GB)
PEARSON (GB)
PEARSON & COX (GB)
PEARSON & SOPWITH (GB)
PEBOK (GB)
PECKETT & McNAB (GB)
PECO (GB)
PEERLESS (GB)
PEERLESS (US)
PEGASO (I)
PENNINGTON (GB)
PENTON (US)
PER (D)
PERFECTA (CH)
PERIPOLI (I)
PERKS & BIRCH (GB)
PERNOD (F)
PERSCH (A)
PETERS (GBM & GB)
PERUGINA (I)
PERUN (CS)
PEUGEOT (F)
PHANOMEN (D)
PHILLIPS (GB)
PHOENIX (D)
PHOENIX (GB)
PIANA (I)
PIATTI (GB)
PIAZZA (I)
PICCOLO (CH)
PIERCE (US)
PIERCE ARROW (US)
PIERME (F)
PIERTON (F)

PILOT (GB)
PIRATE (US)
PIROTTA (I)
PITTY (DDR)
PLANET (D)
PLASSON (F)
P & M (GB)
PMZ (SU)
POINARD (F)
POINTER (JAP)
PONY (D)
PONY (E)
PONY-MONARK (JAP)
POPE (US)
POPET (JAP)
POPMANLEE (JAP)
PORTAL (GB)
PORTLAND (GB)
POSDAM (I)
POSTLER (D)
POUNCY (GB)
POUSTKA (CS)
POWELL (GB)
POWERFUL (GB)
P & P (GB)
PP-ROUSSEY (F)
PRAGA (CS)
PRECISION (GB)
PREMIER (CS)
PREMIER (GB)
PREMO (GB)
PREMOLI (I)
PRESTER (F)
PRESTO (D)
PRIDE & CLARKE (GB)
PRIM (GB)
PRINCEPS (GB)
PRINETTI & STUCCHI (I)
PRIOR (D)
PRIORY (GB)
PROGRESS (D)
PROGRESS (GB)
PROPUL (D)
PROPUL (F)
PUCH (A)
PULLIN-GROOM (GB)
PUMA (RA)
PV (GB)
PZI (PL)

Q

QUADRANT (GB)
QUAGLIOTTI (I)

R

RABBIT (JAP)
RABENEICK (D)
RADCO (GB)
RADIOLA (F)
RADIOR (F)
RADMILL (GB)
RAGLAN (GB)
RALEIGH (GB)
RAMA (F)
RAMBLER (GB)
RAMBLER (US)
RANZANI (I)
RAP (NL)
RAS (I)
RASSER (F)
RATIER (F)
RATINGIA (D)
RAVAT (F)
RAY (GB)
RAYNAL (GB)
READING-STANDARD (US)
READY (B)
READY (GB)
REBRO (GB)
REDDIS (E)
REDUP (GB)
REFORM (A)
REGAL (GB)
REGENT (GB)
REGINA (F)
REGINA (GB)
REH (D)
RELIANCE (US)
RENE GILLET (F)
RENNER-ORIGINAL (D)
RENNSTEIG (D)
REPUBLIC (CS)
REVERE (GB)
REVOLUTION (GB)
REX-ACME (GB)
REX (D)
REX (S)
REX-JAP (GB)
REYNOLDS-RUNABOUT (GB)
REYNOLDS-SPECIAL (GB)
R & F (D)
R & H (GB)
RHONSON (F)
RHONY-X (F)
RICHARD (F)
RICKMAN (GB)
RIEJU (E)
RIKUO (JAP)
RILEY (GB)
RIP (GB)
RIVIERRE (F)
RIXE (D)

RMW (D)
ROA (E)
ROBAKO (D)
ROC (GB)
ROCHESTER (F)
ROCHET (F)
ROCKET (I)
ROCKET (JAP)
ROCKSON (GB)
ROCO (D)
ROCONOVA (D)
ROCVALE (F)
ROEHR (D)
ROES (F)
ROESSLER & JAUERNIG (A)
ROKON (US)
ROLFE (GB)
ROMEO (F)
ROMP (GB)
RONDINE (I)
ROSENGART (F)
ROSSELLI (I)
ROSSI (I)
ROTARY (JAP)
ROULETTE (GB)
ROVA-KENT (AUS)
ROVER (GB)
ROVETTA (I)
ROVIN (F)
ROVLANTE (F)
ROYAL (CH)
ROYAL (F)
ROYAL (I)
ROYAL (US)
ROYAL-AJAX (GB)
ROYAL EAGLE (GB)
ROYAL ENFIELD (GB)
ROYAL MOTO (F)
ROYAL-NORD (B)
ROYAL-RUBY (GB)
ROYAL-SCOT (GB)
ROYAL-SOVEREIGN (GB)
ROYAL STANDARD (CH)
ROYAL-WELLINGTON (GB)
R & P (GB)
RS (D)
RUBINELLI (I)
RUCHE (F)
RUD (D)
RUDGE-WHITWORTH (GB)
RUEDER (D)
RULLIERS (CS)
RUMI (I)
RUNGE (D)
RUPP (D)
RUPP (US)
RUPPE (D)
RUSH (B)
RUSSELL (GB)
RUTER (E)
RWC (A)

RW-SCOUT (GB)
RYS (PL)

S

SACI (BR)
SADEM (F)
SADRIAN (E)
SAGITTA (CS)
SALIRA (B)
SALTLEY (GB)
SANCHOC (F)
SAN CHRISTOFORD (I)
SANGLAS (E)
SAN-SOU-PAP (F)
SANTAMARIA (I)
SANYO (JAP)
SAR (D)
SAR (I)
SARCO (GB)
SARENKA (PL)
SARKANA-SWAIGSNE (LE)
SAROLEA (B)
SARTORIUS (D)
SATAN (CS)
SAXESSORIES (GB)
SCHEIBERT (A)
SCHICKEL (US)
SCHLIHA (D)
SCHNELL-HOREX (D)
SCHURHOFF (D)
SCHÜTT (D)
SCHÜTTOFF (D)
SCHWALBE (CH)
SCHWALBE (D)
SCK (D)
SCOOTAVIA (F)
SCORPION (GB)
SCOTO (F)
SCOTT (GB)
SCOTTA (F)
SCOTT-CYC-AUTO (GB)
SCOUT (GB)
SCS
SCYLLA (F)
SEAL (GB)
SEARS (US)
SEELEY (GB)
SENIOR (I)
SERTUM (I)
SERVICE (GB)
SESSA (I)
SETTER (E)
SFM (PL)
S-FORTIS (CS)
SFW (D)
S & G (D)
SGS (GB)

In the early days of their history (they were later taken over by the BSA group) Sunbeam motorcycles were renowned for quality of manufacture and finish, as is evident in this 1914 example. (M Decet)

SHARRATT (GB)
SHAW (GB)
SHEFFIELD-HENDERSON (GB)
SHIN MEIWA (JAP)
SHL (PL)
SHOWA (JAP)
SHZ (PL)
SIAMT (I)
SIAT (I)
SIC (F)
SICRAF (F)
SIEG (D)
SILK (GB)
SILVA (GB)
SILVER PIGEON (JAP)
SILVER PRINCE (GB)
SILVER-STAR (JAP)
SIM (I)
SIMARD (F)
SIMONCELLI (I)
SIMONETTA (I)
SIMPLEX (GB)
SIMPLEX (I)
SIMPLEX (NL)
SIMPLEX (US)
SIMSON (DDR)
SINGER (GB)
SIPHAX (F)

SIROCCO (CS)
SIRRAH (GB)
SISSY (A)
SITTA (D)
SJK (JAP)
SKF (SU)
SKO (CS)
SKOOTAMOTA (GB)
SLADE-JAP (GB)
SLANEY (GB)
SLAVIA (A)
SLINGER (GB)
SM (PL)
SMART (A)
SMART (F)
SMS (GB)
SMW (D)
S & N (D)
SNOB (D)
SOCOVEL (B)
SOK (S)
SOKOL (PL)
SOS (GB)
SOUPLEX (B)
SOUTHEY (GB)
SOYER (F)
SPA-JAP (GB)
SPARK (GB)

SPARKBROOK (GB)
SPARTA (NL)
SPARTAN (GB)
SPARTON (GB)
SPAVIERO (I)
SPECIAL-MONNERET (F)
SPEED (F)
SPEED-KING JAP (GB)
SPHINX (F)
SPHYNX (B)
SPIEGLER (D)
SPIESS (D)
SPIRIDITS (Latvia)
SPRING (B)
SRM (S)
STABIL (B)
STADION (CS)
STAFFETT (N)
STAFFORD (GB)
STAG (GB)
STAIGER (D)
STAN (GB)
STANDARD (D)
STANGER (GB)
STANLEY (GB)
STAR (B)
STAR (D)
STAR (GB)

STAR-GEM (B)
STEFFEY (US)
STELLA (F)
STELLAR (GB)
STELLBRINK (D)
STERLING (F)
STERVA (F)
STERZI (I)
STEVENS (GB)
STICHERLING (D)
STIMULA (F)
STOCK (D)
STROLCH (D)

STRUCO (D)
STUART (GB)
STUCCHI (I)
STYLSON (F)
STYRIA (A)
SUDBRACK (D)
SUDBROOK (GB)
SUECIA (S)
SULKY (F)
SUMITA (JAP)
SUN (GB)
SUNBEAM (GB)
SUPERBA (I)

SUPERB FOUR (GB)
SUPERIA (B)
SUPERIA (D)
SUPER-X (US)
SUPPLEXA (F)
SUPREMOCO (GB)
SUQUET (F)
SUT (D)
SUZUKI (JAP)
SUZY (F)
SWAN (GB)
SWIFT (GB)
SWM (I)

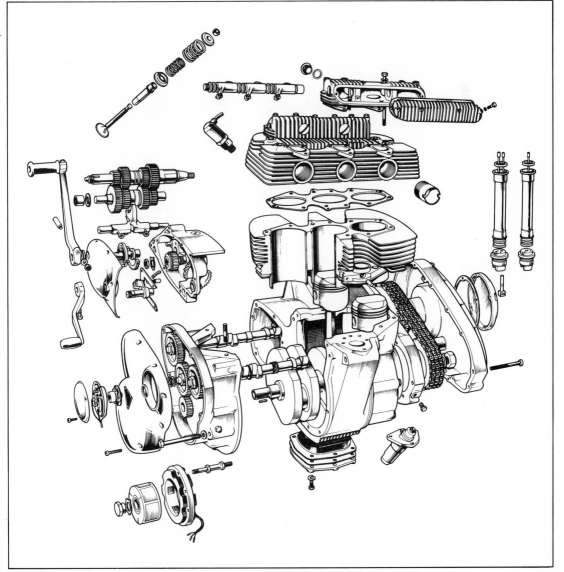

Engine and gearbox of the Triumph 750 cc triple. (Christian Lacombe)

SYMPLEX (GB)
SYPHAX (F)

T

TAC (GB)
TALBOT (F)
TANDON (GB)
TAPPELLA-FUCHS (I)
TAS (D)
TAS (JAP)
TAUMA (I)
TAURA (I)
TAURUS (I)
TAUTZ (D)
TAVERNIER (F)
TECO (D)
TEDDY (F)
TEE-BEE (GB)
TEHUELCHE (RA)
TEMPLE (GB)
TEMPO (N)
TERROT (CS)
TERROT (F)
TESTI (I)
TETGE (D)
THEIN & GOLDBERGER (A)
THIEM (US)
THOMANN (F)
THOMAS (GB)
THOR (US)
THOROUGH (GB)
THUMANN (D)
THUNDER (I)
TICKLE (GB)
TIGER (D)
TIGER (US)
TILBROOK (AUS)
TILL (D)
TILSTON (GB)
TITAN (A)
TIZ-AM (SU)
TMC (GB)
TOHATSU (JAP)
TOMASELLI (I)
TOMOS (YU)
TOREADOR (GB)
TORNAX (D)
TORPADO (I)
TORPEDO (A)
TORPEDO (D)
TORPEDO (GB)
TOWNEND (GB)
TOYOMOTOR (JAP)
TRAFALGAR (GB)
TRAFFORD (GB)
TRAIN (F)
TRAMNITZ (D)

TREBLOC (F)
TREMO (D)
TREMONIA (D)
TRENT (GB)
TRIANON (D)
TRIBUNE (US)
TRIPLE-H (GB)
TRIPLETTE (GB)
TRIPOL (CS)
TRIUMPH (D)
TRIUMPH (GB)
TRIUMPH (US)
TROBIKE (GB)
TROLL (DDR)
TROPFEN (D)
TRUMP (GB)
TSUBASA (JAP)
TULA (SU)
TURKHEIMER (I)
TX (D)
TYLER (GB)
TYPHOON (NL)
TYPHOON (S)

U

ULTIMA (F)
UNIBUS (GB)
UNION (S)
UNIVERSAL (CH)
UNIVERSELLE (D)
URAL (USSR)
URANIA (D)
URS (D)
UT (D)
UTILIA (F)

V

VAGA (I)
VAL (GB)
VALLS (E)
VAN VEEN (NDL)
VAP (F)
VAREL (D)
VASCO (GB)
VASSENA (I)
VATERLAND (D)
VAUXHALL (GB)
VECCHIETTI (I)
VEL AMOS (CS)
VELOCETTE (GB)
VELOX (CS)
VELOSOLEX (F)

VENUS (D)
VENUS (GB)
VERGA (I)
VERLOR (F)
VEROS (I)
VERUS (GB)
VESPA (I)
VIATKA (SU)
VIBERTI (I)
VICKY (NL)
VICTA (GB)
VICTORIA (D)
VICTORIA (GB)
VILLA (F)
VILLOF (E)
VINCENT (GB)
VINCO (GB)
VINDEC (GB)
VINDEC-SPECIAL (D)
VIPER-JAP (GB)
VIRATELLE (F)
VIS (D)
VITTORIA (I)
VOISIN (F)
VULCAN (A)
VULKAAN (NL)

W

WADDINGTON (GB)
WAG (GB)
WAGNER (US)
WAKEFIELD (GB)
WALBA (D)
WALLIS (GB)
WALMET (D)
WALTER (A)
WALTER (CS)
WALTER (D)
WANDERER (D)
WARD (GB)
WARRIOR (GB)
WATNEY (GB)
WAVERLEY (GB)
WD (GB)
WEARWELL (GB)
WEATHERELL (GB)
WEAVER (GB)
WEBER & REICHMANN (CS)
WECOOB (D)
WEE McGREGOR (GB)
WELLER (GB)
WERNER (F)
WERNER-MAG (A)
WERNO (D)
WESTFIELD (GB)
WESTOVIAN (GB)

The touring version of the 1000 cc Vincent was this Rapide. Shown here is the B series with simple girder front fork. (M. Decet)

The 1978/9 Zündapp KS175. (Orbis Publishing)

The 1940/48 Zündapp 751 cc KS750BW, a military integrated motorcycle and sidecar outfit. (Orbis Publishing)

WFM (PL)
W & G (GB)
WHEATCROFT (GB)
WHIPPET (GB)
WHIRLWIND (GB)
WHITE & POPPE (GB)
WHITLEY (GB)
WHITWOOD (GB)
WHIZZER (US)
WICRO-PRECISION (D)
WIGA (D)
WIGAN-BARLOW (GB)
WILBEE (GB)
WILIER (I)
WILKIN (GB)
WILKINSON-ANTOINE (GB)
WILKINSON (TMC) (GB)
WILLIAMS (US)
WILLIAMSON (GB)
WILLOW (GB)
WIMMER (D)
WINCO (GB)
WINDHOFF (D)
WIN-PRECISION (GB)
WITALL (GB)
WITTEKIND (D)
WITTLER (GB)

WIZARD (GB)
WMR (D)
WOLF (GB)
WOTAN (D)
WOOLER (GB)
WSE (D)
WSK (PL)
WULF (D)
WULFRUNA (D)
WURTTEMBERGIA (D)

X

XL (GB)
XL-ALL (GB)

Y

YALE (US)
YAMAGUCHI (JAP)
YAMAHA (JAP)
YAMSEL (GB)

YANKEE (US)
YORK (A)
YOUNG (GB)
YVEL (F)

Z

ZANELLA (RA)
ZEDEL (F)
ZEGEMO (D)
ZEHNDER (CH)
ZEHNER (D)
ZENITH (GB)
ZEPHYR (GB)
ZETGE (D)
ZEUGNER (D)
ZEUZ (A)
ZIEJANUE (D)
ZIRO (D)
ZÜNDAPP (D)
ZURTZ-RECORD (D)
ZWALVE (NL)
ZWEIRAD-UNION (D)
ZWI (IL)
ZZR (PL)

INTERNATIONAL ABBREVIATIONS

A (AT)	Austria	GBM	Isle of Man	RC (TW)	Taiwan (Formosa)
ADN (YD)	Democratic Yemen (formerly Aden)	GBZ (GI)	Gibraltar	RCA (CF)	Central African Republic
		GCA (GT)	Guatemala	RCB (CG)	Congo
AFG (AF)	Afghanistan	GH	Ghana	RCH (CL)	Chile
AL	Albania	GR	Greece	RH (HT)	Haiti
AND (AD)	Andorra	GUY (GY)	Guyana (formerly British Guiana)	RI (D)	Indonesia
AUS (AU)	Australia			RIM (MR)	Mauritania
B (BE)	Belgium	H (HU)	Hungary	RL (LB)	Lebanon
BDS (BB)	Barbados	HK	Hong Kong	RM (MG)	Malagasy Republic (formerly Madagascar)
BG	Bulgaria	HKJ (JO)	Jordan		
BH (BZ)	Belize (formerly British Honduras)	I (IT)	Italy	RMM (ML)	Mali
		IL	Israel	ROK (KP)	Korea (Republic of)
BR	Brazil	IND (IN)	India	RP (PH)	Philippines
BRN (BH)	Bahrain	IR	Iran	RSM (SM)	San Marino
BRU (BN)	Brunei	IRL (IE)	Ireland	RSR (RH)	Rhodesia (formerly Southern Rhodesia)
BS	Bahamas	IRQ (IQ)	Iraq		
BUR (BU)	Burma	IS	Iceland	RU (BI)	Burundi
C (CU)	Cuba	J (JP)	Japan	RWA (RW)	Rwanda
CDN (CA)	Canada	JA (JM)	Jamaica	S (SE)	Sweden
CH	Switzerland	K (KH)	Khmer Republic (formerly Cambodia)	SD (SZ)	Swaziland
CI	Ivory Coast			SF (FI)	Finland
CL (LK)	Sri Lanka (formerly Ceylon)	KWT (KW)	Kuwait	SGP (SG)	Singapore
		L (LU)	Luxembourg	SME (SR)	Surinam (Dutch Guiana)
CO	Colombia	LAO (LA)	Laos	SN	Senegal
CR	Costa Rica	LAR (LY)	Libya	SU	Union of Soviet Socialist Republics
CS	Czechoslovakia	LB (LR)	Liberia		
CY	Cyprus	LS	Lesotho (formerly Basutoland)	SWA	South West Africa
D (DE)	German Federal Republic			SY (SC)	Seychelles
		M (MT)	Malta	SYR (SY)	Syria
DDR (DD)	German Democratic Republic	MA	Morocco	T (TH)	Thailand
		MAL (MY)	Malaysia	TG	Togo
DK	Denmark	MC	Monaco	TN	Tunisia
DOM (DO)	Dominican Republic	MEX (MX)	Mexico	TR	Turkey
DY	Dahomey	MS (MU)	Mauritius	TT	Trinidad and Tobago
DZ	Algeria	MW	Malawi	U (UY)	Uruguay
E (ES)	Spain (including African localities and provinces)	N (NO)	Norway	USA (US)	United States of America
		NA (AN)	Netherlands Antilles	V (VA)	Holy See (Vatican City)
EAK (KE)	Kenya	NIC (NI)	Nicaragua	VN (VD)	Vietnam (Republic of)
EAT (TZ)	Tanzania (formerly Tanganyika)	NL	Netherlands	WAG (GM)	Gambia
		NZ	New Zealand	WAL (SL)	Sierra Leone
EAU (UG)	Uganda	P (PT)	Portugal	WAN (NG)	Nigeria
EAZ (TZ)	Tanzania (formerly Zanzibar)	P (AO)	Angola	WD (DM)	Dominica ⎫ Windward
		P (CV)	Cape Verde Islands	WG (GD)	Grenada ⎬ Islands
EC	Ecuador	P (MZ)	Mozambique	WL (LC)	St Lucia ⎭
ET (EG)	Arab Republic of Egypt	P (GN)	Guinea	WS	Western Samoa
F (FR)	France (including overseas departments and territories)	P (TP)	Timor	WV (VC)	St Vincent (Windward Islands)
		P (ST)	São Tomé and Principe		
		PA	Panama	YU	Yugoslavia
FJI (FJ)	Fiji	PAK (PK)	Pakistan	YV (VE)	Venezuela
FL (LI)	Liechtenstein	PE	Peru	Z	Zambia
GB	United Kingdom of Great Britain and Northern Ireland	PL	Poland	ZA	South Africa
		PY	Paraguay	ZR (ZM)	Zaire (formerly Congo Kinshasa)
		R (RO)	Romania		
GBA	Alderney ⎫ Channel	RA (AR)	Argentina		
GBG	Guernsey ⎬ Islands	RB (BW)	Botswana (formerly Bechuanaland)		
GBJ	Jersey ⎭				

'I cannot praise a fugitive and cloistered virtue, unexercised and unbreathed, that never sallies out and sees her adversary, but slinks out of the race, where that immortal garland is to be run for, not without dust and heat.' John Milton, *Areopagitica*.

SECTION IV

SPORT AND
PLAY

Joe Wright in the saddle of a Brough Superior with the manufacturer, George Brough, standing alongside him. The silencers and exhaust fishtails indicate that the machine is in Brooklands trim: this pattern of silencers was compulsory at the track. (National Motor Museum, Beaulieu)

If you can meet with triumph and disaster,
And treat those two imposters just the same . . .
Giving the new Honda NR500 GP racer its début at the 1979 British Grand Prix, Mick Grant slid on oil left by team-mate
Takazumi Katayama's similar machine. In the ensuing crash, the revolutionary and terribly expensive Honda was burnt out.
(All Sport/Don Morley)

THE WORLD SPEED RECORD

Many are the attempts that have ended in bitter disappointment; several resulted in alarming accidents, some with severe injuries, and, perhaps surprisingly in view of the dangers, only one in death: and there was one attempt that finished almost comically with the rider having set his trousers on fire. It is natural to want to go faster than anybody else, and almost as natural to want to prove it; and so the record books have been packed with onslaughts on the motorcycling speed record for 70 years.

Unfortunately the truth has sometimes been rather difficult to ascertain. Some kind of official recognition of the world land speed record for two wheels has existed since 1909, but doubts have persisted about the proper authentication of the speeds reached. It is not until the 1920s that we can be sure that all the technical requirements for accurate timekeeping, along with other regulations, which include being timed over a stretch of not less than a quarter of a mile (402·3m) — or sometimes a full kilometre — in at least two runs in opposite directions, to be carried out within a certain time to make sure that no unfair advantage is taken of the prevailing wind, have been been observed. Nevertheless, the earlier record attempts were not without merit, and they deserve attention.

The first and slightly dubious period corresponds with the first of three phases in the history of attempts on the world speed record, related to the nature of the course. Prior to 1923, such attempts were usually carried out at one of the recognised racing tracks, most especially Brooklands in England but also at a variety of American venues including the celebrated beach at Daytona. From 1923 until 1956 the record course was almost always a stretch of road, sometimes frighteningly ordinary, sometimes the most modern of German or Italian motorways. The final phase, which has carried us to the present day, has seen all such attempts carried out on the dry salt flats at Bonneville in the USA. It was there in Utah that the record was carried beyond 200 mph (322 km/h) for the first time, and only another 19 years passed before it was raised beyond 300 mph (483 km/h), four times faster than the earliest record ever established.

That honour fell to W E Cook, an Englishman who averaged 75·92 mph (122·16 km/h) over a flying kilometre at Brooklands on 16 June 1909. He was riding a motorcycle known as the NLG (the letters stood for North London Garages, the firm which built it), and it was powered by a 944 cc Peugeot V-twin engine with direct belt drive to the rear wheel. This was the same machine that Cook had ridden to win the very first motorcycle race at Brooklands on 20 April 1908.

Cook pushed the record higher on another NLG later in 1909, this time with the aid of a JAP engine of no less than 2713 cc. Riding this mechanical enormity, Cook reached over 90 mph (144·8 km/h) but did not succeed in setting an official record. Instead it was another Englishman, Charles Collier, who raised the record next, to 80·24mph (129·1 km/h) on 20 July 1910. This 25-year-old Londoner was the son of the founder of the Matchless Company and winner of the first-ever TT in 1907, and it was natural that he should be riding a machine of Matchless make, again powered by a big V-twin JAP engine. In August 1910 he pushed his own speed even higher, to 84·89 mph (136·6 km/h). In 1911 Brooklands was visited by an American rider, Jake (sometimes Jack) de Rosier, the rider of a V-twin-engined Indian which proved capable in the 6 am cool of a July morning at Brooklands of reaching 85·38 mph (137·4 km/h). Before leaving Britain, de Rosier made another record attempt with his 994 cc Indian, succeeding in leaving the figure at 88·87 mph (143 km/h). Hardly had he set sail, however, than Collier brought out his Matchless to Brooklands again and on 4 August did 89·48 mph (144 km/h). On 19 August he took the figure over 90 mph at last, being timed at 91·37 mph (147 km/h), and there for some time the matter lay. Not until 1914 was Collier's record beaten, when on 2 May Sidney George rode the Brooklands kilometre at a speed of 93·48 mph (150·4 km/h), the figure that was to stand unchallenged until the Great War and its aftermath had subsided.

When a sporting rivalry could take the place of those deadly hostilities, the battle for the world speed record was renewed in 1921. Initially there were some exceptionally rapid one-way runs over the Brooklands kilometre — which did not qualify for recognition as world records because of the two-way rule that was by then being enforced; for example Douglas Davidson was the first to be timed at over 100 mph in Britain riding his Harley-Davidson at 100·76 mph

(162·1 km/h) at Brooklands on 28 April 1921. Herbert Le Vack, who had managed 106·52 mph (171·4 km/h) one-way on 29 April then carried out a properly observed two-way sprint which gave him the world record with an average speed of 93·99 mph (151·2 km/h). He was riding an Indian, a 10-year-old eight-valve V-twin that had been christened 'The Camel', nicknames being very popular for machines among the Brooklands devotees in those days.

Le Vack's record did not last long, being taken from him by Claude F. Temple who rode a Harley-Davidson at Brooklands to average 99·86 mph (160·7 km/h). Le Vack came back to answer this challenge in October. He was now riding a JAP-engined Zenith, and with a speed of 102·80 mph (165·4 km/h) he had at last beaten the bogey of 'the magic century'. Or perhaps it had been done already: on the 14 April 1920 an American, Ed Walker, was credited with 103·5 mph (166·5 km/h) — or, according to some, 104·12 mph (167·5 km/h) — riding a 994 cc Indian at Daytona. Any doubts about the exact performance of Walker must be tempered by recognition of his obvious competitiveness, whatever the governing bodies made of his time: in the 1950s we were to see again an American rider evidently the fastest in the world but denied official recognition as such.

Meanwhile, in September 1923 the record was set afresh at a new venue, in conditions which allowed no questioning of its authenticity. F W (Freddie) Dixon took his eight-valve V-twin Harley-Davidson to France for the speed trials at Boulogne. On a closed stretch of road he averaged 171·35 km/h (106·5 mph) and thus began a new era. Only once more would the finishing straight at Brooklands (where the run-in before the timed kilometre and the space available for slowing down after it were becoming too short for such speeds) be the scene of a successful world speed record attempt, when on 6 November 1923 Claude Temple recaptured the record at 174·58 km/h (108·48 mph) riding a 996 cc British Anzani.

Temple's record lasted until 27 April 1924, when Le Vack took it up to 182·59 km/h (113·48 mph) riding a JAP-engined Brough Superior. This was the first such machine to have an overhead-valve engine, a V-twin of 998 cc displacement, but against this advantage Le Vack had to face

the handicap of rain and high winds on a narrow pot-holed road in the Senart Forest, near Paris, where the French Speed Trials were being held. Later that year he went to another stretch of French road near Arpajon, which had been found suitable for high speeds, even for some of the giant cars then attempting to set absolute world land speed records. There Le Vack was able to go faster, and on 6 July 1924 he raised his own record to 191·59 km/h (119·07 mph), again riding the Brough Superior.

Two years passed before his rival, Claude Temple, felt ready to meet that challenge; at Arpajon on 5 September 1926 Temple succeeded, setting a new mark at 195·33 km/h (121·41 mph). This time he was riding a new machine, the 996 cc JAP-engined OEC-Temple, the same one with which 2 days later he set a new record for 1 hour riding non-stop around the banked track at Montlhery near Paris to average 164·1 km/h (102 mph).

Once again 2 years were to pass before another new contender appeared, the British rider Oliver M. Baldwin, riding a 998 cc JAP-engined Zenith on the Arpajon road on 25 August 1928 to average more than 200 km/h for the first time ever, the exact figure being 200·56 km/h (124·62 mph).

There was an exceptional feast of speed at Arpajon in the following year, an almost literal one with 20 000 spectators taking picnics alongside the now famous straight, where all the great names of record-breaking, and a few hopeful contenders, were present. Baldwin, the reigning monarch of two-wheeled speed, was there to defend his crown, while Albert Denly, Freddie Hicks, Bill Lacey, Herbert Le Vack and Joe Wright were there to try to wrest it from him. The date was 25 August 1929, and it saw the world speed record broken no less than four times. Wright and Le Vack were the successful riders, each with a V-twin JAP engine between his knees; but the 996 cc version of the former was in a Zenith frame, the 998 cc power unit of the latter in a Brough Superior that had originally been built for Freddie Dixon. Wright was the first to have a successful run, clocking 202·931 km/h (126·12 mph); minutes later Le Vack responded with a time shorter by a fraction of a second, then Wright did better still, and at last Le Vack emerged the faster, having knocked 0·41 second

So far the smallest capacity class in road-racing has been for 50 cc machines, of which the most consistent world champion rider has been Angel Nieto. (All Sport/Don Morley)

The start at the TT. (All Sport/Don Morley)

Speedway flair demonstrated by Ivan Mauger. (All Sport/Don Morley)

American oval-track flurry shown by Phil McDonald. (All Sport/Don Morley)

Ernst Henne posing with the supercharged 750 cc BMW on which he set a new world speed record in 1930. (Orbis Publishing)

off Wright's opening time to keep the record for the day at 207·330 km/h (128·86 mph). It was the last time that he would ever break the world record, for he was killed in a road accident in Switzerland 2 years later.

Before that mishap, he lost his record to a new rival, the German rider Ernst Henne, who was to become the greatest, the most consistent and the most indomitable record breaker in all the history of high-speed motorcycling.

An earnest and quiet man, Henne had joined BMW in 1925, only a couple of years after they produced the first of their long line of shaft-driven flat-twin-engined motorcycles. In 1928 the fifth production model in the series had been introduced, the R63, the first BMW to have overhead valves, and the first to have a bore substantially greater than its stroke. Henne's record-breaker version was the first to be supercharged, and this forced induction amply compensated for its engine's relatively modest displacement of 734 cc, being the smallest yet to be successful in the pursuit of the world speed record. Henne helped matters along by allowing himself to be streamlined: his helmet had a posterior fairing, another conical aerodynamic infill was strapped to his behind, and in close-fitting white leathers he tucked himself away on his BMW to set a new record at 221·54 km/h (137·68 mph) on a stretch of the new Autobahn running between Munich and Ingolstadt.

Henne threw down this gauntlet on 19 September 1929, and not until 31 August 1930 was anybody ready to take the challenge. Then Wright visited Arpajon again with a JAP-engined OEC-Temple, and with 998 unsupercharged cc to pit against the BMW's blown 735, he was able to hoist the record to 220·99 km/h (137·32 mph) — having had to hire the road privately for the early hours of the morning, after failing in his attempt during the official record session. In 3 weeks, Henne had restored the situation, taking his BMW out again to average 221·4 km/h (137·66 mph) and to make it clear to the whole world that he and BMW were prepared to take on all comers.

He did not go short of challengers. Wright, aided by Claude Temple whose name was now being associated with many OEC motorcycles, prepared a supercharged JAP engine of 995 cc for his OEC-Temple, and another essentially similar 998 cc JAP for his spare Zenith machine. The two were then shipped to Ireland where, on the straight Carrigrohane Road in County Cork, Wright was anxious to capture the record before the London Motorcycle Show opened at Olympia in November 1930. What followed was something of a mix-up, apparently inspired by some slightly commercial disregard for the fine details of the truth. Wright made his first run on the OEC-Temple, and it was a very fast run indeed — quick enough to convince the only photographer present that the record was in the bag, and he rushed away to get his picture off to his agency. In the photographer's absence, Wright had trouble with his OEC and could not complete the return run with it. Instead the Zenith was wheeled onto the road, and with this Wright was successful in posting a new record two-way average of 242·59 km/h (150·74 mph). This was a particularly satisfying result because it represented such a large increment over the BMW's record and because all that still sizeable portion of the world still familiar with Imperial measures could appreciate that 150 mph was a significant milestone. It should have been excellent news for Olympia, but when the show opened it was with a machine labelled 'The Fastest Motorcycle in the World' on the OEC stand. There seems little doubt that OEC knew that the

Zenith was the true record-breaker, but there was no photograph of the Zenith making its run — and the sponsors of the attempt were the engine-makers JAP, who reckoned that since the engines of the two machines were virtually identical, and that OEC would give them better publicity because Zenith were in financial difficulties at the time, there would be no harm in turning a Nelsonian blind eye. The misrepresentation was noticed in the press, however, and not until long afterwards did the resulting controversy abate.

BMW must have been rather shaken by the high speed that Wright reached. It was scarcely considered the done thing in those days to break the record by so large a margin: many record breakers helped to defray their expenses or even to make a profit by accepting bonus payments from the suppliers of fuel, oil, tyres and other components, or even from manufacturers of the complete machines, and there was obviously more money to be made by breaking the record several times by small increments than by taking a large leap forward and reaching one's limit first time out. So almost exactly 2 years were to pass before Henne was to recapture his record (there was a clear assumption that it was his) when on 3 November 1932 he took his BMW to the Tat Road in Hungary, where he was timed at an average of 244·4 km/h (151·86 mph) to begin a 4-year period of supremacy.

On 28 October 1934 he was riding in Hungary again, this time at Gyon, lifting his speed to 246·069 km/h (152·90 mph). In the autumn of the next year he had another go at the title, his last on the 735 cc BMW, riding in Germany again on the Frankfurt–Darmstadt Autobahn to record 256·046 km/h (159·09 mph). The same stretch of road was to serve Henne in the following year, but everything else was changed.

Well, almost everything — his motorcycle was still a shaft-drive flat-twin BMW, but it was a new model with an even smaller engine. In place of the blown 735 cc power unit, there was an even more highly supercharged 495 cc engine, and instead of trying to streamline himself with a tadpole-tailed helmet and an artificially pointed posterior, Henne lay inside a totally enclosed fairing, the first complete streamliner to be seen in the history of the record. The date when he set his new mark was 12 October 1936, and that mark was 272·006 km/h (169·05 mph).

The wonders that Henne had achieved with the 750 BMW faded in comparison with what his dramatic aerodyne accomplished and it might have been supposed that the tremendous speed of the 500 was wholly due to the ovoid aluminium shell, complete with tail fin, within which the whole machine and rider were tucked away from the wind. However, a week before the record shattering run took place, BMW's team manager and engine development specialist Schleicher had said, 'We are finished with the 750 — the blown 500 is already giving much more power'. It very probably was, for there were strong rumours of an unofficial timing of the new streamliner at something like 200 mph (about 320 km/h) during 6-am practice runs on the more sinuous Autobahn running from Munich to Landesgrenze.

Henne's record was set during an officially organised session open to other competitors, and there was a rival on the scene from Britain. This was Eric Fernihough, well known at Brooklands and at the various lesser sprint courses that were popular in Britain, and also with some reputation as a road racer; and he had chosen to enter the fray with a Brough Superior powered by a supercharged 995 cc JAP engine. He could not come anywhere near matching the speed of the new BMW on this occasion, however, but for that matter he was less than favourably impressed by the streamlining of the BMW, which he thought made it dangerously unstable. Some half-hearted attempts had been made to streamline his Brough Superior but these were dispensed with when, 6 months later, he went to Gyon in Hungary for a crack at the record and on 19 April 1937 managed to raise it by a bare 1 km/h to 273·244 km/h (169·786 mph). He then hitched a sidecar to the Brough Superior, ballasted it with 140 lb (63·6 kg) of sand, and set off down the road to take the sidecar record from Henne at a little over 220 km/h (137 mph); but the behaviour of the combination was decidedly comose, and some onlookers considered it a miracle that Fernihough should have survived the experience.

It should have served as a warning to all that the days of brute force and blissful ignorance were finished. No longer could a rider hope to win honours by harnessing the lustiest imaginable engine in the most spindle-shanked chassis capable of lasting the requisite distance. Speeds were now so high that the air was being stirred into a turmoil more violent than many an aeroplane of the day had to endure: as well as imposing a drag or resistance to forward motion, aerodynamic forces at such speeds could engender lateral and vertical lift forces that could promote all kinds of instability. The tail fin on the BMW shell was evidence of some awareness of the dangers, but since even the aviation industry of the time had only a very imperfect understanding of the science of high-speed aerodynamics, it was too much to hope for motorcycle engineers and mechanics to have more than the sketchiest of ideas about the problems likely to be encountered.

The next motorcycle to be presented before the FIM's accredited timekeepers was also very comprehensively streamlined, but in a startlingly different style. The fully enclosed fairing was unconvincingly short and stubby, and ludicrously tall, with an even higher tail fin, and its waisted frontal aspect was so strange that it was nicknamed the 'the flying pillar box'. Inside its aluminium shell lurked a supercharged four-cylinder Gilera and the Italian rider Piero Taruffi.

With a distinguished record as a racing motorcyclist, and later to earn even more fame as a racing car driver, Taruffi had been appointed racing manager for the Gilera team after putting in some very impressive rides himself on the original 4-cylinder supercharged 500 cc Rondine which had appeared in 1935 and was to form the basis of the Gilera when the Rondine was taken over by the Gilera Company. In unstreamlined form the machine had attracted a good deal of attention by being timed at 152 mph (244·6 km/h) on the Autostrada between Firenze and Mare, and that was enough to persuade Taruffi and Gilera that it would be worth building a proper record-breaker. In May 1937 the machine proved its mettle and Taruffi his (not that it was ever in doubt), in an astonishing and successful attempt to take the 500 cc 1-hour record by riding up and down the Autostrada between Brescia and Bergamo. Despite having to come to a virtual standstill when turning round at the end of each leg, Taruffi had succeeded in covering more than 121 miles (194·8 km) in the hour, and this feat gave the team all the encouragement it needed. On 21 October 1937, at dawn on the Brescia road, the 492 cc Gilera carried Taruffi to a new record of 274·181 km/h (170·27 mph) to put Italy into the list for the very first time.

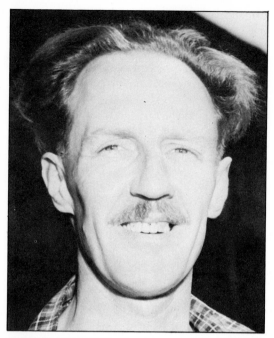

Noel Pope shortly before his unsuccessful attempt to recapture the speed record for motorcycle with a streamlined Brough Superior. (Associated Press)

km/h) somewhat earlier, he tried for a two-way record on Southport Sands, only to be forced to abandon his onslaught by a blazing backside when something went wrong at 120 mph (193 km/h) and set his trousers on fire. There was not to be another challenger until 1949, when a redoubtable former Brooklands rider, Noel Pope, went to the Bonneville salt flats with an old Brough Superior in a new and rather badly designed fairing which upended at about 150 mph (240 km/h), destroying itself comprehensively and bruising its rider severely. Not until 12 April 1951 did Henne, now in retirement, see his record beaten, when he stood by the Munich Autobahn to watch his compatriot Wilhelm Herz race up and down it at an average of 290·322 km/h (180·39 mph), tucked away inside a streamlined shell not unlike the one that the BMW rider had once occupied. However, the machine tucked inside the fairing with Herz was an NSU, a supercharged parallel twin of 498 cc displacement and mechanically elaborate design.

Four years later, a mechanically rather simpler device, a perfectly standard unsupercharged 998 cc Vincent Black Lightning, took the record from the NSU. It was enclosed in a streamlined shell that had been copied from the Herz fairing, but that detracted in no way from the plaudits that the 25-year-old Russell Wright, a New Zealand rider, earned in setting the new record. His mean speed on that 2 July 1955 was 297·640 km/h (184·94 mph) and it was done at Swannanoa in New Zealand on an ordinary wet road.

It was the last time that the world speed record would ever be set on an ordinary road, let alone a wet one, and the last time that it would be set by a completely conventional motorcycle. The place for all future attempts would be the Bonneville Salt Flats, 8 miles (13 km) wide and 15 miles (24 km) long, hard and smooth and high and blindingly obvious. The shape of things to come would be different too, as was demonstrated less than a month after Wright's brave effort in New Zealand. A 22-year-old rider from Texas, Johnny Allen, took a long, low streamliner powered by a 650 cc Triumph engine to the salt lake in Utah and was timed at 193·72 mph (311·7 km/h). It was not an officially recognised record, because his runs were not timed according to the fine detail of FIM requirements, but there was no doubt that he did in fact go so fast, and morally if

No longer could BMW pretend to take no notice. Within 5 weeks Henne had the 493 cc BMW out on the Frankfurt–Munich Autobahn, where he lifted the record to 279·503 km/h (173·67 mph), where it was to remain undisturbed for 14 years.

It did not go untoppled for want of any effort on the part of Eric Fernihough. Once again he took his Brough-Superior to Hungary, once again he launched it along the Gyon road. Alas, it was for the last time: while going at something like 180 mph (about 290 km/h), the Brough suddenly developed a steering wobble and went out of control. Fernihough was killed in the crash.

All the other contenders for Henne's crown had dropped out. An Australian challenger, Arthur Simcock, had managed 153·98 mph (247·81 km/h) on the Tat Road in 1931, but could not manage a satisfactory run in the opposite direction. In 1933 Joe Wright had had another go, this time on an AJS that had been specially built at a cost of £5000: having managed a one-way speed of 167 mph (268

Johnny Allen. (Orbis Publishing)

machine, made great use of the result in advertising, but the record was never officially ratified because once again Allen had not been officially timed by FIM standards.

It was another Triumph-engined streamliner that was first to break the record officially when on 5 September 1962 a 38-year-old truck driver from Los Angeles called William (Bill) Johnson established a new mark at 361·41 km/h (224·57 mph). As in Allen's machine, the vertical-twin engine was the familiar 649 cc pushrod ohv Triumph, but this time the long, low motorcycle was a 'special' built by Joe Dudek. Unlike Allen's it had an enclosed cockpit for the half-supine rider, and raised tail fin to improve directional stability — something that it very nearly failed to do when a side wind set the machine adrift on one run when it was covering the salt at about 230 mph (370 km/h).

The next step was to install two of these Triumph engines in a streamliner, and this was done successfully on 25 August 1966 when a Triumph dealer from Detroit, Michigan reached 395·28 km/h (245·66 mph) in a machine called Gyronaut X-1. The driver (one could no longer call the occupants of these cigar-like projectiles riders) was Robert Leppan.

Next it was the turn of a Yamaha dealer, a Californian named Don Vesco. His streamliner was powered by two twin-cylinder 350 cc 2-stroke Yamaha engines running on pump petrol, and at first it brought him misfortune, crashing at record-breaking speed. Vesco survived unhurt, and on 17 September 1970 he became the first man to pilot a motorcycle at more than 250 mph (400 km/h) going through Bonneville's measured mile for a two-way average of 405·25 km/h (251·92 mph).

This was a splendid achievement, but it remained at the top of the record book for only a few weeks. On 16 October 1970 the record speed was raised to 427·18 km/h (265·43 mph) by America's most gifted road racing motorcyclist, Calvin Rayborn. His machine was outwardly the now conventional streamliner type, but its two engines had a total displacement of 1480 cc and ran on nitromethane fuel. The engines and the backing came from Harley-Davidson, who were to make commercial hay with their record for 4 years before it was plucked from them.

not legally he was for several months the fastest motorcyclist in the world.

His unofficial reign lasted until 4 August 1956 when Herz, now 44 years old, went to Bonneville with the NSU, now very highly supercharged with the aid of a secret compressor which, unknown to the outside world, was a development stage in the evolution of the rotary-combustion Wankel engine on which NSU were then working. It made a highly efficient supercharger, which helped the 499 cc NSU engine to develop no less than 110 brake horsepower; and under that impulsion Herz was able to average a speed that broke through two figurative barriers. It was the first time that a motorcycle had been timed at better than 300 km/h officially, the actual figure being 338·092 km/h (210·080 mph) — and it was the first time that any had exceeded 200 mph, the Imperial equivalent being 210·64 mph.

Allen responded promptly, putting in a couple of runs in his 15-ft (4·5 m) streamliner to average 214 mph (344 km/h). The Triumph Company in England, who had built the engine of Allen's

HOW WORLD SPEED RECORDS ARE MEASURED

The world records that are recognised by the FIM (Fédération Internationale Moto-cycliste — the international governing body) are the following:

with a flying start: 1 kilometre, 1 mile.

with a standing start:

$\frac{1}{4}$ mile, 1 kilometre, 1 mile, 10 km, 100 km, 1000 km, 1 hour, 6 hours, 12 hours, 24 hours.

Flying start records are measured as the mean of two runs in opposite directions over the course, within 1 hour. Only certain specified components (tyres, for example) are allowed to be changed during the interval.

A curious anomaly follows from the FIM rule that the average speed is calculated from the mean time taken for the two runs, not from the mean speed. A simple but exaggerated example will explain this: suppose that a motorcycle capable of 60 mph in neutral conditions were to make timed runs up and down a 1-mile course along which a 30 mph wind was blowing. In the downwind run, the bike would be assisted by the wind and would do 90 mph, covering the mile in 40 seconds. In the opposite direction, the wind would slow it down to 30 mph, so the measured mile would take 120 seconds to cover. Although the average of the two speeds would be 60 mph, the average of the two times would be 80 seconds, equivalent to a speed of 45 mph. Other bodies do not use this method, and when national records are claimed at the same time as world records, it often appears that different speeds are attributed to the same runs. In the USA, where all world speed records have been set for many years, the usual practice is for national records also to be claimed according to the rules of the American Motorcycling Association, and the course used is marked out in $\frac{1}{4}$-mile stages as well as with a measured kilometre. Further confusion is caused when the kilometre begins at one of

the extremities of the measured mile: because the vehicle is usually accelerating all the way through the mile, it will be faster over the kilometre than over the mile in one direction, slower in the other direction — and so the metric average will be different from the speed measured over the mile.

Standing start records are made in one direction only for the longer distances, invariably around an endless track. The front of the motorcycle has to be positioned within 10 cm (3·94 in) of the starting line, and the rider is allowed no assistance in moving off. Any refuelling has to be done with the engine stopped, and if assistants push the machine to restart it they must first pull it back far enough to get it going again before the point at which it stopped, otherwise that lap will be disallowed.

FIM records are supposed always to be expressed in km/h (even for the flying mile!) accurately to three decimal places, calculated from the elapsed time for the run. Record attempts over $\frac{1}{4}$ mile, kilometre and mile must be timed with apparatus accurate to one hundredth of a second, and all others with apparatus accurate to at least one fifth of a second. Timing equipment accurate to one thousandth of a second was first introduced by the German timekeepers observing the record attempt by Ernst Henne with a BMW on the Frank-furt-München Autobahn in 1936. By 1977, when a large Kawasaki team attacked long-distance records in the 750 and 1300 cc classes at Daytona, electronic timing apparatus was employed after certification of its accuracy to within 81 milliseconds over a period of 24 hours or one part in 1 066 667. A second similar timer was even more accurate, its error in 24 hours being only 51 milliseconds. Surveying of the Daytona track was similarly punctilious, the shortest distance around it being certified as 13 045·824 feet, or 2·4708 miles, or 3·9763671 kilometres.

Don Vesco preparing to attack his own world speed record for motorcycles in 1978.

Leppan tried, but was seriously injured when his Gyronaut's front suspension collapsed at 260 mph and the vehicle somersaulted. John McKibben tried, driving a purpose-built Honda streamliner powered by a pair of turbocharged 4-cylinder Honda engines — in fact he tried very often, crashing the Honda Hawk at least ten times, often spectacularly but never suffering more than trivial cuts or grazes. He once managed 286·567 mph (461·184 km/h) one-way — the fastest any two-wheeler had then travelled — but he never captured the two-way record.

Neither did Boris Murray, a drag racer who sought the record in a streamliner propelled by a brace of 850 cc Norton twin-cylinder engines. Even Vesco failed when he tried again in 1974 — not for want of speed, for he was timed at a two-way mean of 281·702 mph (453·355 km/h), but for want of compliance with the regulations. On this occasion his streamliner had been altered to carry two Yamaha TZ700 racing engines, his aim being 300 mph. In fact his fastest run was at 287·5 mph (462·6 km/h), but between the runs he had changed the rubber drive belts (innocently enough), and it turned out that to do so infringed the FIM regulations.

Undeterred, Vesco returned to the salt in 1975 and on 28 September became the first motorcyclist to exceed 300 mph. His machine was the same Yamaha-powered device, christened 'Silver Bird' but it had been furnished with a pair of parachutes to assist in braking from high speed. The aerodynamic perils associated with such velocities were vividly demonstrated when at 270 mph Vesco's machine was blown off course and crashed. Still undaunted he made a fresh start and new history with a speed of 487·515 km/h (302·927 mph).

On Friday 25 August 1978 Vesco was at Bonneville again. His streamliner had been enlarged to accommodate two Kawasaki KZ1000 engines, basically standard production motorcycle machinery but modified to accept turbo-charging and methanol fuel. The streamliner was now called 'Lightning Bolt', and measured 21 ft (6.4 m) in length, but it was only 21 in (533 mm) wide and stood just 32 in (813 mm) high. The total weight with all fuel and rider aboard was about 1200 lb (545 kg), of which Vesco himself, now aged 39, accounted for 155 lb (70 kg). To support all this

was a welded tubular steel frame surrounding a body hand-formed from sheet aluminium 0·065 in (1·65 mm) thick. The wheels were of cast aluminium carrying tyres specially made by Goodyear to suit the anticipated speeds (Vesco was not only a motorcycle dealer but also a tyre wholesaler in San Diego, California) and to stop the machine there was an inboard disc brake assembly to back up the two parachutes. That day they had to stop the 'Lightning Bolt' from a speed higher than any ever before, for with the aid of 250 bhp from the two turbocharged engines Vesco broke his own record at 314·355 mph (505·905 km/h — a new metric landmark).

It was good, but not as good as he had hoped: publicity material issued before the attempt, mainly by the American branch of Kawasaki, spoke of ambitions for 325 mph (523 km/h). Accordingly, 3 days later, Vesco went out on the salt again. His first run at 1.15 pm was north to south, with a 4 mph (6 km/h) tail wind and in an ambient temperature of 92°F (33°C). He entered the speed trap at 314·286 mph (505·794 km/h), departing from it at 322·696 mph (519·328 km/h), making his average speed for the first run 318·330 mph (512·302 km/h). The regulations required that he set his two-way average by completing a second run in the opposite direction within 1 hour, before the wind could change. Had it been a strong wind, Vesco would not have ventured out on the salt anyway: he had commented beforehand 'I am really praying for a windless day at Bonneville. If those damn winds come up you never know where the liner will go. The wind factor plus the chunks in the salt can send me flying off in a rolling tumble. Actually that's happened to me a couple of times in practice'.

As it happened, Bonneville was not quite windless: the 4 mph tail wind had shifted by 2.05 pm when he set off on his second run, south to north, so that once again he had a tail wind, though of a trifling 2 mph. The temperature had gone up to 95° and his average speed went up too, to 318·866 mph (513·165 km/h). That made his overall average and new record, ratified both by the FIM and the National body the AMA, 318·598 mph (512·733 km/h). It was rather less than the 325 mph for which he had hoped, but honour was satisfied in another way, for Vesco's metric average was 509·796 km/h (316·772 mph). This confirmed him in very exclusive company: less than ten men in the world had ever exceeded 500 km/h on land and all the others had done so on four wheels. Vesco was the first motorcyclist to do it.

SPEEDWAY

More gladiatorial than technical, the sport of motorcycle speedway racing began virtually with the century in America, spread to Australia and thence to Britain where, by the late 1970s, it was claimed to be the second largest spectator sport, as well as attracting a lively following elsewhere in Europe.

It had its beginnings on tracks that had originally been laid out for horse trotting and pacing races, which once enjoyed a great vogue. It was literally a case of the motor vehicle replacing the horse, for when motorcar racing became popular in the USA the oval horse tracks were abandoned and fell into decay. Motorcyclists sought to adapt them to their own uses, but the activity was carried out cheaply, with no attempt being made to resurface the courses, and so the expression 'dirt-track racing' was born.

It was by this name that the sport was known when it sprang up in America in the early years of the century. Popularly supported race meetings are known to have taken place as early as 1902, and competition was keen between riders entered or supported by the leading motorcycle manufacturers of America where, in those days, the industry was thriving. Of the scores of early American motorcycle manufacturers, Cleveland, Excelsior, Harley-Davidson, Indian and Peerless were the leading protagonists in dirt-track racing, employing professional riders and making the utmost use of the resulting publicity, notably at the big State Fairs where dirt-track races were great attractions for the public.

Some of these early tracks were unusually long, measuring half a mile or even a mile (1.609 km) to the lap. A few were even longer, up to two miles, but a few were as short as a third or a quarter of a mile. Their loose surfaces often deteriorated into dust bowls, and with little or no thought taken for the safety of the competitors or even of the spectators, accidents were rife and not infrequently fatal.

That was tantamount to ensuring the commercial success of the sport, which encouraged the utmost bravado in the riders. It did nothing to prompt any refinement of their machinery, which was generally over-engined and feeble-framed; and this could be held true even of the speedway motorcycle of today, for this branch of the sport has seen greater technical stagnation than any other, and the machines now in use have far more in common with the track-racing motorcycles of the 1920s than with motorcycles as they are generally accepted today.

Copying the Americans, Australia began to develop dirt-track racing in the early 1920s, most of their tracks being a half or a third of a mile around. Visiting American riders were a popular attraction and one of these, Cecil Brown, is said to have been the first American rider to demonstrate the broadside cornering technique that had become the fashion on American tracks. An interesting development occurred in Australia soon afterwards when the idea of surfacing the track with cinders was tried. The loose surface made even more extravagant riding styles feasible, and a rider named Billy Lamont showed that on cinders it was possible to slide the motorcycle through bends in a single long drift, controlled by pouring enough power through the rear wheel to keep it spinning, and applying a generous measure of opposite lock to the front wheel, while trailing the inside leg on the ground. This dramatic style brought spectators flooding to watch, and the commercial attractiveness of the sport was noted by English travellers who promptly began, on their return to Britain, to promote the idea. Further encouragement to the establishment of the sport in Britain was brought by an Australian promoter, A J Hunting, who used to run the exhibition speedway at Brisbane.

Britain's first dirt-track meeting was held in May 1927 on Camberley Heath, Surrey, though it had little in common with the established form of meetings as conducted in America and Australia. Apart from the fact that the track was undulating and sandy, the competitors were sent off around it clockwise, which would have been an impediment to proper exploitation of the purpose-built machines by then usual in dirt-track racing. These were furnished with a sturdy steel hook upon which the rider could brace his right leg, his left being encased in a stout steel-shod boot, often with a steel toe-cap as well to withstand the punishment it suffered in being dragged sliding through the cinders on the repeated left-hand bends of the oval tracks. Nevertheless, the Camberley meeting succeeded in whetting British appetites, and soon a dirt track came into use at Crystal Palace in South London, followed by one which was developed from a disused cycle track at King's Oak in Epping Forest, Essex.

Before the end of the year it became known that a substantial expeditionary force of speedway riders was coming to Britain from Australia, under the management of Mr Hunting, and when the first meeting was held at King's Oak on 19 February 1928, 30 000 spectators paid for admission. This cost $2\frac{1}{2}$d a head, and the programme cost another $\frac{1}{2}$ penny. The star of the meeting was one Billy Galloway, who had been racing in Australia since 1925, but Hunting did not arrive until the event was half over. Afterwards he showed the organiser, Mr Jack Hill-Bailey, how a correctly shaped track should be planned and built, and pointed out the hazards of allowing spectators to line the track on the inside as well as the outside, without even a safety fence to protect them. Early in the following month a track opened at Manchester and before 1928 was out others had mushroomed all over the country, with no fewer than eight in the London area and several in the Midlands.

Hunting set up a company known as International Speedways Ltd, which promoted eight major competitions of which the Golden Helmet event was the best publicised. Other attractions for the spectators were the League competitions, with teams based on various tracks riding against each other after the pattern of organised football, a development instigated by Jimmy Baxter early in 1929. Prior to this the basis of competition was between individual riders, prominent among whom were several girls. The most outstanding of these was Eva Askquith of Bedale, Yorkshire, who eventually raced internationally in Denmark and South Africa and on occasions beat some of the most renowned male riders in the sport, including the Golden Helmet winner and record breaker at Gosforth in 1929. For the next decade the sport flourished in Britain, becoming so secure that it even continued at Bellevue in Manchester during the World War, when meetings were held on Saturday afternoons.

When the war was over the racing was resumed generally, and the record attendance figures of 1938 were surpassed in 1946, to begin a boom that was not to fade until the 1950s. By 1959 there were only nine tracks still functioning in Britain, but gradually the sport regained its popularity and by 1970 the number had risen again to 36.

In other countries its attractions were beginning to be noticed, notably in Sweden and Eastern Europe, while it remained steady in Australia and underwent a complete metamorphosis in the USA, where dirt-track and short-track racing is still popular but no longer recognisably the same as the undeveloped riot that traditional brawling speedway has remained.

For those addicted to it, the sport promises to change very little. The usual pattern is for four riders to race against each other from a standing start, restrained by tapes until the starting signal is given. They then make a clutch start and complete two laps of the oval shale-surfaced track, which usually measures either 400 m or quarter of a mile (402·3 m) around. Team events and league competitions are sustained by a system of points being awarded to riders according to their successes in these very brief races, and the strictly regulated and commercially organised administration of the sport even goes so far as to relate earnings of these professional riders to the number of points they amass.

The machines they ride scarcely differ one from another, nor change much from year to year or even decade to decade. The invariable pattern is for a very light and spindly frame to carry a large-diameter small-section front wheel and tyre in very slender telescopic forks with skimpy suspension, while the rear wheel has none at all, its spindle being clamped rigidly in the frame. The power comes from a 500 cc single-cylinder 4-stroke engine running on alcohol fuel, with a very high compression ratio but fairly gentle valve timing which ensures tremendous flexibility and ample torque from quite low rates of crankshaft revolution — a necessity since there is no multi-speed gearbox, the transmission consisting merely of chain drive to the rear wheel with only a conventional friction clutch available to engage or disengage the drive. It is usual for the engine's power output to exceed 45 bhp, and the whole motorcycle weighs about 190 lb (86 kg). Exceptionally vivid acceleration is available, for the gearing is quite low, and the emphasis on flexibility and impeccable throttle response throughout an astonishingly wide speed range makes the machines extremely lively, although of course their maximum speeds are seldom much higher than about 80 mph (130 km/h). Their handlebars are very wide, their fuel tanks tiny: with only half a mile to go from start to finish, there is little need for anything else.

DRAG RACING

Originating in America in the late 1940s, drag racing is a sport that developed its own idio-syncratic rules as it went along. Initially it served as an extension of the speed trials popularly held each year on the dried salt lakes of Utah, but it was also a sport that was conducted on the public highway, police turning an occasionally blind eye to the antics of youngsters racing away from the traffic lights because, as they began to organise themselves better, the youngsters began to be less trouble to the populace at large. With further organisation the regulations inevitably proli-ferated, and the sport eventually became an ex-tremely showy one. In this respect, as in all others related to drag racing, America is still supreme.

It does not follow that American drag racing machines have been the fastest sprinters all the time. Sprinting has always been a popular motor-cycle sport in Europe and especially in Britain, where for example the former grass-track racing champion Alf Hagon achieved a time of 9·2 seconds for the standing quarter mile in 1968, which was faster than American riders were then managing. However, there are essential dif-ferences between the two forms of the sport. Both are based on the need to cover a quarter of a mile (402·3 m) as quickly as possible from a standing start, but whereas in traditional Euro-pean sprinting the individual rider competed against the clock, in American drag racing the basic principle was that of a knock-out tourna-ment, with the winner of each heat going though to the next round until the final is run-off between the two most successful riders.

It does not follow that they will be the fastest. Because of the tremendous speeds involved, the timing apparatus has to be very precise, with electronic timing of the passage of the bikes as they break light beams directed at photo-electric cells. The starting procedure introduces an anomaly, however: a sequence of electric lamps flashing in turn on a pole known as 'the Christ-mas tree' warns riders to be ready to go, and finally a green light flashes to give them clearance. As soon as the green lamp is lit, the rider is at liberty to move — but the clock does not start recording the elapsed time until the motorcycle actually moves and breaks the beam. Thus a rider with fast reactions can defeat another with a faster machine. Further compli-cation was introduced to the American sport by some variance of opinion as to whether the elapsed time or terminal speed might be the more important criterion of performance. The knock-out tournament might still survive as evidence of the sporting nature of the activity, but the perfor-mance figures were just as likely to fire the imagination of the paying spectators, and over the years these have been given more and more prominence.

To set these into perspective, the fastest motorcycle in quantity production at the time of writing, the Honda CBX, can cover the standing quarter mile in a little over 11 seconds, reaching 117 mph (188 km/h) over the finishing line. In drag racing there are two basic categories, one of which is for fundamentally ordinary production machines: highly developed versions of these, still running on petrol but very extensively tuned, are known as 'pro-street' in Europe or 'pro-stock' in America, and they can be expected to cover the quarter mile in less than 10 seconds.

It is, however, in the other category, known as 'competition', that the extravagant purpose-built drag racing machines appear and perform their noisy wonders. They are allowed engines of up to 3500 cc displacement, or 2000 cc if super-charged, and in most countries any kind of engine is acceptable, although in America there is a stipulation that it be based on the crankcase of a motorcycle engine. Some of these machines run on petrol, and are known as 'gassers' (the vo-cabulary of the sport is almost entirely American) while those using other substances such as methanol or, most violent of all, nitro-methane, are known as 'fuellers'.

Perhaps the only successful sprint motor cycle to show evidence of having been designed by an engineer, rather than by a mechanic, the Drag-Waye is as elegant structurally as dynamically. The disposition of the major masses (engine and rider) and their relationship to the wheelbase is calculated to give the utmost traction and ample stability. The success of the design is reflected in its capture of the world's standing start record in its class, ridden as shown here by David Lecoq. The official records describe it as a Volkswagen, because that is the origin of the supercharged engine, albeit the least significant item in its specification, the credit for which belongs to designer Clive Waye. (Motor Cycle, London)

Not unnaturally it is the fuel class that provides the pace-setters, but although competitors usually show a predilection for vast power and precious little else in the way of engineering science (aerodynamic aids are very rare indeed) there are some aids to performance that are common to all except the production class. Perhaps most significant is the slick rear tyre, the broad flat expanse of tread of which would be a severe hindrance to the dirigibility of any motorcycle along anything but a perfectly straight course, but provides the utmost in tractive grip. Not only may this grip be enhanced by the tricks of polymer chemistry, producing tread rubbers of exceptional tackiness, but also the effective coefficient of friction between tyre and track may be improved by a technique known as the 'burn-out', in which the tyre is deliberately spun for a few seconds, sometimes in a pool of water or better still domestic bleach, to heat it up to its best operating temperature before the motorcycle is 'staged' on the start line behind the light beam. Moreover, the most successful and commercial drag racing stadia have had their tracks surfaced with the best available of modern aggregates to give the utmost coefficient of friction, and with these aids performance standards have risen rapidly during the 1970s.

It was in 1971 that a time of less than 9 seconds was first recorded for the quarter-mile drag, by the American rider Joe Smith riding a 1700 cc Harley-Davidson. Later that same year Boris Murray also beat 9 seconds riding a double-engined Triumph on which he was the first to be timed at more than 170 mph (273·5 km/h) across the finish line. In fact both of these performances were rivalled by that of one E J Potter, popularly nicknamed the 'Michigan Madman', who during the middle 1960s made several appearances at drag events riding a machine between the wheels of which a vast 6-litre Chevrolet V8 car engine (the biggest ever fitted into a motorcycle) lay transversely. This engine made Potter's machine ineligible for organised competition, but did not bar him from making demonstration runs, which were highly welcomed (and highly paid) by race promoters. The entertainment Potter offered was invariably appreciated but not entirely consistent: he built six of these contraptions, and is reported

Russ Collins on the world's fastest Dragster, his twin engined Sorcerer, in 1978.

to have fallen off every one of them at some time or another — but when all went well the thing went fast, and he was timed at 8.8 seconds and 180 mph (289·6 km/h) before anybody else.

The first drag racer to run the quarter mile in under 8 seconds on a machine that complied with the regulations was American Russ Collins, proprietor of a Los Angeles firm specialising in the tuning of Honda engines. Three such engines, each a 750 cc 4-cylinder motor enlarged to 1100 cc, figured in a spectacular monster christened the Atchison, Topeka and Santa Fe — a station for each engine, so to speak, and with a wheelbase so long that the device almost resembled a train, the machine was wittily named. It weighed 858 lb (389 kg), cost $21 000 to build, and occupied nearly 2 years of Collins' time in being readied for competition; but at the sport's most important event, the National Hot Rod Association's Supernationals held in 1976 at Ontario Motor Speedway, California, Collins broke the 8-second barrier with a time of 7.86 seconds, reaching a terminal speed of 178 mph (286 km/h). In June of the same year he crashed the bike, replacing it in due course with an even faster one with two engines and an enormous supercharger.

Collins' greatest rival since 1973 has been Tom Christenson, familiarly known as TC. In 1973 he introduced a major technical innovation in the form of the slipper clutch, devised by his Wisconsin friend John Gregory. Previously, most of the leading drag bikes had single-gear transmissions, relying on wheel spin to get away from the starting line; but Gregory realised that this was inefficient and built a clutch designed to slip a certain amount at the start of a run, locking up progressively as the bike gathered speed. With the aid of this, Christenson's bike could profit from a two-speed gearbox, and with two Norton engines to propel it the TC bike, called Hogslayer (hog being a slang term for a certain kind of Harley-Davidson), became the most successful motorcycle in the history of drag racing, winning every major event at least once. Christenson began in 1973 by taking no less than half a second off the existing record time for the quarter mile, eventually leaving it at 7.93 seconds with a terminal speed of 176 mph (283·2 km/h).

In 1976, when Collins bettered these figures, some interesting demonstration runs were made by another American rider, Larry Welch, astride a rocket-powered machine. The rocket was one of the liquid-propellant type, the principal fuel being hydrogen peroxide; and as is characteristic of such devices, it demonstrated increasing efficiency as the speed of the machine grew higher. Thus, although Welch's elapsed time for the quarter mile was 7·9 seconds, his terminal speed was almost 200 mph (322 km/h). Incidentally E J Potter also appeared on a drag strip with a jet-propelled machine, a three-wheeler which crashed after reaching 150 mph (241 km/h); it was Potter's last ride on the strips.

Russ Collins has now clocked 7·62 seconds and 199·55 mph (321·14 km/h) at the Winston World Finals on 7 October 1978 on his 2000 cc 8-cylinder Honda 'Sorcerer'.

ICE RACING

Although technically interesting, in that the motorcycles used are mechanically very similar to speedway machines and yet do not behave like them (a paradox in that ice racing machines skid less although ridden on a much more slippery surface), the outstanding characteristic of ice racing is that it is rough, rumbustious and frighteningly dangerous. Sheet steel guards and welded tubular steel cages around the more obviously dangerous parts of the machines notwithstanding, riders still get hurt — and when their injuries come, as is often the case, from the flesh-scouring spikes set in the tread of a fast-spinning tyre, the consequences can be ugly and painful. The dulling of sensation due to the deep-freezing temperatures in which such races are held may serve as some kind of opiate for an injured man, just as it appears to dull the critical faculties of spectators; but the most immediate and obvious consequence of an ambient that may run down to minus 40° is that the motorcycles have to be warmed up for 15 minutes before racing. This warming is done in the pits, which are centrally heated — and yet a blow torch is necessary!

The sport began on the ice of frozen lakes in Sweden in the early 1920s, when it was supposed that the idea of speedway and dirt-track racing, born earlier in the USA, might be imported and suitably translated. They even tried marking out tracks on the frozen Baltic Sea, but inland venues were not unnaturally more popular, making use of the facilities provided by sundry small sports arenas already dotted around the country. This was how the oval 400 metres became standardised, as it had done by 1932; but in the beginning the tracks were sometimes much longer, often 800 m and occasionally even as much as 3000 m.

Racing was originally done in pairs, but against the clock rather than following the more time-consuming rules of a knock-out tournament. Slowly they learned how to adapt to the necessities of the ice. Instead of riding their machines broadside into corners they improved tyre grip by the use of home-made spikes, 8 to 10 mm (0·3 in–0·4 in) long, and so they began to slide less and to steer more conventionally. Within a few years the spikes had grown to 16 mm (0·6 in) in length and by 1934 each tyre would be bristling with 200 of them.

It was a year earlier, on 3 March 1933, that a new riding technique was publicly displayed for the first time at the Altstadion in Stockholm. The rider Torsten Sjoberg had been training privately and discovered that he could bank his Douglas more steeply by riding with his inner leg trailing behind instead of maintaining the usual seated position that had been conventional. This dramatic-looking development seemed to bring new vitality to the sport, and 1934 saw the first motorcycles designed and built specifically for ice racing. Previously they had been adapted road machines of any convenient make, but Sjoberg and Torsten Fogelberg built their own special ice racer in 1934, and in 1935 Sweden began to import JAP machines from England. By 1947 competitors and meetings were numerous enough to justify further engineering investment and the Swedish firm of SRM introduced a complete new ice racer (based on an engine from Husqvarna) to be followed in another decade by the Jawa which accompanied the development of the sport in Russia.

Some international interest had already been stimulated when a trio of English riders went to Sweden at the beginning of the 1950s. The most successful was Bruce Semmens, who was competitive with the best of the Swedes, but although ice racing began to spread into other parts of Europe it went into a temporary decline in Sweden, not being revived until 1963. Meanwhile the sport had taken off in Russia, and when a championship for European riders was instituted

for the 1963 season, it was a Russian, Gabdrakham Kadirov, who became the first European champion, with the best Swede, Westlund, in ninth place. In the next 10 years Kadirov, who came from Ufa, in the Ural mountains, carried off the world championship six times; it was not until 1970 that the title was won by any non-Russian. An Englishman had reached the world championship finals in 1969 (the status of the championship had been upgraded in 1966 when Kadirov won it) but in the final of 1969 it was Kadirov again, the Englishman Andy Ross finishing twelfth. The highest he ever reached was fifth in the following year when the title went to the Czechoslovakian rider Antonin Svabb. Another Czech won the world championship in 1974, a mechanic named Milan Spinka, then aged only 22. The first to win the world title three times in succession was the Russian Sergei Tarabanko, who did it in the years 1975, 1976 and 1977.

As practised today, the sport has a greater degree of standardisation than might have been contemplated in its infancy. Most of the tracks are speed-skating stadia built to Olympic standards, though in some countries ordinary speedway tracks are flooded with water which is then frozen. The spiking of tyres is now standardised with 105 spikes on the rear tyre and 86 on the front, 65 of which are on the left side where most of the work is done since all races are run in an anti-clockwise direction. The spikes are 28 mm (1·1 in) long, conical and sharpened by hand for each race. Amongst the safety provisions are a steel toe cap for the rider's left boot, a piece of car tyre cut open to fit over the left leg from ankle to thigh, and a metal belt or wrist strap attached by cable to an ignition cut-out on the machine so that if a rider falls he can (or may automatically, by being separated from his motorcycle by a sufficient distance) stop the engine and thus check the spinning of those lacerating wheels. The spikes are judged by the riders worth the dangers they entrain: with their aid a phenomenal grip may be obtained, allowing the motorcycle to be banked through as much as 55° from the vertical, which puts the tip of the left handlebar a mere 4 in (101 mm) from the ground. Because of this it is usual for the handlebars to be asymmetrical, the one on the right being straight and the one on the left being bent upwards to give a better steering position for the rider.

Alf Hagon with his 1260 cc JAP on which he covered a 1/4-mile from a standing start in 9·432 seconds on 2 June 1968.
(G. Forsdyke)

SPRINTING

The object of this branch of sport is to cover a short set distance in the shortest possible time. Basically it is a test of acceleration from standstill, the usual distance being a quarter of a mile (402·3 m), although there have been some famous half-mile sprints in the past (that along the sea front of Brighton used to be one of the best) and there is also the kilometre as an alternative distance. The sport has enjoyed a long history in Britain, where record attempts over short measured distances have been numerous since the beginning of the century. The governing body of the sport in Britain, The Auto-Cycle Union, defines sprinting as 'A race from point to point in a straight line and on a metalled surface, approximately level and not exceeding one mile in length, between two or more competitors or individually against time'.

In this definition may be seen the essential distinction between sprinting and the American

This supercharged 650 cc Triumph set a world standing start record in 1972.

equivalent which is known as drag racing. The latter is mainly a form of knock-out tournament, in which one competitor beats another and then goes on to be matched against the victor of a similar duel. Today the elapsed time for the distance — almost invariably a quarter of a mile in drag racing — is accorded more importance than used to be the case, but the terminal speed (measured with accurate modern apparatus over a short distance at the flying finish of the quarter mile) is also accorded prominence. In sprinting, British style, the rider competes strictly against the clock, and the best performance of the day is the briefest.

As in drag racing, sprints are simple one-way affairs, the conditions being the same for everybody at a given meeting. Official records are organised differently: runs in opposite directions

along the course are required, and they have to be completed within a period of 2 hours. Between runs no fundamental changes can be made to the machine, although there is limited scope for some adjustment and other mechanical work. The usual distances are a quarter of a mile, a kilo-metre and a mile, and there are categories for motorcycles with engines ranging in displacement from 50 to 2000 cc.

Although sprinting became popular in Britain in the early 1900s and was one of the mainstays of motorcycle sport in the 1920s, it was not until 1958 that a National Sprint Association was formed in Britain. This organisation set out to arrange regulated competitions, and its example has been followed in Germany, Sweden and especially in Holland.

MOTOCROSS

Motocross grew out of the sport of trials riding. The two therefore have something in common, the acceptance of difficult off-highway cross-country courses as the basic obstacle to be overcome. Everything else is different, but in essentials trials riding is a balancing act, whereas motocross is racing. The motocross rider gains no marks for keeping his feet up no matter how difficult the going, or for maintaining way rather than coming to a halt and making a fresh start: his object is simply to go faster than all his rivals over the same course, and it does not matter how untidily he does it. In fact the whole thing can be a bit of a scramble.

'A rare old scramble' is what competitors were promised in the first such event, held in Britain which was the birthplace of the sport. From the 1920s, when it began, the sport continued to be known for a quarter of a century as scrambling; but when its popularity spread to Europe a new name was given it: assembled from the components of the French word for 'motorcycle' (*motocyclette*, generally abbreviated to *moto*) and the operative part of 'cross-country', motocross became the word and now it is used almost invariably even in England.

The sport was born in a works outing organised by Alfred Scott, proprietor of the Scott Motorcycle Company, for his employees and their friends. It had most of the elements of the popular one-day sporting trial, sometimes called a reliability trial, with difficult stretches of rough country forming the course, but what distinguished it from other trials was that competitors had to ride against the clock. The Scott Trial has endured since its beginnings in 1914 as one of the most difficult classic events in the trials-riding calender, but it also represented the first stage in the evolution of scrambling. All that was necessary was to do away with the system of penalty points incurred for stopping or losing one's balance. Instead the event became strictly speed-oriented, and from the beginning was accepted as demanding physical strength and stamina of the rider as well as skill.

Early scrambles were exhausting affairs, but gradually races were shortened, as much to allow more competitors to ride as to make it more feasible for them to finish. Another change was from the time-trial basis, according to which the

Brian Stonebridge leads a field of scrambling experts in 1957. (All Sport/Don Morley)

riders started off individually and raced against the clock, to a massed-start race which offered more obvious attractions to spectators. The outcome today is an event in which the rider will race around a circuit 1 or 2 miles (about 2–3 km) long, in the course of which he will have to deal with steep gradients, bumps, jumps, sand pits, ditches, mud holes, water splashes and all the filth flung in his face by the spinning wheels of his competitors' machines.

In the early days, he would simply have to race for a certain number of laps of the course, the first to complete that number being the winner. When the sport spread to Europe in the years immediately after World War II, a much more complex system of marking was introduced, one which must have made an appreciation of the event's progress very difficult for the now large crowds of spectators to acquire. The idea was that the race would be run for a certain length of time, generally about 40 minutes, whereupon a marker would be shown to the riders informing them that they had only two more laps of the circuit in which to make their final bids for victory. This would not have been so bad were it not that the Continental system envisaged two races or heats for each event: if he were to win, a rider had to finish in as high a position as possible in each heat. Should he finish first in the first heat and second in the second, swopping positions with a rival in the process, then obviously there would be a tie, in which case it would be resolved by combining the riders' times for the two heats, the victor being he who had covered the total distance at the higher average speed.

It took a lot of pressure on the FIM, the international governing body of the sport, before this complicated and ponderous arrangement was revised. It had sometimes produced unfair results, because of the necessity to finish in both heats if a rider were to score points in the championship series of which the race might form part. If he had fared badly in the first heat, it would not be worth his while bothering with the second; if he did badly in the second, it made his efforts in the first a waste of time no matter how successful they had seemed then. The riders did not like the arrangement, and neither did the spectators. Instead, a points system was devised in which the first ten finishers in each heat were awarded a number of points according to their finishing posi-

Jeff Smith, nine times British and twice world champion. (All Sport/Don Morley)

World Trials champion Mick Andrews riding a Matchless in the 1962 Lincolnshire Grand National scramble.
(All Sport/Don Morley)

tions: in this way the winner of the event would be he who had gained the greatest number of points. At the end of the season the winner of the appropriate championship would likewise be the rider who had amassed the largest total number of points from all the races counting towards the title. Only in France was this new proposition rejected, possibly because in that country motocross is regarded less as a sport than as a form of entertainment, highly commercialised and thus subject to its own commercially inspired rules — which may or may not have something to do with the fact that, prosper though the sport may in that country, France has never produced a world champion.

Neighbouring Belgium, on the other hand, has been exceptionally successful in nurturing motocross champions, and as recently as 1975 all three world champions (125, 250 and 500 cc categories) were Belgian. The staunchest of their European rivals have always been the British, who have never been out of contention, but from Scandinavia the Swedes were exceptionally prominent in the 1960s and produced many

champions in that period. Some Italian riders and machines have figured in the sport's fairly recent history too, as have riders from East Germany, Finland and Czechoslovakia; but the greatest boom has been in America.

There is plenty of room for it in the USA, plenty of people looking for the excitement it offers and apparently plenty of money to be spent on making it as thrilling for those with a financial interest in its popularity as for those whose interest is more active. With so much commerical encouragement (not to mention the indirect encouragement offered by legislation that severly inhibited the pleasures to be derived from riding motorcycles on the public highways of the USA) motocross in the USA enjoyed intense cultivation in the 1970s, particularly in the western states where the leading Japanese motorcycle manufacturers used the sport as a vehicle for sales promotion on a very large scale.

The organisation of the sport follows the same general rules in most countries, where it comes under the aegis of the national governing body. The country may be divided into regions known

An unusual view of the leap at Ballaugh Bridge on the IoM TT course. (All Sport/Don Morley)

Broadside cornering at very high speeds is a feature of American oval-track racing, illustrated by Gary Scott. (All Sport/Don Morley)

Russian ice-racing champion Sergei Tarabanko. (All Sport/Photographic Ltd)

Trials: Martin Lampkin riding a Bultaco. (All Sport/Don Morley)

First European motocross champion, Les Archer on his 500 cc Norton in 1957. (All Sport/Don Morley)

as centres, and motorcycle clubs recognised by the national body are permitted to organise motocross events within their centres and invite entries from suitably qualified riders. A meeting might be restricted to riders within that centre, in which case it is described as 'open to centre', or entrants may be invited from surrounding centres in which case the meeting will be described as 'regional restricted'. In a national event, riders belonging to any recognised club in the country can enter. At an international event, which will be organised by one of the clubs on behalf of the national body, representatives of the FIM will attend to supervise. The riders must hold competition licences of the appropriate grade, beginning as novices (known patronisingly as juniors) and eligible to be upgraded to expert status after winning a race. If an expert reaches one of the top three positions in his national championship, he is guaranteed an entry for international Grand Prix events which count towards the world championships.

The characteristics of motocross machinery have grown more marked in the 1970s, power being sought after as urgently as ever, but far greater emphasis being placed on suspension design than ever before. Originally, scrambles motorcycles were scarcely distinguishable from those used in trials, but increasing specialisation gradually brought about divergences in design and preparation. Flexibility and responsiveness in the engine were still important in scrambling, but so was ample power, and the compromise between tractability and tractive effort has seen a gradual shift of emphasis to the latter. During the 1960s 2-stroke engines began to predominate, large-capacity single-cylinder 4-strokes and the occasional twin having previously been the rule. The motorcycles have become lighter in weight and more easily manhandled, and at the same time suspension design has grown very much more sophisticated. Long wheel travel is now considered essential, and the complexities of springing and damping grow steadily more baffling for riders and development engineers alike. Chain tensioning devices, pneumatic springing, gas-recuperated dampers and elaborate rear suspension mechanisms have all been

Jeff Smith on a BSA. (Press Association)

assiduously cultivated in the 1970s in the search for the utmost traction in conditions of the utmost difficulty, while plastics, light alloys and other modern materials of high strength-to-weight ratio are enjoying increasing use.

Despite all this mechanical refinement, moto-cross is still perhaps the most physically demanding of all sports. Because speeds are seldom very high, and the scenery usually fairly soft, very serious injuries are infrequent and fatalities are surprisingly rare; but hard knocks are commonplace, and even the dust, sand and mud that fill the air can be very trying for the rider. A measure of the strain to which he is sub-jected is that his pulse rate will remain above 100 per minute, quite often reaching 200, throughout the event's two heats, each of which may last up to 45 minutes, amid the press of perhaps 30 rivals. All this he must endure under the scrutiny of spectators who are likely to number no less than 3000 and may come in crowds of as many as 100 000; the gate is always at least 15 000 for a Grand Prix.

The profits from the box office are consider-able, because overheads are so low (tracks do not have to be specially and elaborately built for example), and it thus is commercially feasible for the organisers to pay the riders quite handsomely. The top men, whose services are in demand to help publicise the products of the great motor-cycle manufacturers, earn carefully concealed but evidently very substantial incomes — and of course that in turn makes the sport more popular still. Unfortunately, it remains a young man's sport, the physical strain of competing being so great that it is unusual for a rider's career to be protracted long after his 30th birthday.

TRIALS

Trials riding — a sport which involves riding a motorcycle non-stop and feet-up across difficult and acclivitous country — is now a world-wide business, but until recent years it was almost exclusively British. Its origins go back to the very beginning of motorcycling, in the form of simple reliability trials in which points would be deducted from riders for any unscheduled stops. The inclusion of freak hills was merely a consequence of improvements in motorcycle reliability, which made more difficult routes necessary in order to separate the sheep from the goats. A goatlike competence on steep gradients and bad surfaces became more and more requisite, with the result that the purpose-built trials motorcycle has emerged as a type in its own right, no more appropriate to riding on the public highway than the intemperately powerful road racer of today.

Britain's governing body of the sport, the Auto-Cycle Club (later the Auto-Cycle Union) ran its first quarterly trial in 1906. Supported mainly by motorcycle manufacturers, the event soon began to attract private entrants. In the early years it always followed the same course, starting from the Checkers Hotel in Uxbridge and travelling via Banbury, Berkhamsted and Beaconsfield back to the starting point. It was a one-day event which by the spring of 1907 was attracting more than a score of entries, and for the first time several competitors managed to make non-stop runs over the required sections of road including the steepest hill, which incorporated a gradient of 1 in $7\frac{3}{4}$. From then on, the course would have to be made more vigorous.

In that same year a Lightweight class was introduced for machines weighing no more than 110 lb (49·9 kg) excluding stand, horn, tool bag, tools, lamp, petrol and oil. The tank had to contain at least $\frac{1}{2}$ gallon (2·3 litres) and the rider had to carry ballast if he weighed less than 161 lb (73 kg). The tyres had to be at least $1\frac{3}{4}$ in (44·5 mm) in section, metal mudguards and the usual accessories had to be carried, and quietness, cleanliness and smoothness of running were taken into account in awarding the prize.

As motorcycles proliferated, local clubs were set up to run their own road trials. As the machines improved, trials became more difficult: the stiffest test yet in 1909 was laid on by the Edinburgh Motorcycling Club in the form of an event over 5 days, covering a road mileage of 758 (1220 km). This Scottish 5-days trial, forerunner of the Scottish Six Days which to this day is a highlight of the world trials calendar, ran from the Murrayfield Tram Terminus in Edinburgh to John O'Groats and back, and attracted 33 entrants of whom 26 riders started. None of them achieved a clean climb of Amulree Hill, so naturally it figured again in subsequent events. Most notable of these was the 6-day trial introduced in 1910 by the Auto-Cycle Union. The course ran from Land's End to John O'Groats, taking in Amulree on the way, and attracted 83 entries. In 1913 foreign entries were invited, and so the event became the International Six Days Trial for the first time. Even as early as 1910, trials were becoming so popular that there was justification for the ACU being split up into regional centres, with clubs being affiliated appropriately thereto. Some of the trials they ran were scheduled to last 12 hours, almost all incorporated a time factor of some sort, and observation tests on hills were equally common. Team events between clubs were also introduced in 1910, the ACU Inter-Club Team championship being staged on roads in Derbyshire on 8 September in that year. In the following year there was a Scottish Six Days Trial with 36 starters, while the ACU Six Days Trial set a new pattern in being based on a single location (Harrogate) from which daily routes clawed through the surrounding hills to places as remote and forbidding as the Lake District, where the first International Six Days Trial (the initials ISDT were to become familiar jargon) was held in 1913.

By that time, trials had become a popular recreation for hundreds of otherwise ordinary motorcyclists, but there were still some innovations to be introduced before the sport was brought to a temporary stop by the outbreak of the Great War (1914). These innovations were characteristic of the new Scott Trial, run in Yorkshire shortly before the war. Alfred Scott, proprietor of the eponymous motorcycle factory which had its workshops on the edge of Ilkley Moor noticed how his workers enjoyed romping around on rough ground on motorcycles during their lunch breaks, and he proposed a works' picnic to be held along similar lines. The Scott Trial was thus laid out to include sections over bogs and through streams, and it has been one of

Britain's toughest trials ever since, even though the venue was later transferred from the Pennine Moors of the West Riding to the North Yorkshire moors. The event, which went so well that the ACU's Yorkshire centre eventually took it over and fostered it, was responsible for two new features of motorcycling sport: one was the use of observed sections in rough country as opposed to on the road, the other was that the time factor was given such priority that the event became a kind of race and was thus the progenitor of motocross.

The sport did not recover from the Great War until 1919, with the 120 miles Victory Trial which saw the first appearance of several secretly-developed new motorcycles. Manufacturers were already treating trials as a serious and useful testing ground for the development of new components and designs; in the years that followed, motorcycles improved so greatly that the off-highway 'observed section' became the normal ingredient of a trials course, the road sections becoming practically meaningless and literally pointless. By the 1930s, the craze for trials riding was having a discernible affect on motorcycle styling as well as on detail design: upswept exhaust pipes became fashionable, even on purely road-going machines, because deep-water fords had become a regular trials hazard. Knobbly tyres were likewise popular, so that by 1938 the possibly unfair advantages conferred by such tyres became a matter of concern, even to their being banned from all events on the public highways. In the London Motorcycle Show of that year there had been several purpose-built trials motor-cycles, such machines having begun to emerge from the factories in the latter half of the decade. The first to specialise wholly in the production of off-road motorcycles was H P Baughan, whose machines were powered by Blackburne engines.

Then, just as the sport was promising — or threatening — to become a thoroughly business-like and technically fruitful activity, it was checked by the outbreak of the World War in 1939. The stop was more theoretical than real, for many events staged by the armed services, ostensibly as military training for despatch riders, were thinly disguised sporting trials. At any rate the real thing reappeared as soon as the war was over in 1945; in the following year, with most of

Martin Lampkin. (All Sport/Gary Morley)

the well-known clubs active again, lightweight 2-stroke machines began to put in an appearance. The large-capacity (350 or 500 cc) single-cylinder 4-stroke engine, tuned or perhaps detuned with low compression ratio, heavy flywheel and modest valve timings to offer the utmost in flexibility and back-up torque at low crankshaft rates, was still the dominant type, popular with the leading riders. However, the increasing severity of trials courses made a lightweight machine attractive on account of its easy handling, and this trend continued throughout the 1950s. Almost as slow was the revolution in frame design: although sprung rear wheels had become commonplace on roadsters and mandatory in racing motorcycles, trials riders obstinately insisted on unsprung rear wheels in the belief that they could secure better traction and control. Only in the latter 1950s was rear suspension established as normal in trials motorcycles.

It was at about this time that the most outstanding rider in the history of the sport began his long and distinguished career, and kept the big 4-stroke single-cylinder engine supreme long after it had failed all other riders. This man was the legendary Sammy Miller, still riding in 1978 with over 900 trials victories behind him. His almost equally legendary 497 cc Ariel (now in the National Motor Museum at Beaulieu, still wearing its famous number plate GOV 132) was a masterpiece of specialised development engineering, supervised and largely executed by Miller himself. Winning the British Experts Trial of 1959, 1961, 1962, 1963 and 1964, Miller cast his Ariel in the teeth of reason and prejudice, retaining his supremacy more by virtue of his riding ability than of his machine's unquestionable excellence. The turning point came in November 1964 when Miller and Ariel parted, the rider transferring his allegiance to Bultaco and bringing that Spanish make a similar round of victories — and incidentally inspiring the rival Spanish factories of Montesa and Ossa to enter the arena as well.

The sport had spread to Europe, where small-capacity lightweight motorcycles had always been popular in difficult country, and where the traditions of other sports such as pedal cycling encouraged the emergence in the motorcycling sport of a new kind of professionalism. Trials had hitherto been considered an amateur's sport, despite the generous support offered by the trade and the substantial number of riders kept in employment by the competition departments of the various participating manufacturers; but as the sport spread throughout Europe, with a championship to be determined each year, the rewards grew more substantial and the competition more grim. With the upsurge of interest in all kinds of motorcycling, but especially the off-highway variety, in the USA, there was every reason to promote the European championship into a world championship, and the mechanism of trials organisation became more professional too, with such refinements or corruptions as a punched-card system whereby to verify riders' scores.

In the 1970s the Japanese manufacturers recognised the importance of the sport and began to take it seriously. Suzuki had been the first, developing some single-cylinder trials machines from their road motorcycles. Then Yamaha engaged Mick Andrews, formally a star of the Ossa team, as a development rider; Kawasaki signed another British rider, Don Smith, to do likewise for them; Suzuki began to market purpose-built trials motorcycles featuring British-made frames; finally, if not conclusively, Honda engaged Sammy Miller to develop a four-stroke trials machine for them. So successful was he that by 1976 the 306 cc Honda trials machine had established itself as the most competent of them all. Not that it won everything: in 1977 it was a Bultaco that was ridden to a world championship by Yrjo Vesterinen, a Finnish rider who was the first non-British competitor to take the title. No explanation has yet emerged for the dismissal by Honda of Miller at the end of the same year; he went to Italy to do similar work for SWM, but with such a fund of talent among the younger riders of the late 1970s — such as Malcolm Rathmell, Sidney and Martin Lampkin, Rob Edwards and Rob Shepherd — there is no telling whither or by whom the next trend will be led.

WORLD CHAMPIONSHIPS

The more bloated the frog, the bigger the puddle that he tries to dominate. It is natural for a sportsman to seek recognition as the master in his particular activity, and it is a measure of the popularity and importance of a sport that it should acknowledge some world champion. In motorcycling sport, however, the title of world champion has sometimes not been earned world wide, has sometimes not been instituted at the time of the sport's world-wide spread, and has not always been given official recognition even when it has been popularly accepted.

There was a World Trophy in motorcycling sport as early as 1913, when the Six Days Trial became international. It is essentially a team event, and in that respect differs from the other world championships — just as the event differs in its character from straightforward trials or motocross, containing elements of both.

Although **moto-cross** began in Britain in the 1920s, it did not become sufficiently international to support any international championships until after World War II. A team competition at international level was inaugurated in Europe in 1947, to be known as the Moto-Cross des Nations. Britain, France, Holland and Belgium entered five-man teams, but it was not until 1952 that a championship for individual riders evolved from this series. It was then for the 500 cc class only, the first European champion being Victor Leloup of Belgium riding an FN. In 1957 a 250 cc European championship was inaugurated, and at that point the 500 cc category was elevated to world status, the first championship title going to the Swedish rider Bill Nilsson. The 250 cc championship was upgraded from European to world status in 1963, being first won by another Swedish rider, Torsten Hallman. Sidecar motocross events have never risen above European championship level, but the 125 cc solo class which was added to the European programme in 1973 achieved the status of a world championship in 1975 when it was won by the Belgian Gaston Rahier.

As for **trials**, this sport was for so long confined to the British Isles that there was no question of any world championship or even a European championship until the latter was instituted in 1968. Only in 1975 was a world trials champion recognised in Martin Lampkin.

In these championships, individual performances in a series of qualifying events are evaluated by some more or less arbitrary system of points scoring in order to determine the final outcome. The method of assessing a champion in **speedway** is somewhat different, the title going to the best performer at a specific world championship meeting for riders who have qualified to participate. The speedway world championship was instigated in 1936, under the aegis of the FIM, being held at Wembley, England. Riders came from America, Australia, Canada, Denmark, France, Germany, Great Britain, New Zealand, South Africa, Spain and Sweden, the Australian rider Lionel Van Praag winning an extra tie-deciding race from the British rider Eric Langton. The speedway title did not, however, enjoy official status until 1949, when the British rider Tommy Price won it.

The same year saw the beginnings of **road racing** world championships, which have ever since been the most widely recognised and glamorised titles in motorcycle sport. Once again the championship sprang from a more modest European title, which was organised by the then FICM (forerunner of today's governing body, the FIM or Fédération Internationale Motocycliste) in 1938. The results were based on the outcomes of eight of the most important races in Europe, and appropriate titles were awarded in the 500, 350 and 250 cc classes, being won for the first time by Georg Meier of Germany on a BMW, by Ted Mellors of Britain on a Velocette, and by Ewald Kluge of Germany on a DKW, respectively. Most interestingly there was also an overall title of Champion of the Year, which went to the rider who scored more points during the season than any other in any of the classes, and in 1938 this most successful of competitors was again Kluge. He repeated his success the following year (as did Mellors) but the idea of a 'champion of champions' did not survive the World War, after which the championships were elevated to world status, as already mentioned, in 1949. By that time there was a 125 cc class as well, and another for sidecars: the 50 cc title was not added until 1962.

Because there is a healthy body of opinion which considers that motorcycle racing should be a contest between machines rather than a contest between men, there has also been another kind of world championship for constructors, though it has attracted far less attention. More often than not, the factory entering the world champion rider has also carried off the constructor's laurels, but there have been occasions when one make of machines was dominant but when, due to the differing fortunes of individual members of the team, the title has gone to the rider of a different make of machine. These exceptions to the general rule which can be followed in the individual world championship tables are as follows:

In the 50 cc class, the champion constructor of 1966 was Honda, though the world champion rode a Suzuki.

In the 125 cc class the champion constructor in 1953 was MV Agusta, although the individual champion rode an NSU.

In the 250 cc class the constructors' title went to MV Agusta in 1955 and to Yamaha in 1974, when the individual championships were won by riders of NSU and Harley-Davidson respectively.

In the 350 cc class the champion constructor of 1957 was Gilera, though the individual title went to the rider of a Guzzi. In 1973 the constructors' title went to Yamaha, though the individual one was captured on an MV Agusta. In 1976 the top constructor was again Yamaha, though the individual title was won by the rider of a Harley-Davidson.

Similarly in the 500 cc class, the constructors' title went to Norton in 1950, to Honda in 1966, and to Yamaha in 1974, although the individual titles were won by riders of a Gilera in 1950 and an MV Agusta in 1966 and 1974.

In the sidecar class the constructors' championship went to BMW in 1968 and 1971, and to König in 1974 and 1975; but the champion individual piloted an URS in 1968, a Münch in 1971, a BMW-engined Busch in 1974 and a König-engined Busch in 1975.

Champion of Champions
Ewald Kluge on the supercharged 250 cc DKW during his winning ride in the 1938 Lightweight TT, when he achieved the first 250 cc lap at over 80 mph. (Orbis Publishing)

Helmut Fath with passenger Wolfgang Kalauch. (Orbis Publishing)

THE TOURIST TROPHY

The way that motorcycle racing developed at the very beginning of this century caused widespread dissatisfaction, not only among participants but also among spectators and all others interested. Organised motorcycle competition grew virtually in the shadow of pedal-bicycle racing, but this produced petty, small-track races that seemed pointless or at least dead-ended, because the machines encouraged for racing were monstrously inept as motorcycles. There were also some brief and tragically unhappy experiments with the most genuine and realistic road racing in the form of the great races between great European cities: in these events there were classes for two-, three- and four-wheelers, which sometimes became inappropriately mingled on roads that were scarcely fit for any of them. The organisation fell somewhere short of what was possible, let alone of the impossibly high standard that would have been necessary to make them safe, so they were inevitably dangerous and doomed to end in disaster. That end arrived in the course of the 1903 race from Paris to Madrid, fated to be stopped long before the course was completed because of the number and severity of the accidents that occurred on the route.

Thereafter attempts were made to organise a new type of race over a closed circuit with an international field arranged by restricting the entries to teams of three from each country. This was the International Cup Race, open to all countries and organised by the country of which the previous year's winner was a national. Because France played such a pioneering part in the development of all forms of motoring sport in those days, it seemed appropriate that the host country initially should be France, but it was a questionable hospitality that the French offered. Britain sent a team consisting of a JAP, a Lagonda, and a Quadrant, but they and all the other foreign entrants were frustrated by the transparent chicanery of the organisers which was intended to secure a French victory — all so obviously that the event was declared a nullity.

Apart from these malpractices, the International Cup Race was broadly similar in nature to the race for the Gordon Bennett Trophy which was for cars. Britain had been decently represented in these, but enthusiasm in Britain was greater for a motor race designed to encourage the development of practical touring cars rather than of outright racers, and this event was known as the Tourist Trophy. Thus, when Britain's motorcycle enthusiasts sought a major competitive event that would be better than the International Cup, they had a good precedent to follow.

On 17 January 1906 the idea was mooted at the annual dinner of the Auto-Cycle Club (later the Auto-Cycle Union or ACU). While proposing a toast to 'the sport and pastime' the representative of the magazine *The Motorcycle* mentioned during his speech the hope that a competition could be arranged for motorcycles using the Tourist Trophy races for cars as a model. He suggested that engines be limited to maximum bore and stroke of 80 mm each, which with a single cylinder would have given a displacement of 402 cc, and that the machines weigh no more than 130 lb (59 kg). Arbitrary these proposals may have been, but the basic idea was a good one, and from it sprang the motorcycle TT races.

There was virtually no choice of venue. The laws of Britain imposed a speed limit of 20 mph (32 km/h) on road traffic, and forbade the closure of the roads for racing. Across the water, however, lay Ellan Vannin, Mona's Isle, the Isle of Man: call it what you will, it could be recognised, then as now, as a place enjoying a certain proud independence. It had its own government, it had no general speed limits, and it allowed its roads to be closed for racing. Indeed the Manx authorities had already provided facilities for motor racing, for the eliminating trials for the Gordon Bennett Trophy race were held there, as well as the motor car Tourist Trophy; and as recently as 1905 the Auto-Cycle Club had been allowed to run its eliminating trials for the International Cup on the Island. The Manx authorities were the obvious ones to ask, particularly noting their desire to give a profitable boost to their tourist industry, and they showed themselves ready to co-operate.

At that time it seemed unlikely that the motorcycles of the day were competent to undertake the lengthy and difficult road circuit followed by the cars, which included the stiff climb up Snaefell mountain (2034 ft (620 m)) in their tour of the island. A shorter and easier

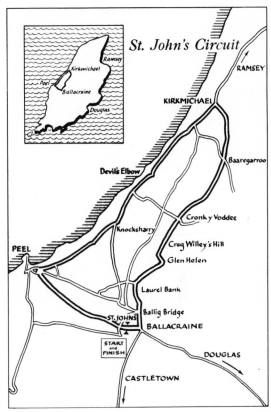

The original Isle of Man TT circuit, known after the place of the start and finish at St Johns. (BP)

course was chosen, starting and finishing in St Johns and going by Ballacraine, Kirk Michael, and then down the west coast to Peel, the triangular lap measuring 15 miles 1430 yd (25·442 km). Entries of touring motorcycles were invited for the first race, to take place in 1907 — which by coincidence was the same year as saw the opening of the Brooklands banked track, where a completely different kind of racing was promoted. For the event on the Manx roads, it was found difficult to define a touring motorcycle, and eventually the matter was left rather vague in the regulations — a problem which has persistently denied the race its intended character ever since. All that could be agreed was that a touring motorcycle should have two brakes and a silencer, a tool bag and a proper saddle. More fundamental design features caused disagreement, fuel tank requirements being particularly difficult to settle. Eventually it was decided, only in the month before the race, that there would be two races: one would be for single-cylinder machines, the other for those with two-cylinder engines. The former would have to be capable of 98 mpg (2·9 litres per 100 km), the latter of 75 (3·8).

These restrictions on the amount of fuel that could be consumed were meant to emphasise the tourist element implicit in the race's title. A fairly complete freedom in design was otherwise allowed, with no engine capacity limit and no weight limit. The winner of each of the two separate classes would receive £25, the runners-up £15 and the third finishers £10 each. For trophies, the winner of the multi-cylinder class would receive a trophy donated by Dr Hele-Shaw (inventor of the eponymous multi-plate clutch), while the winner of the single-cylinder race would take the Tourist Trophy itself. This was in the form of a silver figure of Mercury poised on a winged wheel, the whole statuette and mount standing 34 in (86 cm) high. This is the trophy that is now awarded to the winner of the Senior TT, winners of the other races getting replicas of the original Tourist Trophy, which was presented to the ACU in 1907 by one of the most enthusiastic of motorcycling pioneers, the Marquis de Mouzilly St Mars.

> More than 200 different makes of motorcycles have been ridden in the Tourist Trophy races since the first event in 1907.

It is with that trophy in 1907 that the recorded history of the event begins with the single-cylinder race won by a JAP-engined Matchless ridden by Charlie Collier, one of the pair of brothers (the other being Harry) who were to become famous by racing motorcycles of this make, in the early tradition of bosses who were also riders. At the end of ten laps, a pair of Triumphs followed 10 minutes behind the Matchless. As for the multi-cylinder race, this was won by a Peugeot-engined Norton ridden by 'Rem' Fowler, who finished no less than half an hour ahead of the second-placed Vindek despite a fall, belt drive problems, and a couple of punctures, with the third man 20 minutes further behind him still. In fact Fowler's Norton was very much faster than any of the other bikes, and averaged 43 mph (69 km/h) for one non-stop lap, but its troubles with tyres and

driving belts reduced its overall speed to 36 mph (57·9 km/h), as against Collier's 38 mph (61·1 km/h). It was the overall speed that mattered, or rather the time taken to complete the course, and not who finished ahead of whom. Vehicles were sent off in pairs at regular intervals, the effect being not exactly that of a race but rather like that of a time trial.

Thus each man pitted himself against the road and his mount, rather than confusing the issue by introducing the strategies and tactics appropriate to a massed-start race, when there is the danger that the event may become a race for men rather than a test of machines. The idealism of the TT's founders insisted on the latter.

In any case the riders had much to contend with in the starkly realistic conditions created by racing on public roads in the Island. Rutted, narrow and dusty, the roads were also affected by extraordinary fickle weather. It may be at its best in June, when the Isle of Man may be seen as 221 square miles of green valleys and gorse-clad hillsides; but it may not be seen at all, for mists and fog are rife, and rain prolific and chill. In such changeable and treacherous conditions, racing on ordinary roads can be terribly arduous. Worse still is covering the same course at racing speeds during the practice periods, which are held in the early hours of the morning before the sun is properly up to dispel the misty mordant cold.

Despite these problems, speeds mounted rapidly. By 1909 the TT was being won at 49 mph (78·8 km/h) this time by the other Collier brother, Harry. That year saw the first major changes in the regulations: pedalling gear was proscribed and the fuel restrictions were discarded. Most constructively, the event became a single race by the elimination of any distinction between singles and multi-cylinder engines.

In 1911 the most important developments took place, when the St John's circuit was abandoned. Instead the TT was staged over the full-length mountain circuit. This course was sometimes referred to as 'the 4-inch course' because the RAC rules governing the car races held there since 1905 limited the cylinder diameter in the cars' engines to 4 in, as well as limiting the number of cylinders to four so as to impose a maximum piston area and, by implication, a maximum probable power output. The organisers of motorcycle sport were perhaps less well versed

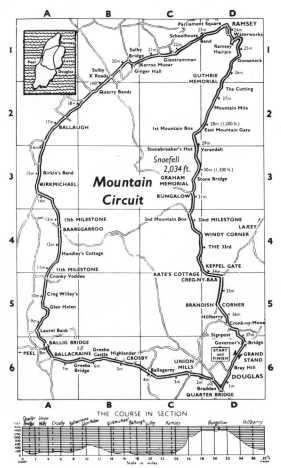

The full modern 'mountain' circuit for the
Isle of Man TT. (BP)

were a little slower then previously: Frank Philipp, a cousin of manufacturer Alfred Scott, established (on a Scott, of course) the new record for the daunting mountain lap at 50·11 mph (80·63 km/h), a clear 3 mph slower than the record lap of the St John circuit set in 1910.

The new course was not yet finalised, as it happened, and in the meantime there were other innovations. In 1913, for example, the races were held over two days: on the first the 350 cc Juniors covered two laps in the morning and the 500 cc Seniors three laps in the afternoon, while on the second day those who were still running were sent off together to cover another four laps. The experiment was not repeated. The Great War then intervened, and when racing was resumed in 1920 another alteration was made to the course: where riders had gone from Hillberry to Bray Hill by way of Willaston Corner, they now veered left at Cronk-ny-Mona and proceeded to Bray Hill by way of Signpost Corner, Glencrutchery Corner (nowadays called Bedstead), the Nook, Governor's Bridge and the Glencrutchery road. In 1922 a private road running from Parliament Square in Ramsey to the foot of May Hill was substituted for the previous detour in the town, and at last the course was finalised. One lap amounted to 37·733 miles (60·712 km), involved something like 265 significant corners and bends, and yet could be lapped even in far-off 1922 at nearly 60 mph. In fact the new record lap was set at 59·99 mph (96·54 km/h) by Irish-Canadian RAF officer Alec Bennett. The first 60-mph lap was put in by the brilliant J H (Jimmy) Simpson in 1924, on a 350 AJS. In 1926 he set the first 70 mph lap on a 500 AJS, and in 1931 pushed the record beyond 80 mph riding a 500 Norton. It was on a Norton, too, that F L (Freddie) Frith established the first 90 mph lap in 1937, and it was to be a very long time indeed before the next two increments of 10 mph were made.

> The first overhead-camshaft engine in a TT winner was the 348 cc Velocette ridden by Alec Bennett in 1926.

Meanwhile the experiments and changes continued. They have always been a feature of the TT series, and not without good reason. There was a certain monotony in the races, because the

in engine technology, for they made the classic mistake of establishing limits on piston displacement, an error that has been universally perpetuated. Thus for the first time in 1911 the races were divided into Senior and Junior classes. It was also the first time that a foreign machine won a TT race, and the first time that one make scored a 1-2-3 victory, when in the Senior race a team of Indian machines finished in that order. These American motorcycles were of some technical interest, having amongst other advanced features two-speed gearboxes, and this provision was scarcely less than a necessity in view of the hill-climbing demands made by the new circuit. From Ramsey at sea level the road climbs 1000 ft (300 m) in the course of a couple of miles and carries on to peak at nearly 1400 feet (425 m) near the Bungalow on the side of Snaefell. Lap speeds

Walter Handley sets off at the start of the 1932 Senior TT, only to crash and thus put the name of Handley's Cottage on the TT map. (Orbis Publishing)

machines coming under starter's orders tended to be very similar to each other: with the exception of the two 'Golden Ages' in the late 1930s and the mid-1950s, there was very little originality or variety in design. To make matters worse, the difficulties of the circuit made it a great leveller, extravagant power being as much a liability as an asset. The Manx authorities doubted the appeal of such repetitive races to the holiday-makers whom they wished to attract to the Island; what was wanted was a solid body of holiday makers who would feel justified in making a full week of it, since the tourist trade would not make much profit out of day trippers and weekenders — but the week would have to contain events sufficiently attractive in their variety if those holiday makers were to come, to stay, and to return another year.

Some new formula for success has always been sought, and the search still goes on.

Only once has a 350 cc machine won the Senior TT, in 1921 when Howard R Davies (who gave his initials to the HRD) won the 500 cc race on an AJS.

The novelty in 1922 was a new class, the Lightweight, for machines of up to 250 cc. Bikes of this engine displacement had been competing for the past 2 years in the Junior event, not with much hope of winning it but with the consolation of the Motorcycle Cup, a separate award for the best performer in this race within a race. In 1923 a Sidecar event was introduced, but the sidecar manufacturers did not approve, feeling that the pictures of wildly gymnastic crews so popular in the press were bad publicity for them, tending to act as a deterrent to the sales of passenger sidecars. Under this commercial pressure the organisers capitulated, and the Sidecar TT was abandoned after 3 years, not to return for another 30 years.

The new gimmick for 1924 was the Ultra Lightweight TT for 175 cc bikes. That event actually contained another gimmick, for it featured the first massed start in a TT, an experiment that was not repeated until 1948. The 175 class turned out to be poorly supported and the race for it was abandoned after only two seasons. The pattern thereafter reverted to the classical one of three races (Lightweight, Junior and Senior) and it remained so until 1947. In that long interval only one new idea was introduced — and that a merciful one: 1935 was the first year in which engines were allowed to be warmed up for a period prior to the beginning of the race. Previously, the races had been started with cold engines, and since there were few riders who could discipline themselves to use the throttle with restraint for the first few miles, early seizures were numerous and some of them led to injurious accidents.

> The last pushrod-engined machine to win a TT (other than Clubman events) was the New Imperial 250 cc ridden by Bob Foster in 1936. it was also the last occasion when a British machine won the Lightweight race.

By the time that the World War erupted in 1939 to put an end to racing over The Mountain for the time being, factory-entered machines were lapping remarkably quickly in the hands of star riders. The lap record stood to the credit of Harold Daniell on a Norton at 91 mph (146·4 km/h) in the course of winning the 1938 Senior TT, while the record race average was achieved in the 1939 Senior by Georg Meier on a supercharged BMW at 89·38 mph (143·8 km/h).

When racing was resumed in 1947, after the war, speeds were lower. Quite apart from all the ravages of the war and its effects on industry and

Harold Daniell riding a 500 cc Norton into fifth place in the 1937 Senior TT. (National Motor Museum, Beaulieu)

Helmut Fath driving the winning BMW in the 1955 TT. (All Sport/Don Morley)

upon a strained economy that had to do some things in the most parsimonious ways, there were some changes in the regulations that were to have far-reaching effects. Most important were the banning of supercharging, and the insistence on the use by all competitors of ordinary commercial grade petrol — at that time a noisome brew known as Pool and mustering a research octane number of somewhat less than 80. In the circumstances it was to everybody's credit that speeds should be as high as they were. The Senior was won by H L Daniell, again on a Norton, at 82·81 mph (133·2 km/h) his team mate A J (Artie) Bell and Velocette-mounted rival P J Goodman tying for fastest lap at 84·07 mph (135·2 km/h).

In the post-war years, full of reformatory zeal, innovations were to be expected. A new type of event was introduced in the form of the Clubman's TT, with classes for roadster-based or roadster-related machines of 250, 350 and 500 cc. There were fears ventilated that ordinary Clubmen could not safely be sent racing over so notoriously difficult a course, but these fears proved ill founded. The only trouble with the Clubman's races was that they attracted so little variety of machinery. Thus when a race of 1000 cc machines was introduced it rapidly became a race for Vincents and, since the riders were in no way stars, the public found little to hold their interest. Gradually the same began to apply to the Senior and Junior Clubman's events (the Lightweight was short-lived) as the entry list became dominated by the virtually purpose-built BSA Gold Star. This monotony brought about a gradual demotion of the Clubman's events until, as we shall see, an excuse was finally found to get rid of them altogether.

In the meantime the organisers found other tricks to play. For the 1948 Lightweight TT they brought back the massed start, and enforced it again for 1949 and 1953. In 1951 they introduced an Ultra Lightweight race of 125 cc limit and then — as though to deny the importance of this new venture — they transferred it, together with the revived Sidecar TT, to the new little Clypse circuit in 1954.

The Clypse course was a small and shallow travesty of the real thing, only 10·7 miles (17·2 km) around, barely 700 ft (213 m) from bottom to top, and embodying only a very small part of

George Meier on his winning ride in the 1939 Senior TT on a supercharged 500 cc BMW. (Orbis Publishing)

the Mountain Circuit. It was generally and deservedly unpopular, although it might have seemed impressive if it had not suffered comparison with the grandeur of the Mountain Circuit. Even the Lightweight TT was transferred to the Clypse course in 1955, as though to dignify the petty circuit, but the precedent was followed only for a few years.

> The rider with the longest history of competing in the Isle of Man Tourist Trophy races is C W Johnston, who retired when riding a New Imperial in his first attempt there, the 1922 Lightweight TT, and finished 16th on a Sun in his last, the 1951 125 cc TT. In the course of those 30 years he started in a total of 32 TT races and finished in 13 of them, scoring one victory — on a Cotton in the 1926 Lightweight TT.
>
> His nearest rival in time-span was J W Beevers, who rode in solo and Sidecar TT races from 1935 to 1960 inclusive. During that time he started in 42 races and was classed as a finisher in 32 of them, his highest place being in his very last race — the 1960 Sidecar TT, in which he was 7th on a BMW.
>
> Another rider whose TT career, like that of Beevers, embraced 26 years was C Tattersall, who took part in 22 races from 1928 to 1953 inclusive and finished in 8, his highest placing being 5th on a CTS in the 1932 Lightweight TT. Thirteen of his entries were on CTS machines, the initials standing for C Tattersall Special.

A far more welcome innovation was noted in 1954 when Inge Stoll-Laforge, riding as a passenger in the revived Sidecar TT, was the first woman ever to take part in a TT race. Another hopeful sign was given in 1956 with the introduction of a clutch start for the Sidecar race.

In another year it was time for the Tourist Trophy to celebrate its Jubilee. This required so much organisational effort, said the organisers, that it would not be possible to run the Clubman's race that year, so that once promising event was quietly disposed of, disappearing to the mainland. The Jubilee TT races that were held in 1957 were splendid affairs, especially the senior event which

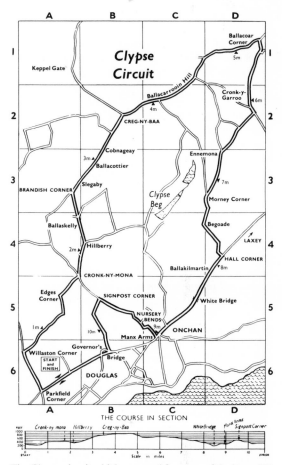

The Clypse circuit which was used for some of the lesser TT races. (BP)

was extended for that one year to cover eight laps of the mountain instead of the usual seven, amounting to a race of 302 miles. The field was a scintillating one and so was the win: R. McIntyre, who had first raced in 1953 on a Junior AJS, now rode a works-entered Gilera to win at a record average speed of 98·99 mph (159·3 km/h), putting in the first lap at over 100 mph and setting a new lap record at 101·12 mph (162·7 km/h).

In the following year we saw that the Golden Jubilee had brought the end of a golden age. Rules now came into force limiting the streamlining to the skimpy but now familiar 'dolphin' fairing in place of the full 'dustbin' type that had acquired such elegance on the best machines from Italy and Germany. Inevitably, the 1958 runners were slower and the racing less distinguished, due to the withdrawal of the leading Italian factories from racing. In the following year the ACU found a means of making the races easier to follow and more exciting for the spectators, by seeding the riders on the basis of their known abilities. The top five seeds drew lots for the honour and advantage of starting first, while the rest of the field followed in their seeded order singly at 10-second intervals. This meant that there would be plenty of stimulating battles between riders of equal ability to be seen, and the public approved wholeheartedly. This seeding only affected the Senior and Junior races, the others being doomed to the Clypse circuit and to a massed start.

To cater for those who criticised the extravagantly-engineered factory racing specials as too irrelevant to motorcycling in general and to the traditional objects of the Tourist Trophy in particular, a new kind of race for what were described as 'standard production racing motorcycles' was introduced in 1959. In practice these two so-called 'Formula 1' races were for Manx Nortons and 7R AJS machines, though many of them were more than a little non-standard. As might have been expected, these races were boring, and the apathy of the public hastened their demise.

More drastic changes occurred in 1960. At last the Clypse circuit was abandoned, the Lightweight, Ultra-Lightweight and Sidecar races moving back to the proper mountain circuit, the only one that really counted. The whole week was reorganised so that racing took place on the Monday, Wednesday and Friday, and the seeding process was further improved by starting the riders in pairs at 10-second intervals.

That 1960 season really marked the beginning of modern times in the Isle of Man. It saw the first serious entry by Honda (following their tentative but successful team entry in the 125 cc race the previous year), heralding an era in which new and technically adventurous Japanese machines began methodically to take over the whole world of motorcycle racing. With so much engineering progress suddenly being made, organisational changes in the TT races became less significant, but some of the racing was outstanding. It was in 1960 that the course was first lapped by a single-cylinder machine at over 100 mph (160·9 km/h); Derek Minter achieved this distinction seconds

before Mike Hailwood performed the same feat. By 1967 Hailwood had raised the lap record to 108·77 mph (175·0 km/h) on a ferociously powerful and fearsomely misbehaved 500 cc Honda, and that record stood unbroken for 9 years until at last the new magic of 109.82 mph was displayed by Mick Grant on a Kawasaki. There had been other innovations, such as the introduction of a 50 cc class which saw some astonishing pieces of engineering virtuosity, starting with the twelve-speed Kreidler and culminating in the magnificent twin-cylinder Honda and Suzuki racers. Eventually this tiny class was dismissed from the Island (later the 350s went, and the Lightweight race became known as the Junior), and in 1977 a new class of races for Formula 1, 2 and 3 machines was introduced. Still controversial, this should have been one of the best ideas yet, for it allowed virtually complete freedom of chassis design while requiring that the engine, carburettors and transmission be fairly substantially based on production, road-going motorcycles. The authorities tried to give the first such event artificial importance by arranging for it to have the status of a world championship: since it was the only race in that category during the year, Phil Read in winning the Formula 1 race (on a Honda) automatically became a world champion yet again.

The Island has also seen races for 750 or even 1000 cc machines of the so-called 'superbike' category, and prodigiously fast they have been. So welcomed were some of these that there are even hopes that this still young race will supplant the Senior and eventually become the most important of TT week. In 1978 this event, called the Open Classic, justified such optimism by proving the fastest TT ever, won at 112·4 mph (180·8 km/h) by Mick Grant, whose 750 Kawasaki carried him to a new absolute lap record, breaking the 20 minutes barrier for the first time to average 114·33 mph (183·9 km/h). That lap record survived intact after the 1979 TT week, but the race speed for the Open Classic was a new record, Alex George covering six laps in 2 hours 7 seconds to average 113·08 mph (181·98 km/h) on his 998 cc Honda. Close behind him rode Mike Hailwood in his last race, setting a new 500 cc lap record of 19 minutes 50 seconds (114·14 mph, 183·69 km/h) on a Suzuki 500.

TABLES

STANDING START WORLD RECORDS

Category	Distance (or time)	Rider	Machine
50 cc solo	$\frac{1}{4}$ mile	A. Toerson	Kreidler
	1 km	A. Toerson	Kreidler
	1 mile	A. Toerson	Kreidler
	10 km	R. Kunz	Kreidler-Meo
75 cc solo	$\frac{1}{4}$ mile	O. Buscherini	Minarelli
	1 km	O. Buscherini	Minarelli
	1 mile	R. Sullivan	Yamaha
	10 km	P. Cava	Minarelli
	100 km	P. Cava	Minarelli
	1 hr	P. Cava	Minarelli
100 cc solo	$\frac{1}{4}$ mile	P. Bianchi	Minarelli
	1 km	P. Bianchi	Minarelli
	1 mile	P. Cava	Minarelli
125 cc solo	$\frac{1}{4}$ mile	D. Heckle	Yamaha
	1 km	D. Heckle	Yamaha
	1 mile	D. Heckle	Yamaha
175 cc solo	$\frac{1}{4}$ mile	O. Buscherini	Minarelli
	1 km	O. Buscherini	Minarelli
	1 mile	P. Irons	Montaco
250 cc solo	$\frac{1}{4}$ mile	M. Hand	Honda
	1 km	M. Hand	Honda
	1 mile	D. Heckle	Yamaha
	1000 km	T. Robb, S. Graham, B. Smith, M. Hodder	Suzuki
	6 hr	T. Robb, S. Graham, B. Smith, M. Hodder	Suzuki
	12 hr	T. Robb, S. Graham, B. Smith, M. Hodder	Suzuki
350 cc solo	$\frac{1}{4}$ mile	M. Hand	Honda
	1 km	J. Balchin	BSA
	1 mile	L. Julian	Triumph
	10 km	W. Herz	NSU
	24 hr	E. Crooks, F. Whiteway, B. Ball, H. Anscheidt	Suzuki
500 cc solo	$\frac{1}{4}$ mile	P. Miller	Triumph
	1 km	J. Hobbs	Triumph
	1 mile	B. White	Triumph
750 cc solo	$\frac{1}{4}$ mile	D. Hocking	Triumph
	1 km	D. Hocking	Triumph
	1 mile	P. Windross	Triumph
	10 km	S. McLaughlin	Kawasaki
	100 km	C. Neilson	Kawasaki
	1000 km	C. Neilson, W. Fulton, S. McLaughlin, R. Cleek	Kawasaki
	1 hr	G. Romero	Yamaha
	6 hr	C. Neilson, W. Fulton, S. McLaughlin, R. Cleek, P. MacDonald	Kawasaki
	12 hr	W. Cooley, K. Code, J. Hateley	Kawasaki
	24 hr	R. Hagie, L. Hindle, H. Klinzmann, D. Cox, S. Moses, R. Milligan, R. Cleek, M. Kidd	Kawasaki

Capacity (in ccm)	Cylin- ders	Time (or distance)	Speed in km/h (mph)	Date set
49·61	1	15·5685 sec	93·034 (57·809)	05-10-68
49·61	1	30·3185 sec	118·739 (73·781)	06-10-68
49·61	1	44·392 sec	130·510 (81·095)	06-10-68
49·80	1	3 min 19·131 sec	180·785 (112·335)	23/5-10-65
74·72	1	14·535 sec	99·649 (61·919)	06-11-75
74·72	1	28·56 sec	126·050 (78·324)	06-11-75
72·865	1	49·305 sec	117·500 (73·011)	24-09-72
·73·5	1	4 min 32·80 sec	131·964 (81·999)	19-11-66
73·5	1	44 min 05·80 sec	136·064 (84·546)	19-11-66
73·5	1	135·769 km (84·363 m)	135·769 (84·363)	19-11-66
99·666	1	14·785 sec	97·964 (60·872)	13-10-73
99·666	1	28·195 sec	127·681 (79·337)	13-10-73
99·666	1	43·485 sec	133·232 (82·787)	03-10-71
124·889	2	13·245 sec	109·354 (67·949)	25-09-71
124·889	2	25·06 sec	143·655 (89·263)	25-09-71
124·889	2	36·54 sec	158·555 (98·522)	03-10-71
174·148	1	12·415 sec	116·660 (72·489)	06-11-75
174·148	1	24·425 sec	147·381 (91·578)	06-11-75
173·628	1	37·0 sec	156·570 (97·288)	24-09-72
247·0	2	10·50 sec	137·950 (85·718)	22-09-73
238·32	2	21·71 sec	165·820 (103·036)	23-09-72
246·50	2	33·26 sec	174·189 (108·236)	29-09-70
247·34	2	6 hr 35 min 19·6 sec	151·786 (94·315)	01-08-68
247·34	2	907·919 km (564·155 m)	151·319 (94·025)	01-08-68
247·34	2	1791·674 km (1113·295 m)	149·306 (92·774)	01-08-68
253·1	2	10·255 sec	141·230 (87·756)	23-07-77
349·8	1	20·125 sec	178·881 (111·152)	04-10-75
343·47	2	32·425 sec	178·677 (111·025)	03-10-71
347·285	2	2 min 38·829 sec	226·658 (140·839)	18-08-66
256·59	2	3496·521 km (2172·637 m)	145·688 (90·526)	01-08-68
489·25	2	9·935 sec	145·770 (90·577)	30-09-72
490·88	2	19.545 sec	184·190 (114·450)	02-10-71
492·448	2	28·58 sec	202·720 (125·964)	24-09-72
738·029	2	9·78 sec	148·090 (92·019)	23-09-72
646·141	2	18·81 sec	191·387 (118·922)	25-09-72
649·30	2	28·165 sec	205·703 (127·818)	03-10-71
748·642	3	2 min 25·09 sec	248·120 (154·175)	18-03-77
652·120	4	27 min 52·772 sec	215·211 (133·726)	15-03-77
652·120	4	4 hr 51 min 20·187 sec	205·946 (127·969)	16-03-77
694·87	4	242·07832 km (150·420 m)	242·0783 (150·420)	03-04-74
652·120	4	1232·673 km (765·948 m)	205·446 (127·658)	16-03-77
652·120	4	2288·129 km (1421·777 m)	190·676 (119·481)	15-03-77
652·120	4	4523·875 km (2811·006 m)	188·494 (117·125)	15-03-77

STANDING START WORLD RECORDS

Category	Distance (or time)	Rider	Machine
1000 cc solo	$\frac{1}{4}$ mile	H. Vink	Kawasaki
	1 km	H. Vink	Kawasaki
	1 mile	J. Hobbs	Triumph
	10 km	A. Gossutti	BMW
	100 km	A. Gossutti	BMW
	1000 km	G. Mandracchi, R. Patrignani, F. Trabalzini	Guzzi
	1 hr	A. Pagani	Guzzi
	6 hr	D. Beinhauer, H. Dahne, M. Milan, A. Gossutti, E. Zanini, A. Clerieuzio	BMW
	12 hr	D. Beinhauer, H. Dahne, M. Milan, A. Gossutti, E. Zanini, A. Clerieuzio	BMW
	24 hr	D. Beinhauer, H. Dahne, M. Milan, A. Gossutti, E. Zanini, A. Clerieuzio	BMW
1300 cc solo	$\frac{1}{4}$ mile	H. Vink	Kawasaki
	1 km	H. Vink	Kawasaki
	1 mile	G. Brown	Vincent
	10 km	S. McLaughlin	Kawasaki
	100 km	S. McLaughlin, W. Fulton	Kawasaki
	1000 km	B. Farnsworth, S. Moses, S. McLaughlin, K. Kiefer, W. Fulton	Kawasaki
	1 hr	S. McLaughlin, W. Fulton	Kawasaki
	6 hr	B. Farnsworth, S. Moses, S. McLaughlin, J. Corpe, K. Kiefer, W. Fulton	Kawasaki
3000 cc group F	$\frac{1}{4}$ mile	J. Hobbs	Weslake
	1 km	B. Jones	Volkswagen

Capacity (in ccm)	Cylin- ders	Time (or distance)	Speed in km/h (mph)	Date set
963·0	4	9·255 sec	156·490 (97·238)	23-07-77
963·0	4	16·68 sec	215·820 (134·104)	24-07-77
998·56	4	26·395 sec	219·496 (136·388)	01-10-72
981·984	2	2 min 50·09 sec	211·652 (131·514)	29-10-77
981·984	2	27 min 11·09 sec	220·711 (137·143)	29-10-77
758·0	2	4 hr 51 min 21·40 sec	205·933 (127·961)	30-10-69
797·50	2	217·040 km (134·862 m)	217·040 (134·862)	31-10-69
981·989	2	1150·052 km (714·609 m)	191·675 (119·101)	29-10-77
981·989	2	2290·449 km (1423·219 m)	190·870 (118·601)	29-10-77
981·989	2	4067·203 km (2527·243 m)	169·466 (105·301)	29-10-77
1140·6	4	8·805 sec	164·490 (102·209)	23-07-77
1018·0	4	18·425 sec	195·360 (122·391)	04-10-75
1145·0	2	27·979 sec	207·067 (128·665)	22-10-67
1030·5594	4	3 min 6·496 sec	193·032 (119·945)	17-03-77
1030·5594	4	31 min 8·080 sec	192·710 (119·744)	17-03-77
1030·5594	4	5 hr 15 min 41·697 sec	190·055 (118·095)	17-03-77
1030·5594	4	191·511 km (118·999 m)	191·511 (118·999)	17-03-77
1030·5594	4	1135·7758 km (705·738 m)	189·2958 (117·623)	17-03-77
1684·7	4	9·165 sec	158·030 (98·195)	24-07-77
1475·3	4	22·37 sec	160·920 (99·991)	24-07-77

STANDING START WORLD RECORDS

Category	Distance (or time)	Rider	Machine
250 cc sidecars	$\frac{1}{4}$ mile 1 km 1 mile	A. Reynard A. Reynard A. Reynard	Royal Enfield Royal Enfield Royal Enfield
350 cc sidecars	$\frac{1}{4}$ mile 1 km 1 mile	N. Hyde N. Hyde E. Hurley	Triumph Triumph Norton
500 cc sidecars	$\frac{1}{4}$ mile 1 km 1 mile	C. van Dongen N. Hyde N. Hyde	Honda Triumph Triumph
750 cc sidecars	$\frac{1}{4}$ mile 1 km 1 mile	P. Harman N. Hyde N. Hyde	Triumph Triumph Triumph
1000 cc sidecars	$\frac{1}{4}$ mile 1 km 1 mile	J. Jansen N. Hyde G. Brown	Kawasaki Triumph Vincent
1300 cc sidecars	$\frac{1}{4}$ mile 1 km 1 mile	G. Brown G. Brown G. Brown	Vincent Vincent Vincent

(m — in the Time (or distance) column stands for miles)

Capacity (in ccm)	Cylin-ders	Time (or distance)	Speed in km/h (mph)	Date set
247·821	1	14·61 sec	99·135 (61·560)	25-09-71
244·61	1	28·295 sec	127·230 (79·057)	02-10-71
244·61	1	42·13 sec	137·517 (85·449)	02-10-71
348·0	2	13·643 sec	106·164 (65·967)	05-10-68
348·0	2	26·373 sec	136·503 (84·819)	06-10-68
348·0	1	38·720 sec	149·629 (92·975)	21-10-67
493·3	4	11·925 sec	121·450 (75·466)	24-07-77
498·0	2	24·940 sec	144·346 (89·686)	11-10-69
498·0	2	34·640 sec	167·252 (103·926)	12-10-69
746·9	2	10·035 sec	144·335 (89·686)	30-09-72
736·06	3	21·87 sec	164·609 (102·283)	25-09-71
739·32	3	32·015 sec	180·965 (112·446)	03-10-71
938·1	4	11·255 sec	128·690 (79·964)	24-07-77
823·11	3	21·285 sec	169·130 (105·093)	29-09-72
997·52	2	30·346 sec	190·916 (118·630)	02-11-66
1147·0	2	11·746 sec	123·310 (76·621)	21-10-67
1147·0	2	21·625 sec	166·470 (103·440)	04-11-66
1147·0	2	31·057 sec	186·548 (115·916)	03-11-66

FLYING START WORLD RECORDS

Category	Distance (or time)	Rider	Machine
50 cc solo	1 km	H. van Kessel	Kreidler
	1 mile	R. Kunz	Kreidler
175 cc solo	1 km	A. Venturi	Minarelli
	1 mile	A. Venturi	Minarelli
750 cc solo	1 km	D. Vesco	Yamaha
	1 mile	D. Vesco	Yamaha
1300 cc solo	1 km	F. Cooper	Triumph
	1 mile	F. Cooper	Triumph
1300 cc solo Group C	1 km	D. Vesco	Yamaha
	1 mile	D. Vesco	Yamaha
3000 cc solo Group F	1 km	D. Vesco	Kawasaki
	1 mile	D. Vesco	Kawasaki
250 cc sidecars	1 km	A. Reynard	Royal Enfield
	1 mile	A. Reynard	Royal Enfield
750 cc sidecars	1 km	N. Hyde	Triumph
	1 mile	N. Hyde	Triumph
1000 cc sidecars	1 km	N. Hyde	Triumph
	1 mile	N. Hyde	Triumph
1300 cc sidecars	1 km	G. Brown	Vincent
	1 mile	G. Brown	Vincent

Capacity (in ccm)	Cylin-ders	Time (or distance)	Speed in km/h (mph)	Date set
49·863	1	16·2623 sec	221·586 (137·687)	06–09–77
49·80	1	27·821 sec	208·247 (129·399)	23–10–65
173·62	1	18·67 sec	192·822 (119·814)	02–10–71
173·62	1	30·13 sec	192·287 (119·482)	03–10–71
747·964	4	9·299 sec	387·138 (240·556)	28–09–75
747·964	4	14·955 sec	387·404 (240·722)	28–09–75
1298·0	4	11·94 sec	301·507 (187·348)	25–09–71
1284·421	4	19·66 sec	294·690 (183·112)	24–09–72
1495·928	8	7·391 sec	487·078 (302·656)	28–09–75
1495·928	8	11·884 sec	487·515 (302·928)	28–09–75
	8	7·062 sec	509·796 (316·775)	28–08–78
	8	11·290 sec	512·731 (318·866)	28–08–78
247·821	1	20·335 sec	177·034 (110·004)	29–09–71
247·0	1	32·392 sec	178·859 (111·138)	27–09–70
736·06	3	14·83 sec	242·751 (150·838)	25–09–71
739·32	3	24·445 sec	237·006 (147·269)	03–10–71
823·11	3	13·825 sec	260·39 (161·799)	24–09–72
828·82	3	25·41 sec	227·99 (141·666)	01–10–72
1147·0	2	14·939 sec	240·972 (149·733)	03–11–66
1147·0	2	28·073 sec	206·372 (128·234)	03–10–70

CHRONOLOGICAL TABLE OF ABSOLUTE WORLD SPEED RECORDS FOR MOTORCYCLES RECOGNISED BY THE FIM

Year	Course	Rider	Machine	Capacity (in ccm)	Speed km/h	mph
1920	Daytona, USA	Ernest Walker	Indian	994	167·670	104·12
1923	Brooklands, GB	Claude F Temple	British Anzani	996	174·580	108·41
1924	Arpajon, F	Herbert Le Vack	Brough Superior – JAP	867	191·590	118·98
1926	Arpajon, F	Claude F Temple	OEC – Temple	996	195·330	121·30
1928	Arpajon, F	Oliver M Baldwin	Zenith JAP	996	200·560	124·55
1929	Arpajon, F	Herbert Le Vack	Brough Superior	995	207·330	126·75
1930	Arpajon, F	Joseph S Wright	OEC – Temple	994	220·990	137·23
1930	Ingolstadt, D	Ernst Henne	BMW	735	221·540	137·58
1930	Cork, IRL	Joseph S Wright	OEC Temple JAP	995	242·590	150·65
1932	Tat, H	Ernst Henne	BMW	735	244·400	151·77
1934	Gyon, H	Ernst Henne	BMW	735	246·069	152·81
1935	Frankfurt-München Autobahn, D	Ernst Henne	BMW	735	256·046	159·01
1936	Frankfurt-München Autobahn, D	Ernst Henne	BMW	495	272·006	168·92
1937	Gyon, H	Eric Fernihough	Brough Superior – JAP	995	273·244	169·68
1937	Brescia autostrada, I	Piero Taruffi	Gilera	492	274·181	170·27
1937	Frankfurt-München Autobahn, D	Ernst Henne	BMW	495	279·503	173·57
1951	Ingolstadt, D	Wilhelm Herz	NSU	499	290·322	180·29
1955	Christchurch, NZ	Russell Wright	Vincent HRD	998	297·640	184·83
1956	Bonneville, USA	Wilhelm Herz	NSU	499	338·092	211·40
1962	Bonneville, USA	William A Johnson	Triumph	667	361·410	224·57
1966	Bonneville, USA	Robert Leppan	Triumph Special	1298	395·280	245·60
1970	Bonneville, USA	Don Vesco	Yamaha	700	405·25	251·66
1970	Bonneville, USA	Calvin Rayborn	Harley-Davidson	1480	410·37	254·84
1970	Bonneville, USA	Calvin Rayborn	Harley-Davidson	1480	426·40	265·49
1975	Bonneville, USA	Don Vesco	Yamaha	1496	487·515	302·92
1978	Bonneville, USA	Don Vesco	Kawasaki	2032	512·731	318·87

THE WORLD CHAMPIONSHIPS: MOTOCROSS

Year	Champion rider	Country	Champion manufacturer
	125 cc		
1977	Gaston Rahier	Belgium	Suzuki
1978	Akira Watanabi	Japan	Suzuki
	250 cc		
1962	Torsten Hallman	Sweden	Husqvarna
1963	Torsten Hallman	Sweden	Husqvarna
1964	Joel Robert	Belgium	CZ
1965	Victor Arbekov	USSR	CZ
1966	Torsten Hallman	Sweden	Husqvarna
1967	Torsten Hallman	Sweden	Husqvarna
1968	Joel Robert	Belgium	CZ
1969	Joel Robert	Belgium	CZ
1970	Joel Robert	Belgium	Suzuki
1971	Joel Robert	Belgium	Suzuki
1972	Joel Robert	Belgium	Suzuki
1973	Hakan Andersson	Sweden	Yamaha
1974	Gennadi Moisseev	USSR	KTM
1975	Harry Everts	Belgium	Puch
1976	Heikki Mikkola	Finland	Husqvarna
1977	Gennadi Moisseev	USSR	KTM
1978	Gennadi Moisseev	USSR	KTM
	500 cc		
1957	Bill Nilsson	Sweden	AJS Crescent
1958	Rene Baeten	Belgium	FN
1959	Sten Lundin	Sweden	Monark
1960	Bill Nilsson	Sweden	Husqvarna
1961	Sten Lundin	Sweden	Lito
1962	Rolf Tibblin	Sweden	Husqvarna
1963	Rolf Tibblin	Sweden	Husqvarna
1964	Jeff Smith	Great Britain	BSA
1965	Jeff Smith	Great Britain	BSA
1966	Paul Friedrichs	East Germany	CZ
1967	Paul Friedrichs	East Germany	CZ
1968	Paul Friedrichs	East Germany	CZ
1969	Bengt Aberg	Sweden	Husqvarna
1970	Bengt Aberg	Sweden	Husqvarna
1971	Roger de Coster	Belgium	Suzuki
1972	Roger de Coster	Belgium	Suzuki
1973	Roger de Coster	Belgium	Suzuki
1974	Heikki Mikkola	Finland	Husqvarna
1975	Roger de Coster	Belgium	Suzuki
1976	Roger de Coster	Belgium	Suzuki
1977	Heikki Mikkola	Finland	Yamaha
1978	Heikki Mikkola	Finland	Yamaha

THE WORLD CHAMPIONSHIPS: ROAD RACING

Year	Champion rider	Champion manufacturer
500 cc		
1949	Leslie Graham (British, AJS)	AJS
1950	Umberto Masetti (Italian, Gilera)	Norton
1951	Geoff Duke (British, Norton)	Norton
1952	Umberto Masetti (Italian, Gilera)	Gilera
1953	Geoff Duke (British, Gilera)	Gilera
1954	Geoff Duke (British, Gilera)	Gilera
1955	Geoff Duke (British, Gilera)	Gilera
1956	John Surtees (British, MV Agusta)	MV Agusta
1957	Libero Liberati (Italian, Gilera)	Gilera
1958	John Surtees (British, MV Agusta)	MV Agusta
1959	John Surtees (British, MV Agusta)	MV Agusta
1960	John Surtees (British, MV Agusta)	MV Agusta
1961	Gary Hocking (Rhodesian, MV Agusta)	MV Agusta
1962	Mike Hailwood (British, MV Agusta)	MV Agusta
1963	Mike Hailwood (British, MV Agusta)	MV Agusta
1964	Mike Hailwood (British, MV Agusta)	MV Agusta
1965	Mike Hailwood (British, MV Agusta)	MV Agusta
1966	Giacomo Agostini (Italian, MV Agusta)	Honda
1967	Giacomo Agostini (Italian, MV Agusta)	MV Agusta
1968	Giacomo Agostini (Italian, MV Agusta)	MV Agusta
1969	Giacomo Agostini (Italian, MV Agusta)	MV Agusta
1970	Giacomo Agostini (Italian, MV Agusta)	MV Agusta
1971	Giacomo Agostini (Italian, MV Agusta)	MV Agusta
1972	Giacomo Agostini (Italian, MV Agusta)	MV Agusta
1973	Phil Read (British, MV Agusta)	MV Agusta
1974	Phil Read (British, MV Agusta)	MV Agusta
1975	Giacomo Agostini (Italian, Yamaha)	Yamaha
1976	Barry Sheene (British, Suzuki)	Suzuki
1977	Barry Sheene (British, Suzuki)	Suzuki
1978	Kenny Roberts (American, Yamaha)	Yamaha
350 cc		
1949	Freddie Frith (British, Velocette)	Velocette
1950	Bob Foster (British, Velocette)	Velocette
1951	Geoff Duke (British, Norton)	Norton
1952	Geoff Duke (British, Norton)	Norton
1953	Fergus Anderson (British, Moto Guzzi)	Moto Guzzi
1954	Fergus Anderson (British, Moto Guzzi)	Moto Guzzi
1955	Bill Lomas (British, Moto Guzzi)	Moto Guzzi
1956	Bill Lomas (British, Moto Guzzi)	Moto Guzzi
1957	Keith Campbell (Australian, Moto Guzzi)	Gilera
1958	John Surtees (British, MV Agusta)	MV Agusta
1959	John Surtees (British, MV Agusta)	MV Agusta
1960	John Surtees (British, MV Agusta)	MV Agusta
1961	Gary Hocking Rhodesian, MV Agusta)	MV Agusta
1962	John Redman (Rhodesian, Honda)	Honda
1963	John Redman (Rhodesian, Honda)	Honda
1964	John Redman (Rhodesian, Honda)	Honda
1965	John Redman (Rhodesian, Honda)	Honda
1966	Mike Hailwood (British, Honda)	Honda
1967	Mike Hailwood (British, Honda)	Honda
1968	Giacomo Agostini (Italian, MV Agusta)	MV Agusta
1969	Giacomo Agostini (Italian, MV Agusta)	MV Agusta
1970	Giacomo Agostini (Italian, MV Agusta)	MV Agusta
1971	Giacomo Agostini (Italian, MV Agusta)	MV Agusta
1972	Giacomo Agostini (Italian, MV Agusta)	MV Agusta
1973	Giacomo Agostini (Italian, MV Agusta)	MV Agusta
1974	Giacomo Agostini (Italian, Yamaha)	Yamaha
1975	Johnny Cecotto (Venezuelan, Yamaha)	Yamaha
1976	Walter Villa (Italian, Harley-Davidson)	Yamaha
1977	Takazumi Katayama (Japanese, Yamaha)	Yamaha
1978	Kork Ballington (South African, Kawasaki)	Kawasaki

Year	Champion rider	Champion manufacturer
	250 cc	
1949	Bruno Ruffo (Italian, Moto Guzzi)	Moto Guzzi
1950	Dario Ambrosini (Italian, Benelli)	Benelli
1951	Bruno Ruffo (Italian, Moto Guzzi)	Moto Guzzi
1952	Enrico Lorenzetti (Italian, Moto Guzzi)	Moto Guzzi
1953	Werner Haas (West German, NSU)	NSU
1954	Werner Haas (West German, NSU)	NSU
1955	Hermann Müller (West German, NSU)	MV Agusta
1956	Carlo Ubbiali (Italian, MV Agusta)	MV Agusta
1957	Cecil Sandford (British, Mondial)	Mondial
1958	Tarquinio Provini (Italian, MV Agusta)	MV Agusta
1959	Carlo Ubbiali (Italian, MV Agusta)	MV Agusta
1960	Carlo Ubbiali (Italian, MV Agusta)	MV Agusta
1961	Mike Hailwood (British, Honda)	Honda
1962	Jim Redman (Rhodesian, Honda)	Honda
1963	Jim Redman (Rhodesian, Honda)	Honda
1964	Phil Read (British, Yamaha)	Yamaha
1965	Phil Read (British, Yamaha)	Yamaha
1966	Mike Hailwood (British, Honda)	Honda
1967	Mike Hailwood (British, Honda)	Honda
1968	Phil Read (British, Yamaha)	Yamaha
1969	Kel Carruthers (Australian, Benelli)	Benelli
1970	Rod Gould (British, Yamaha)	Yamaha
1971	Phil Read (British, Yamaha)	Yamaha
1972	Jarno Saarinen (Finnish, Yamaha)	Yamaha
1973	Dieter Braun (West German, Yamaha)	Yamaha
1974	Walter Villa (Italian, Harley-Davidson)	Yamaha
1975	Walter Villa (Italian, Harley-Davidson)	Harley-Davidson
1976	Walter Villa (Italian, Harley-Davidson)	Harley-Davidson
1977	Mario Lega (Italian, Morbidelli)	Yamaha
1978	Kork Ballington (South African, Kawasaki)	Kawasaki
1979	Kork Ballington (South African, Kawasaki)	Kawasaki
	125 cc	
1949	Nello Pagani (Italian, Mondial)	Mondial
1950	Bruno Ruffo (Italian, Mondial)	Mondial
1951	Carlo Ubbiali (Italian, Mondial)	Mondial
1952	Cecil Sandford (British, MV Agusta)	MV Agusta
1953	Werner Haas (West German, NSU)	MV Agusta
1954	Rupert Hollaus (Austrian, NSU)	NSU
1955	Carlo Ubbiali (Italian, MV Agusta)	MV Agusta
1956	Carlo Ubbiali (Italian, MV Agusta)	MV Agusta
1957	Tarquinio Provini (Italian, Mondial)	Mondial
1958	Carlo Ubbiali (Italian, MV Agusta)	MV Agusta
1959	Carlo Ubbiali (Italian, MV Agusta)	MV Agusta
1960	Carlo Ubbiali (Italian, MV Agusta)	MV Agusta
1961	Tom Phillis (Australian, Honda)	Honda
1962	Luigi Taveri (Swiss, Honda)	Honda
1963	Hugh Anderson (New Zealander, Suzuki)	Suzuki
1964	Luigi Taveri (Swiss, Honda)	Honda
1965	Hugh Anderson (New Zealander, Suzuki)	Suzuki
1966	Luigi Taveri (Swiss, Honda)	Honda
1967	Bill Ivy (British, Yamaha)	Yamaha
1968	Phil Read (British, Yamaha)	Yamaha
1969	Dave Simmonds (British, Kawasaki)	Kawasaki
1970	Dieter Braun (West German, Suzuki)	Suzuki
1971	Angel Nieto (Spanish, Derbi)	Derbi
1972	Angel Nieto (Spanish, Derbi)	Derbi
1973	Kent Andersson (Swedish, Yamaha)	Yamaha
1974	Kent Andersson (Swedish, Yamaha)	Yamaha
1975	Paolo Pileri (Italian, Morbidelli)	Morbidelli
1976	Pierpaolo Bianchi (Italian, Morbidelli)	Morbidelli
1977	Pierpaolo Bianchi (Italian, Morbidelli)	Morbidelli
1978	Eugenio Lazzarini (Italian, MBA)	MBA

Year	Champion rider	Champion manufacturer
50 cc		
1962	Ernst Degner (East German, Suzuki)	Suzuki
1963	Hugh Anderson (New Zealander, Suzuki)	Suzuki
1964	Hugh Anderson (New Zealander, Suzuki)	Suzuki
1965	Ralph Bryans (Irish, Honda)	Honda
1966	Hans-Georg Anscheidt (West German, Suzuki)	Suzuki
1967	Hans-Georg Anscheidt (West German, Suzuki)	Suzuki
1968	Hans-Georg Anscheidt (West German, Suzuki)	Suzuki
1969	Angel Nieto (Spanish, Derbi)	Derbi
1970	Angel Nieto (Spanish, Derbi)	Derbi
1971	Jan de Vries (Dutch, Kreidler)	Kreidler
1972	Angel Nieto (Spanish, Derbi)	Kreidler
1973	Jan de Vries (Dutch, Kreidler)	Kreidler
1974	Henk van Kessel (Dutch, Kreidler)	Kreidler
1975	Angel Nieto (Spanish, Kreidler)	Kreidler
1976	Angel Nieto (Spanish, Bultaco)	Bultaco
1977	Angel Nieto (Spanish, Bultaco)	Bultaco
1978	Ricardo Tormo (Spanish, Bultaco)	Bultaco
Sidecars		
1949	Eric Oliver (British, Norton)	Norton
1950	Eric Oliver (British, Norton)	Norton
1951	Eric Oliver (British, Norton)	Norton
1952	Cyril Smith (British, Norton)	Norton
1953	Eric Oliver (British, Norton)	Norton
1954	Wilhelm Noll (West German, BMW)	BMW
1955	Willy Faust (West German, BMW)	BMW
1956	Wilhelm Noll (West German, BMW)	BMW
1957	Fritz Hillebrand (West German, BMW)	BMW
1958	Walter Schneider (West German, BMW)	BMW
1959	Walter Schneider (West German, BMW)	BMW
1960	Helmut Fath (West German, BMW)	BMW
1961	Max Deubel (West German, BMW)	BMW
1962	Max Deubel (West German, BMW)	BMW
1963	Max Deubel (West German, BMW)	BMW
1964	Max Deubel (West German, BMW)	BMW
1965	Fritz Scheidegger (Swiss, BMW)	BMW
1966	Fritz Scheidegger (Swiss, BMW)	BMW
1967	Klaus Enders (West German, BMW)	BMW
1968	Helmut Fath (West German, URS)	BMW
1969	Klaus Enders (West German, BMW)	BMW
1970	Klaus Enders (West German, BMW)	BMW
1971	Horst Owesle (West German, URS)	BMW
1972	Klaus Enders (West German, BMW)	BMW
1973	Klaus Enders (West German, BMW)	BMW
1974	Klaus Enders (West German, BMW)	BMW
1975	Rolf Steinhausen (West German, König)	König
1976	Rolf Steinhausen (West German, König)	König
1977	George O'Dell (British, Yamaha)	Yamaha
1978	Rolf Biland (Swiss, Beo-Yamaha and TTM-Yamaha)	Yamaha
Formula 750*		
1973	Barry Sheene (British, Suzuki)	—
1974	John Dodds (Australian, Yamaha)	—
1975	Jack Findlay (Australian, Yamaha)	—
1976	Victor Palomo (Spanish, Yamaha)	—
1977	Steve Baker (USA, Yamaha)	—
1978	Johnny Cecotto (Venezuelan, Yamaha)	Yamaha

*FIM Trophy until 1977 when awarded World Championship status

OVERSEAS STATISTICS

	1973 (†)	1974	1975	1976	1977
Moped Production					
Austria	203·8	215 347	181 389	189 667	247 020
Czechoslovakia	—	—	95 670	118 997	(1)
France	1 216·2	1 381 480	1 073 105	985 010	962 705
Germany (West)	226·7	242 318	211 016	254 109	340 005
Italy	685·0	785 000	590 000	770 000	880 000
Netherlands	63·0	63 800	45 500	61 200	68 300
Spain	174·4	200 396	181 444	189 333	203 850
Switzerland	—	24 727	18 885	23 645	40 390
Yugoslavia	69·3	64 825	69 866	57 376	60 551
Motorcycle Production					
Austria	12·3	14 244	10 746	11 119	9 006
Czechoslovakia	—	—	118 566	110 557	(1)
France	8·7	9 038	8 513	9 715	7 463
Germany (West)	84·4	66 911	74 660	73 356	79 032
Italy	206·6	255 250	243 750	246 500	280 500
Japan	2 683·7	4 509 420	3 802 547	4 235 112*	5 577 359*
Spain	54·2	60 253	58 351	52 122	63 379

(1) Data not available

* includes moped production

† 1973 figures in thousands

Source: ANCMA — Milan

	Mopeds	Motorcycles & Scooters	Total
Two Wheeled Vehicles in use — 1977			
Austria	515 815	82 211	598 026
Belgium	553 574	99 888	653 462
Denmark		36 500	36 500
France	6 100 000	500 000	6 600 000
Germany (West)	1 800 000	300 256	2 150 256
Greece			90 715
Japan	8 194 957	750 435	8 945 392
Netherlands	1 650 000	68 000	1 718 000
Norway	113 321	21 801	135 122
Spain	—	—	1 142 439
Sweden	—	28 396	28 396
Switzerland	666 499	93 639	760 138
USA	—	4 916 000*	4 916 000*

* Source: Motorcycle Industry Council — Motorcycle Statistics Annual 1978

Source: ANCMA — Milan

THE UK MARKET

	1971	1972	1973	1974	1975	1976	1977	1978
UK Sales — New Registrations by Engine Size								
Mopeds	36 691	52 140	78 108	81 245	90 834	83 768	77 409	48 449
Scooters	12 365	6 653	5 539	4 714	4 500	2 866	3 073	3 407
Motorcycles								
Below 50 cc				13 727	17 325	11 296	8 018	7 058
51–100 cc				26 541	44 552	43 881	37 187	36 513
101–150 cc				16 069	31 344	29 198	30 988	23 409
151–200 cc				19 030	28 842	30 469	24 634	22 385
201–250 cc	78 866	93 726	109 965	18 060	26 582	36 265	35 469	40 787
251–350 cc				2 553	5 070	2 258	2 197	2 064
351–500 cc				3 475	10 571	19 167	15 474	18 320
501–750 cc				3 557	7 379	11 289	17 583	15 812
Over 751 cc				1 854	3 086	4 804	4 481	7 747
Total Motorcycles	78 866	93 726	109 965	104 866	174 751	188 627	176 031	174 095
Total 2 Wheelers	127 922	152 519	193 612	190 825	270 085	275 261	256 513	225 951
Total 3 Wheelers	13 153	13 407	11 255	14 392	15 182	11 677	8 622	6 187

1971–73 statistics obtained from DOE

1974–78 statistics obtained from MCRIS

	1974 %	1975 %	1976 %	1977 %	1978 %
Origin of New Registrations					
Mopeds					
British	0·6	0·2	1·9	3·8	4·3
W. European	63·5	51·7	36·5	29·0	29·3
E. European	0·8	0·9	0·2	0·7	1·1
Japanese	35·1	47·2	61·4	66·5	65·3
Total	100·0	100·0	100·0	100·0	100·0
Motorcycles					
British	3·2	2·9	2·2	2·0	2·2
W. European	4·7	3·8	3·2	3·1	6·4
E. European	9·4	7·4	5·3	7·3	5·5
Japanese	82·7	85·9	89·3	87·6	85·9
Total	100·0	100·0	100·0	100·0	100·0

Source: MCRIS

THE UK INDUSTRY

	1974	1975	1976	1977	1978
Production (Thousands)					
Mopeds	0·9	0·5	2·5	4·3	3·3
Motorcycles	26·5	26·4	19·0	14·4	23·9

	1971	1972	1973	1974	1975	1976	1977	1978
Imports (Thousands)								
Mopeds	28·5	53·5	59·3	87·5	89·5	78·3	60·1	56·2
Scooters	11·6	6·6	4·8	6·3	4·5	2·2	3·8	3·3
Motorcycles	79·4	105·3	138·6	149·8	184·6	228·3	184·6	224·8
Exports (Thousands) — including re-exports								
Mopeds	0·8	0·4	—	0·4	0·4	0·9	1·3	1·2
Scooters	0·1	0·3	0·1	—	—	0·1	0·1	0·1
Motorcycles	47·2	45·6	49·6	23·2	21·5	14·8	10·9	19·9

Source: Customs & Excise

	1971	1972	1973	1974	1975	1976	1978
Total Two Wheeled Vehicles in use (Thousands)							
Mopeds					297	383	377
Motorcycles	448	454	487	509			
Below 50 cc					250	154	94
51–150 cc	258	243	244	250	289	314	330
151–250 cc	195	177	175	184	214	239	255
251–350 cc					21	20	15
351–500 cc	119	109	100	99	32	42	56
Over 501 cc					58	66	75
Total	1020	983	1006	1042	1161	1219	1202

Source: Department of Transport
(Statistics for 1977 were not compiled due to Department of Transport re-organization)

INDEX

Page numbers in italics refer to illustrations

OTHER GUINNESS SUPERLATIVES TITLES

Facts and Feats Series:

Air Facts and Feats, *3rd ed.*
John W R Taylor, Michael J H
Taylor and David Mondey
Rail Facts and Feats, *3rd ed.*
John Marshall
Tank Facts and Feats, *2nd ed.*
Kenneth Macksey
Car Facts and Feats, *3rd ed.*
edited by Anthony Harding
Yachting Facts and Feats
Peter Johnson
Motorboating Facts and Feats
Kevin Desmond

Business World
Henry Button and Andrew
Lampert
Music Facts and Feats
Robert and Celia Dearling with
Brian Rust
Art Facts and Feats
John FitzMaurice Mills
Soccer Facts and Feats, *2nd ed.*
Jack Rollin
The Guinness Book of Antiques
John FitzMaurice Mills

Animal Facts and Feats
Gerald L. Wood FZS

Plant Facts and Feats
William G Duncalf

**Structures – Bridges, Towers,
Tunnels, Dams . . .**
John H Stephens

Weather Facts and Feats
Ingrid Holford

Astronomy Facts and Feats
Patrick Moore

Guide Series:

**Guide to French Country
Cooking**
Christian Roland Délu

Guide to Freshwater Angling
Brian Harris and Paul Boyer

Guide to Saltwater Angling
Brian Harris

Guide to Field Sports
Wilson Stephens
Guide to Equestrianism
Dorian Williams
Guide to Motorcycling, *2nd ed.*
Christian Lacombe
Guide to Bicycling
J. Durry and J B Wadley

**Guide to Waterways of Western
Europe**
Hugh McKnight
Guide to Water Skiing
David Nations OBE and
Kevin Desmond
Guide to Steeplechasing
Richard Pitman and
Gerry Cranham

Other Titles:

Guinness Book of Answers,
edited by Norris D. McWhirter

The Guinness Book of Records
edited by Norris D. McWhirter

The Guinness Book of 1952
Kenneth Macksey

The Guinness Book of 1953
Kenneth Macksey

The Guinness Book of 1954
Kenneth Macksey

Kings, Rulers and Statesmen
Clive Carpenter

Derby 200
Michael Seth-Smith
and Roger Mortimer

History of Land Warfare
Kenneth Macksey

History of Sea Warfare
Lt-Cmdr Gervis Frere-Cook
and Kenneth Macksey

History of Air Warfare
David Brown, Christopher
Shores and Kenneth Macksey

English Pottery and Porcelain
Geoffrey Wills

Antique Firearms
Frederick Wilkinson

AAA Centenary
Peter Lovesey

**The Guinness Guide to Feminine
Achievements**
Joan and Kenneth Macksey
The Guinness Book of Names
Leslie Dunkling
100 Years of Wimbledon
Lance Tingay
**The Guinness Book of British
Hit Singles,** *2nd ed.*
edited by Tim and Jo Rice, Paul
Gambaccini and Mike Read
**The Guinness Book of World
Autographs**
Ray Rawlins
**The Guinness Book of
Winners and Champions**
Chris Cook